Melinda Ann
Secrets of Kingsley Mansion

Books by Modenia Joy Kramer

The following three books are the Kingsley Family Trilogy

Lilly Going West – A Young Woman's Journey

Melinda Ann – Secrets of Kingsley Mansion

Orchard-Kingsley Brothers – The End of the Line

Mother's Memories – Days to Remember

Sunrise - Sunset – Book of Poems

Melinda Ann
Secrets of Kingsley Mansion

Modenia Joy Kramer

ARPress
ILLUMINATING IDEAS
EMPOWERING VOICES

ARPress
45 Dan Road Suite 15
Canton MA 02021

Hotline: 1(800) 220-7660
Fax: 1(855) 752-6001

Ordering Information:
Quantity sales. Special discounts are available on quantity purchases by corporations, associations, and others. For details, contact the publisher at the address above.

Printed in the United States of America.

ISBN-13:   Softcover   979-8-89676-090-0
            eBook   979-8-89676-091-7

Library of Congress Control Number: 2020923979

Dedicated to
John Haydn Kramer
My beloved husband and
dear friend,
…for his encouragement and
faith in this book.

ACKNOWLEDGMENTS

*The author wishes to acknowledge the Invaluable
assistance of the following people:*

*Marilyn Brown, Heidi Bailey, Paul Cooper, Kathy Grosso, Dorrie Mongold-
Guyan, Muriel Haege, Sam Hobel, Robert Emmett Hodges, Sharon Heath,
Annabel Johnson, Elizabeth King, Sid Kramer, Hugo Lackman, Holley Gene
Leffler, Chrissie Bales, and Lois Voltz.*

I appreciate all your interest and support. Thank You!

PROLOGUE

I had my whole life planned now it was being shattered by this news. As I sat in the taxi with the crumpled cablegram in my lap I reread these words:

COME HOME AT ONCE STOP
THIS IS TOO MUCH TO BEAR STOP
AUNT GINNY

As the taxi turned up the road I saw the old Kingsley mansion, chiseled-stone maker. Even though it was covered with a green vine and I could barely read it, I knew what it said. It brought back a flood of memories. When I saw the house I could hardly believe my eyes. I was so shocked everything else was a blur. The blackened walls still stood with sagging windows hanging in their frames, and the great pillars which stood in the front of the house were nothing, but burned stumps.

As I sat looking out the window Mr. Jenkins' face was full of concern. "Miss Melinda Ann, I hate to leave you out here all alone."

I was alone. Yes all alone. Oh Stephen, I miss you so much. Will I ever see you again?

CHAPTER ONE

I had just turned fifteen when my mother and I were talking about my future. That was the day that changed my life. It was the first time I talked back to her, and probably the first time I really took a good look at my mother. She was always sick or pretending to be. I didn't pay much attention to her. Now, I realized, the woman was as pale as a sheet with dark rimmed eyes, and sunken cheeks. She was extremely frail. I didn't understand her. One minute she seemed completely normal, and then she would fly off and go into a fit of anger. She was sitting in her chair with a throw over her outdated dress. She glared at me with her eyes flashing and mouth twisted. I'll never forget that day because her outburst was so hurtful.

"Melinda Ann, you seem to delight in causing me to be unhappy. You're just like your brother Charles Harley, he went off on his own and broke my heart, and now you want to leave, too! Why can't you be more like your cousin Birdie? She doesn't bristle at everything I say."

"Mother, please! Have you ever asked me how I feel about being here and being like a servant to all of you? No, not once! You're unreasonable. I wish you would listen to me. I want to do something different with my life. I want to become a nurse."

"Why, you're just a child. You're too young to do such a thing, and what do you really know about nursing? You have done precious little to show me that you would ever finish something like going into nurses' training. Your place is here! You don't need to be someplace caring for who knows who, taking care of nasty, dirty strange people in some hospital. You have a tradition to uphold. You are a Kingsley, and you need to stay with your own class. I am telling you, you're not going anywhere!"

"Mother, I won't sit here and listen to you one more minute. You don't care how I feel! You think the highest calling in the world for a woman is to be the mistress of a plantation. Well, I don't agree. I hate it here and I hate being told what to do and what not to do. You don't even know who I am. You say I am very mature for my age, but you don't really believe it. And another thing, I'm not upset if someone is dirty or even that the color of their skin is different from mine. People everywhere suffer from sickness and I want to help them. I wish just for once you could understand me."

"Melinda Ann, calm down and hush. I've heard enough from you. You can't talk to me this way. You know those nursing schools cost money and how do you think you can pay for it? I will not take money out of my household funds. You are not going off to some wild place and get into trouble. You will not bring shame on the Kingsley name! Do you understand me?"

"Oh, is that all you think of? I'm sick of being a Kingsley! I'll do as I please, and I will leave here, and I will become a nurse, you'll see! I'll speak to Father when he comes home. He is always more understanding than you. He'll give me the money to pay for it whether you like it or not!"

"Who knows what will happen to you or how you will live on your own! I'll not have it! The matter is closed!"

"No, Mother, the matter is not closed! I will not change my mind no matter what you say."

"For heaven's sakes, Melinda Ann, you have everything you want living right here! Why do you insist on pushing me so far?"

Before I could answer her, she began coughing, feigning sickness as she always did, and then suddenly changed her tone as she spoke. "Go ahead and leave! All you do is upset me with your ridiculous ideas and constantly asking me questions I won't answer. If you're so anxious to leave then do it, but I won't lift a finger to help you. When you fail, don't you dare come running back home to me? Birdie and I can manage just fine without you."

"As far as Birdie and you managing the household, I'm sure you can do without me."

Birdie! It was always Birdie. Why was she so perfect? Why did she hate me so much? What had I done or not done to her? I always knew Birdie resented me but I never knew why - one of those unanswered questions.

"Daughter, you have said too much. You haven't the slightest idea about living in the real world or how hard it is to survive out there. Go to your room and stay there until you can think clearly. And as far as Birdie is concerned it's none of your business. She has been like a daughter to me. I'll rely on her from now on, and I'll never ask for anything again."

"Birdie, come in here right now! You can help me to my room. Melinda Ann, you have given me a dreadful headache, and I'm so upset my hands are shaking."

I moved toward Mother. She screamed at me. "No, don't you dare come near me. Birdie! Birdie, come here at once! I want you to take me to my room. I must lie down."

As usual, Birdie, was just outside the parlor door listening. She burst in, all of five feet tall and every inch of her angry. Her dark eyes flashed hatred as she passed me. Her brown hair was pinned up on the back of her head in a bunch of curls. Her olive complexion was flawless. The dress she wore was much too fancy. She looked like a southern woman wearing fashions of the late 1800's, down to the small white gloves she always wore, so out of place for the early 1900's. As she moved toward Mother she extended her arms which Mother eagerly grabbed.

As I watched Mother and Birdie leave the room arm in arm, I wondered why she was so fond of Birdie.

CHAPTER TWO

I t wasn't much of a surprise when I think about it now. Father saw my desire to leave as an opportunity for me to break away from my mother's grasping hands. He listened to my hopeful plan and came to the conclusion it would be good for me to learn a skill, and nursing was one of the best for women. He provided the money and sent me off to a new nursing school in West Virginia, called St. Francis Hospital Nursing School.

Going to school in Charleston, West Virginia was a dream come true and wildly exciting for me. I was younger than most of the other girls. Teachers and the administrator didn't believe I would ever finish the training. I was just a child to them and incapable of concentrated study, but they didn't know me and how determined I was to become a nurse. Maybe it was because I was the youngest in the class that my classmates teased me. I never let them know how hurtful it was. I had the nastiest jobs. At the plantation I never had to clean any floors, wash walls, or empty bedpans.

Part of the school housed an infirmary where we practiced on real patients. We learned how to bath bodies, make them comfortable and administer certain medications.

Since I loved reading I spent my free time in the library reading medical books and journals. I was determined to be the best nurse possible and acquire the knowledge I would need to choose my specific area of nursing. Caring for children appealed to me since I'd had a great deal of experience caring for my brothers. When our instructors told us that nurses would not have any trouble getting jobs in most any hospital in the country, I paid attention.

Our group was the first graduating class in 1916 and we were all very excited. None of my family ever visited me during my time in school neither did any of them attend the graduation. I received my school's unique nurses' cap and pin, and was told I would be doing my internship at a hospital in Charleston, South Carolina. Hip-hip hooray! I had finally finished my training.

It was there that I met the well-known, Mrs. Harriett Camp Lounsberry, who became my mentor. She had served in the United States Army during the Spanish-American War, and I wanted to be just like her. We became friends and after my internship was completed she recruited me as a military nurse. But I was unable to go into the service at that time due to receiving an urgent telegram from home. It informed me Mother was quite ill and I should return home immediately. Since I was sixteen and the youngest in the group, I was advised to return home and care for my mother. Yes, I was going home, not as a failure, but as a certified nurse!

Once home I found I could not step back into the old routine. I had changed. When I saw Mother I could see the telegram had been a ruse. She was fairly well. She thought she had won and planned to keep me under her control as long as possible. When I asked her why she had insisted that I come home, she simply replied. "You're much too young to be on your own, out in the world being exposed to all sorts of temptations. And since you're home now, you might as well make the best of it."

Well, she was right, I'd been out in the world and I knew some of those temptations, and yes, I was young, but she was dead wrong thinking she could keep me with her for the rest of my life. The longer I remained at home the more resentful I became, and it showed. It was impossible to be around me. I didn't care. Soon after my arrival Mother called me into the parlor.

"Melinda Ann, I am weary of your rude behavior making everybody in this household miserable."

"But I'm the one who is miserable. I had a chance to travel and to work in a hospital and you insisted that I come home. You took an excellent opportunity away from me and I want to know why. There is nothing for me to do here."

"It does not matter why, Melinda Ann. I don't see what you're trying to prove by leaving. You didn't learn anything at that fancy school. You just wasted our money. You think you're smarter because you have a graduation certificate. Well, I assure you, nothing has changed."

"Yes, it has, I've grown up! I worked hard and I did earn my nurses' certificate and am now qualified to work in a hospital."

Before I could utter another word Birdie dashed into the parlor and assisted Mother as she rose from her chair. Then Birdie looked at me with so much anger that I knew I was right, this was no place for me.

Birdie looked me straight in the eyes and in her high pitched voice told me, "Just leave this house and give us some peace. You don't want to be here, so get out and good riddance! Look what you have done to your mother. She is terribly upset and it's entirely your fault. Get out of my way!"

Oh, I would leave soon because I knew how much Birdie hated me. She had always tried to take my place with my mother, but the fact was, I was Mother's only daughter whether she liked it or not. I knew I could not leave immediately because I needed to talk to Father. I was sure he would understand, and I needed to tell him the truth about this incident. I wanted to explain why I was leaving. When I did that, he understood.

I began to notice that Mother looked well one day and the next she was pale and seemed to withdraw into herself. Birdie made sure I was never alone with Mother. I wanted to push Birdie out of my way, but what good would that do? She had no intention of leaving the plantation but I was determined to leave!

I was sleeping in my own room and in my own bed, but I slept fitfully and dreamt disturbing dreams. Dreams I could not understand. There were loud noises, strange voices, yelling and screaming. I felt somehow the dream was about Charles Harley. So without decent sleep I was extremely tired.

In the next few days I went against Mother's wishes and applied for a hospital job in Roanoke. I was hired on the spot. Moving to the nurses' quarters on the hospital grounds provided the relief from the plantation that I'd longed for. On April 6, 1917, while leaving the hospital and heading for my room I noticed newspaper boys on the streets yelling and waving the papers. I bought a paper, read the headline, WILSON DECLARES WAR.

The problems with my family had been the center of my attention. The chilling truth suddenly ran through my mind. The whole country had a much bigger problem. I wondered if my brothers would have go to war, and since I'd already been recruited into the military I was sure I would be called to serve, but I didn't know when. I knew nurses would be needed and I was ready.

CHAPTER THREE

In February, 1918 I was working at the hospital in Roanoke, on my regular shift, when I heard the hospital administrator talking to the head nurse. "Well, the news came today. The Surgeon General has put out a call for nurses to do duty in cantonments or camp hospitals in the United States.

I'm sure we will be losing some of our nurses, especially the ones who have already been recruited, but any others who volunteer are free to go."

Most nurses, like me, eagerly responded and many others would soon follow. Those who responded were assigned to duty at various major hospitals in the United States, like Walter Reed General and the Ft. Sam Houston in Texas.

That was all I needed to hear. This was my opportunity to leave Virginia and see the world. I waited for specific placement. The war had started for the Americans in April of 1917 and here we were in February of 1918 just beginning to get ourselves organized and ready to join the war effort. I received a letter saying I had been attached to Base Hospital Unit 48. Later I learned that all the nurses who were attached to this unit were well-trained and most had worked in private practices or in Army hospitals. I was eager to receive my orders for mobilization and to prepare for my trip overseas.

On July 15th I received my orders to report to New York City by the 21st of July. Since I wasn't far from the plantation I made a short trip home to tell my family good-bye. While I was there I found out what my brother Charles Harley had done since he left home. One afternoon I was looking through papers on Mother's desk when I found some letters tied up with a blue ribbon. I was shocked that she had not shared them with me. The return address showed they were from Charles Harley. I was delighted and wondered why Mother had not told me about receiving them. I eagerly read each one, the first one written from Baltimore, Maryland in April of 1913 to the last in June of 1917. In his early letters he wrote of his experiences in New York City, trying to get on the stage and how proud he was of being a Kingsley from Virginia. He assured us he was able to take care of himself and we were not to worry. In the last one he said he had joined the United States Army and was stationed in France. From that last letter I learned that he had been assigned to the Remount Station, earlier called The Cavalry, because of his experience with horses. He told about his life in the Army, the terrible food, the cold rainy weather, and that he had slept many a night with the horses, because the hay in the stalls was the warmest and driest place he could find.

His closing remark really stuck with me. "We need to get the Americans over here and whip the pants of these Krauts." These letters haunted me. He said he was in France. What was he doing there?

Was he behind the lines, had he been in the regular fighting, had he been wounded or even worse killed? No letter had come since June. I needed answers to my questions so that very evening when the family was in the parlor, I told them I'd read the letters, and that I'd been having nightmares concerning my brother. I told them how worried I was, and soon I would be going overseas. Once there I would try to find him despite all odds.

Mother immediately became hysterical and Father looked straight ahead in that stoic manner of his. Edward expressed concern, but showed little emotion. Edwin seemed oblivious to the fact that our brother was in any danger in Europe. Aunt Ginny was not there, but Miss Birdie glided into the room typically overdressed in her old-fashioned ruffles and frills. And her fists were clinched in her small white gloves. She irritated me to death. Birdie always dressed and acted like she was the mistress of the plantation and not my Mother. She pretended to be deferential to all the family, except me, because I knew it was only an act. She did a little curtsey and looked very humble as she spoke to Father.

"Sir, all of the help would like to know what has happened to Master Charles Harley. We all love him very much and wish him well."

Father almost choked hearing her say this. He looked at Birdie in amazement. "Oh, Birdie! Come on, Charles Harley is more like a brother to you than a master. Didn't he always treat you well and like one of the family?"

"Yes, Sir. He always treated me like a sister and that is more than I can say for some of this family."

Hearing and seeing Mother in her condition, Birdie, quickly went over to her, grabbed her arms and assisted her to a standing position.

Mother was a bit startled, but quickly turned to Birdie. "Birdie, help me! Help me get to my room!"

So Mother went to bed and stayed there the rest of the time I was home. I was concerned, of course, and went to her bedroom several times, but got only a glimpse of her from the doorway. When I tried to enter her room she yelled at me to leave and not come back. At these times Birdie would appear, rush past me and go to my Mother's side. The day I had to leave I went to Mother's bedroom one last time hoping to see her. As I entered the door Birdie came rushing toward me and this time I stuck out my foot and tripped her. It was a glorious sight, seeing Birdie sprawled out on the floor, kicking and sputtering at me. I stepped over her and went to the side of my mother's bed. I did want to know what was wrong with her, and I wanted to say, "Good-bye." I knew I would not be able to live with myself if I didn't try to speak to her. Mother saw me and quickly turned her head toward the wall and covered her face. I knew it was of no use trying to reason with her so I leaned over, told her good-bye, and left the room.

As I walked out Father was standing in the hall and he spoke to me. "Melinda Ann, I am glad you came home. I wish things were different here, but I understand when Uncle Sam calls, you have to go. Just know I'm always here for you. By the way, if you do get to London and need funds I will give you a letter to give to my solicitor, and he will get the money you need. There is plenty of currency in the Kingsley Family account." I thanked him for his generosity and went to my room.

Before I left I said my farewell to Edward in private and advised him to go easy with his flirtation with Birdie. My exact words were. "Edward, you need to meet a nice girl and get married. You would be a great dad and you don't need to get involved with our cousin Birdie. It is shameful to think of you marrying her. You have already established yourself as the number two man around here. Father needs your help and besides you're the only one he trusts."

"Melinda Ann, it is none of your business who I marry and I'll marry whom I please and you can accept it or not because I really don't care! I know what you think of Birdie and if I love her it's none of your concern. I'll be glad when you're gone, and by the way I hope you enjoy yourself in Europe and never mind about us! We will do just fine without you or Charles Harley for that matter! And yes, I am the most suited to be master of this household!"

Later that same day I spoke with Edwin. "Well brother, It's time for me to say good-bye. I know we have never gotten along very well, but I do care about you, and I do wish you would consider leaving here."

"Sis, I'm sorry you're leaving. I know going overseas will be tough. You are one smart girl and I know you can handle anything that comes your way. I wish I were more like you, daring and independent. I'm itching to join the Army, but Dad won't let me. Says the Army wouldn't take me anyway because of my poor health. I guess he is right, but we'll see what happens. I guess I'll be stuck in Virginia for the rest of my life."

"Edwin, it's good to know you care about what happens to me, but I'm shocked that you believe you will be stuck here forever. You know it is your choice to stay or leave. Surely you do not lack the gumption to get out of here, or is it that you're so attached to Mother and Father that you can't leave?" He looked at me in a strange way. "No need to talk about it now." He just walked off leaving me standing in the hallway.

On the 17th, I took the train out of Roanoke headed north and on the 21st, reported to the Nurses' Home at the Metropolitan Hospital of New York City. I would be living there for the next few weeks. I'd grown-up quickly tending to patients and being exposed to the daily life of working in a hospital. Day after day, seeing sick, hurting and dying people helped make me tough. I was sensitive to their needs, but did not have to be involved in their personal lives.

The following two weeks of training were hectic. Our instructors ran us through daily marching drills which they said would build up our bodies, but to tell you the truth, it nearly killed me. Every muscle in my body ached! Then the group had to do singing exercises and we all agreed that was fun, but for the life of me I could never figure out why singing was required. Later, I learned that the leaders found it helped us speak more clearly, losing our local accents.

I understood having our photograph taken and being finger-printed, but writing our last will and testament made me a little uneasy. I'd not thought much about my future. All I knew was that I was not going back to Virginia. I couldn't even think of anything I really owned, and as far as my earnings going to someone if I died, well that made me laugh. When we were told to take out a life insurance policy it made me wonder just what my life was worth to anyone. I'd pretty much cut all ties with my family, but almost as an afterthought I put Charles Harley's name on the policy.

That summer in New York was so hot we wore our whites and hoped we would never have to wear our wool dress uniforms. That hope was dashed when we were told they planned to take a group photograph in our dress uniform. Sure enough, we had no choice and while we waited for the picture to be taken we sweated like a bunch of Indians in a sweat lodge. Most of us had long hair pinned in a bun on the nape of our neck and with our low set brimmed hats and high neck blouses we were dripping wet. The wool suits made us itch and the body odor was overwhelming. Being crowded together like sardines in a can, I wondered why they bothered to take our picture in the first place. Later when we did get a glimpse of the photo we could not tell one person from another.

Finally we received our orders and shipped out of New York Harbor on August 8th on the USS Olympic also known as the U.S. Transport No. 527. Leaving the harbor was a little sad as we moved slowly by the Statue of Liberty. Most everybody rushed to the rail to view the magnificent lady.

I'd never been on a big ship before and I hoped I would not be seasick. Once we were out at sea we literally took our hair down. At that moment I felt a freedom I had never known. I was at last on my own!

CHAPTER FOUR

We docked at Southampton, England on August 16, 1918, but were not allowed to leave the ship until the next day. I was so excited I walked around the ship most of the night. That morning we were loaded on two small hospital boats that took us across the English Channel, and when we finally landed on French soil it was with great relief. On the 19th we were in La Havre. There were 100 nurses and six civilians in our contingent. We were divided into two groups, each with an interpreter. Having been told we were on our way to Paris, all of us were extremely thrilled.

It was night when we arrived in Paris and because of the constant air raids, all lights were out. There was total darkness yet the city hummed with activity. How the motorized ambulances and other traffic moved around the city without a speck of light was a mystery to me. The traffic moved and people went about their business, totally accustomed to the dark. They had had a lot of practice.

Our group was hustled off to the Hotel Regina where I had a brief night of sleep and I do mean brief. It seemed I'd just gotten comfortable in the soft Parisian bed when I was awakened at dawn. Just lying there I thought of running away and seeing this historical city for myself. Touring Paris excited me no end, but I knew that adventure would have to wait. I went to the window and looked out over the city. I couldn't see much except in the distance there was a white building towering over Paris. Later I was told it was the Basilica of the Sacred Heart, *Baslique du Sacre-Coeur*. It was a glistening white church sitting on the tallest hill in the city. It is one of the most familiar sights in Paris with its huge bell tower and onion-shaped dome.

By six o'clock a.m. the Red Cross ambulances pulled up and we were called out. We were taken to the train station and sent on our way to Roane, France. On the way I saw beautiful chestnut trees lining the city's famous avenues. My head was turning from side to side, because I was so afraid of missing something. While enjoying the scenery, I couldn't miss the rumors of our destination that flew around us. The news was that Base Hospital No. 48, would be stationed in Roane, but that did not happen. On August 20th we found ourselves in the town called Mars-sur-Allier. It was fun to be there because I ran into some nursing friends I'd worked with in the United States, but we never had time to really catch up.

Our duties started immediately and for four months we worked endless hours. I thought I knew what it meant to be cold, but it was nothing like what I experienced in those first months. The weather was unpredictable most of the time, and pneumonia was rampant. Three of our nurses contracted the disease and died. Morale was as low as could be. We never expected to lose any of our own to sickness. I was one of the lucky ones. I never had the sniffles. We were cold because of the weather, and we were hungry because we were not familiar with French cooking. Oh, what I would have given for a good southern breakfast!

Day after day there was a steady stream of soldiers pouring into the base hospital. These were some of the bravest men I've ever seen and they were so very grateful for any care received. They came to us bloody with parts of their once sturdy bodies shot away and many with empty looks in their eyes, shocked by the constant sound of bombs exploding around them. All brave men, but not whole men any longer.

I was totally involved in my work and never thought I would be detached from the unit, but then it happened. I was sent with several other nurses to a hospital in Nancy, France. It was disappointing to leave those of whom I'd become so fond.

Even before I left the United States and especially since I'd been in Europe, I had a recurring dream that haunted me. It was about my brother, Charles Harley, in a soldier's uniform. I dreamt there was a loud explosion which sounded like a freight train rolling by, followed by a large cloud of gray/black dust or smoke. Then I would hear my brother, Charles Harley's voice calling to me from a distance just like he had done when we were kids. I knew it was his voice and I knew he needed my help, but where was he? I had the feeling there was something terribly wrong with him. Then I would wake up.

From one of the letters I'd read at home, I knew he was in the Army, but where? If my dream was true and he had been wounded, how could I ever find him?

CHAPTER FIVE

Once I was established at the hospital in Nancy, I found the work overwhelming with very little chance to relax. I worked steadily side-by-side with the doctors. One morning I recall hearing a lot of commotion taking place outside the hospital. It was a courier sharing the news with some folks passing by. When the doctor in charge heard him, he yelled, "What is that courier saying? Go out there, Nurse Kingsley, and bring him inside. We are as hungry for news in here as anyone!"

When the courier entered he spoke directly to the doctor. "I've good news, Doc! The American troops are pushing the Germans back and our guys, along with the English, are heavy into the fight!" Then he added his own opinion. "I betchya' that will get those Krauts attention. They'll wish they never started this damn war. This will scare the hell out of them!"

Once he spotted me in the room, he began to stammer and bow his head holding his cap to his chest. "Oh pardon me, ma'am. I didn't know there was a woman present." I guess he thought I'd left the room.

Hearing him, the hospital doctor almost laughed, then exclaimed, "Aw, hell man, she isn't a lady, she's a nurse!" And I was just that and so were the other young women nurses. We were indispensable to the doctors and the patients, as well as a welcome sight to the troops, too. When we were not working in the hospital, we were busy passing out doughnuts and coffee in the canteen, giving a smile and chatting with the boys passing through. I believe, as the men looked at us they were reminded of home, apple pie, their mothers, and their sweethearts.

There was hardly any time for rest because we worked night and day catching a little sleep whenever possible. My back ached and my hands were raw from the harsh soap, but that was no reason to give in.

As the days passed, I'd not given up my desire of finding Charles Harley. Every time I checked a list of new patients I was relieved that his name wasn't there. Of course, there were some men with no dog tags and no way of identifying them. I tried to find someone who might have known my brother. I described him in detail, but all they would do is nod their heads and with sad eyes say they had not seen him.

When I told the head nurse, Mrs. Gilbert, about my concern for my brother, she explained that all the patients with broken limbs and amputees had been sent to the annex behind the main hospital. I had never had the opportunity to go to that place. I was stunned to think my brother might be right here under my nose and I'd not realized it. Nurse Gilbert was most understanding and arranged for me to leave my duties and visit the annex. If I found him I was to let her know and if he was there she would see to it that I received a lighter work duty so I could spend time with him.

At the next opportunity I found my way to the annex and proceeded to look for Charles Harley. I held to the hope that he had to be here. If he had been wounded early in the fighting and had a broken limb this would be the place I should find him. Being realistic I wondered how I ever thought I would find him among the hundreds of thousands of soldiers in France, but I had hopes.

I walked the partitioned annex dorms carefully looking at every patient. Each time I would get my hopes up I was disappointed. There were so many soldiers to look at. In one dimly lit ward I stopped by a young man lying on his side with his back toward me. In gasping breaths he was groaning. I knew he was in a lot of pain. The back of him did look familiar so I moved closer to his bed and gently touched his shoulder. I spoke to him in a soft reassuring voice. "Charley Harley, is that you?"

When the man heard my voice he tried to turn over and I realized he was unable to move so I went to the other side of the bed. As I did, he reached out and grabbed my hand clutching it tightly in his. I couldn't believe my eyes! It was my brother!

"I don't believe it. Sis, is that you? Is it really you? Thank God you have found me. I've been calling for you over and over again. I need you! I was hoping you would find me. I'm scared! These crazy doctors tell me they are going to amputate my leg in the morning. I can't stand for that to happen! I won't let them! You can't let them. You know what my leg means to me! For God sakes, Melinda Ann, help me! I know you can do something!"

After this outburst he turned his face to heaven and said in a cry that made my skin crawl. "Please, God, don't let them cut off my leg!" He was exhausted, in tears, and had a frantic look in his eyes like a cornered wild animal. I knew he would rather die than have one of this legs cut off. All of his life he had dreamed of being in show business. His heart was in the theater and with one leg missing he would have no chance at all.

I had seen many leg wounds in my nursing days, and if what I suspected had happened he would most probably lose his leg. I had to do something because he was going to get his leg amputated unless I could pull off a miracle.

I leaned over him and grabbed both of his wrists and pinned him down. "Charles Harley, stop this ranting at once! Yes, I'm here, and now that I've found you I will not leave you, I promise. Just try to calm down and let me do what I can to treat you."

As I quickly looked at his leg, the odor was putrid and gangrene had set in. In nurses training I remembered reading about an old remedy of using a dry mustard plaster to draw out puss and infection.

"Charles Harley, I'm going try an old treatment on your leg, but I can't promise you it will work." Saying this, I went to a nurse, and asked her if she could arrange to get some dry mustard for me. She said there was a tin in one of the storage cabinets I could use. Then I went to the kitchen and asked for a slab of raw fat. The cook was a little puzzled, but he gave it to me anyway.

I threw off my cape and set to work. I was appalled at what I saw. My brother's leg was swollen and looked like it was ready to burst. On the piece of fat I spread a thick mixture of dry mustard and water, applied this to his leg and covered it with a clean piece of bandage. After applying the mustard plaster, I waited until the plaster dried and then repeated the whole process over and over.

I found a small wooden chair out in the hall and brought it inside the ward. Sitting beside my brother's bed I put his hand in mine, smoothed his hair out of his eyes, and with a gentle voice I told him to go to sleep.

He slowly relaxed and did as I asked. He looked like the little boy I remembered lying helpless and all alone – but he was not all alone. I was with him!

As I kept my vigil I remembered so many things about him as a child, how he walked holding himself up straight like a little toy soldier, strutting around like a general, or reciting poems at Christmas, standing before the brightly lit tree. I remembered how he had stood on a raft floating in the pond declaring he was the greatest sea captain in the world. I also prayed, because I believed nothing was impossible with God. I'd done what I could and now I would rely upon God's help to save Charles Harley's leg.

Sitting in the ward waiting I heard the other soldiers call out for help. I could not stand doing nothing so as I moved through the ward I tended to their needs as best I could. There were many doughboys in the beds that lined the walls of the ward. There were not enough nurses to provide the essential basic care they needed. Only a single nurse was stationed at the door, but the sheer number of patients was overwhelming. In the middle of the night I did see some Sisters of a Holy Order offering care to the patients.

As dawn approached, the hospital became quiet again except for an occasional groan or even a muffled scream from one of the delirious patients. I sat in the semi-darkness with only moonlight streaming through the high, bare glass windows. Every hour I changed the mustard plaster. At first the bandages were covered with puss and blood that oozed from the multiple leg wounds. By candlelight I could see the red squiggly line that had been moving toward his groin, as I'd feared it would do. By six o'clock in the morning, dear Charley was resting comfortably and appeared to be out of pain. I was anxious for a doctor to arrive and take a look at his leg.

The surgery was scheduled for seven o'clock that morning, but I knew things would move slowly especially if there were any critical patients who needed immediate attention. I said my prayers and thought of what a miracle it was that I had found my brother. I realized this was what my dream had been telling me. He had cried out for my help and somehow I'd heard him. Against all odds, God had brought me to my brother.

CHAPTER SIX

Around 7:30 in the morning the head surgeon arrived. He was prepared to tell my brother the worst. He would be taking off his leg, and my brother, like so many others, would plead and beg for the doctor not to do it. I'd heard it all before. The doctor would tell Charles Harley he would learn to live with only one leg.

The doctor's manner was confident, but impersonal. He had grown hardened by working day after day with brutal war injuries. Yet, he stopped to chat along the way with a couple of the other soldiers and then stopped abruptly at the end of Charley's bed, pulled up the chart clamped on the end of the bed, and began to read.

Looking at me and then at what I'd carefully written on the chart he spoke in a rather gruff voice. "What is this?" Who authorized this treatment and why the outdated procedure of a mustard plaster? Young woman, I don't recognize you. I can see you are a nurse, but what are you doing in this annex? This boy's leg is infected and gangrene has set in. His leg has to come off!"

"Doctor, I'm his sister and I've been looking for him…"

"Well, never mind. Let's have a look at the leg." With that he flipped back the sheet and gently raised the mustard plaster. "I don't believe this. I saw this young man's leg yesterday morning and I knew it needed to come off then, but I decided to give him one more day to get used to the idea. It is not an easy task cutting off a man's leg, but when it needs to be done to save his life, it must be done."

"Yes, I know, Doctor. And yes, I'm an American nurse serving here in the main hospital. This is my brother, Private Charles Harley Kingsley.

About the mustard plaster I can explain. It seemed to be the best option to try and I had to do something. I didn't mean to interfere, but I couldn't just stand around and let a doctor cut off my brother's leg."

"Nurse, quit acting like a dim-witted female and know that you did exactly what you should have. I don't know why I didn't think of it myself. Sometimes the old remedies are better than our more modern methods. The plasters have drawn out most of the infection. Young lady, your action has saved your brother's leg. Now it would be best to continue the treatment and anytime you want to work in the annex let me know. We are understaffed over here and we need all the help we can get."

"Doctor, would it be possible for me to be assigned to take care of my brother until he is out of danger and through his convalescence?"

"I think that could be arranged since you're already assigned to this hospital. I'll speak to your supervisor right away."

"What is your name Nurse?"

"My name is Melinda Ann Kingsley, Sir."

With a grin on his face the doctor exclaimed, "Private Charles Harley Kingsley, you're one lucky doughboy. We will be shipping you back to the United States before long. Now you better thank your sister. It was her knowledge of an old-time remedy that saved your leg. I will be telling this story for some time to come."

The Doctor leaned down closer to my brother and with a very serious tone in his voice. "You'll limp for a time and will need to use a cane, but after a while you will be able to walk without it and maybe even dance again!"

Those were beautiful words to both Charley and me. At that moment my brother, with tears in his eyes, tried to sit up and salute the doctor. "Thanks, Doctor. This is the best news I've had in weeks!"

"Come here, Sis!" He reached up and grabbed me with both arms and pulled me down, giving me a warm hug. He was still weak, but totally happy and at peace.

It took several days for the swelling to go down and the redness to fade. When the infection had cleared he had surgery to set the bones in his leg. I was there when he was sedated, holding his hand. He was so grateful to know he would keep his leg, and soon would be going home that he gladly went into a peaceful sleep.

My request to work in the annex and care for my brother was granted. I would be able to look after Charley until he was shipped home. I, too, truly wanted to go back to America, to forget about this destructive war! So many British and French lives had been lost as well as many of our American troops. I was sick of war. It was not as I'd thought it would be. There was no glory in it. The posters portrayed something completely different. Instead, war was destruction, pain and innocent blood shed, and for what? They told us it would make a better world and it would put an end to all wars. If that was the truth, then it was worth being overseas and fighting for our country, but only time would tell.

When Charley was discharged from the hospital, he wanted to return to his outfit. But that was out of the question. He was still limping badly so his request was denied, which I was sure it would be. He was scheduled to be shipped home soon. The Armistice was officially signed on November 11, 1918 at eleven o'clock a.m.! That was a time for great rejoicing. Europe was free of the oppressor, but much of it was in ruins. There were many American soldiers awaiting transport to our beloved country, but due to things moving slowly we were sure we would not be returning home immediately.

CHAPTER SEVEN

Though Charley had been discharged, I was still volunteering at the Annex so he stayed with me. Each day we took walks over the grounds, first with me pushing him around in the wheelchair and then later using his cane.

One day when we were in the Annex resting, one of his Army buddies came for a visit. A big strong man name Jake. When Charley saw him he was delighted.

"By golly, Jake, it's good to see you! Can you stay awhile? When are you guys shipping out? Have they told you?"

"Who knows? You know how the Army works. Everything takes more time than they plan. Our unit hasn't received any orders, yet! Oh, by the way, buddy, I brought you something I carved, a cane from a wooden propeller of one of those crashed German planes. The metal knob is from the cockpit of the same plane.

"Well I'll be, Jake. How did you know that's just what I need? Look! It fits me perfectly!"

"Good, it's just a little something to remind you of me."

I do believe that gift was one of the best things Charley could have received. When he pulled himself up out of the wheelchair he stood taller and began to limp less.

When Jake was ready to leave he grabbed my brother, shook his hand and gave him a warm hug. "Best of luck, buddy, hope to see you again someday. Take care of yourself Charles Harley, and that sister of yours. She's a pretty smart gal."

Since the Army was not moving troops home as fast as we had hoped, we decided to cable our parents. When Charley was missing in action the Army had notified the family, but there was no mention of his being wounded. On the way to the cable office, Charley spoke to me. "Melinda Ann, I want to ask you one thing. Will you please not tell our parents about my leg injury? I don't want any of the family to know I have been wounded or how serious it was. They'll carry-on something awful. Promise me, won't you?"

"Of course, you can trust me. I won't tell them anything. Besides, by the time we get home you'll be walking just fine."

There were at least a hundred American military people hanging around the cable office. We knew it was a good idea to send word home, but it was hopeless, so we gave up and returned to the hospital. I did cable them later that week. The fact that we were together was all that mattered to me.

It occurred to both of us how quiet it was now that the war was over. For the first time in several years there was no artillery fire in France. The countryside was peaceful.

CHAPTER EIGHT

While we were still in France, Charles Harley received mail from home. In one letter Mother mentioned that Aunt Ginny still wanted to breed horses like the Kingsley ancestors did. We had heard it all before. It had always been Aunt Ginny's dream to be like our Great-great-grandmother Felice Stewart Kingsley. She had wanted to have the best line of horses in the state of Virginia and so did Aunt Ginny. Our Aunt Ginny was an excellent rider and knew good horse stock when she saw it. Mother's letter gave us food for thought. What if we could find that special breed of horse?

"Charley, do you remember the portrait of Great-great-grandmother Felice with her hand resting on the side of her beautiful prize horse? It was hanging at the top of the grand staircase at home. I was just thinking maybe we could make Aunt Ginny's dream come true."

Charley's eyes brightened. "Sure, I remember the painting, and do you have the same idea I do? I've been thinking we could look around Europe for that special breed of horse. Since there has been a war, horses have been used by all sides. My question is how would we begin and where?"

"Oh, I don't know, but I've been thinking about this. I've asked around and was told that many fine breeds of horses were saved by the French farmers. They were stabled in a forested section south of the major seaport of Bordeaux. No one seems to know if these horses are still there or not, but it is worth a try."

"I'm for it, Sis. Let's make arrangements to get there as soon as possible. There isn't any sense of us waiting around here any longer. It could be months before we're shipped home."

To make a long story short, we did make arrangements to visit this lovely place south of Bordeaux. We found no horses that looked like the one we remembered in the painting. These horses were heavy harness coach horses. They were big animals weighing 1,200 to 1,400 pounds and at least 16 hands high. We were disappointed but not surprised, so we returned to Nancy.

Several nights later we were sharing a light supper when the thought occurred to me that we were looking in the wrong place. "Charley, what have we been thinking? Our great-great-grandparents came to America from England, not France. It's only logical that they brought their fine breed of horses from there. Don't you agree?"

My brother became excited. "You've got it, Melinda Ann! Now, all we have to do is some tall talking to convince our superiors that we need a pass to make another trip, and this time to England."

"But we won't have to do that, our orders came today. Our troop ship will not be leaving for home until after February, so that gives us plenty of time to get to England and return. I've never been so excited in all my life. Wouldn't it be great fun to actually find that special horse?"

"That's great news! It might be a shot in the dark, but we have to try. I'll get us a ride to Cherbourg and from there we can book passage on a small ship to cross the English Channel." We really had no idea what breed of horse we were looking for, but we did know what the horse looked like. We also knew the main reason horses were brought to Virginia from England was their strength and ability to jump fences during the fox hunts. We were looking for a refined English breed.

As Charley and I talked, we realized how much we both wanted to bring the former Kingsley line of horses back to Virginia.

Before we left for England we talked about our ancestors, our Great-great-grandmother Felice, born in Scotland, and her husband, Edward Philip Kingsley, born in England. We imagined them boarding a ship and leaving England with their prize horses located below somewhere in the hold of the ship. As the story was told to us, Felice was a horsewoman and tough as leather – strong-willed and independent. She was raised on a large estate with horses. Her family wasn't poor by any means. They said she learned to sit a horse when she was only three. When she was grown she met an English gentleman named Kingsley and they were married. Both had dreams of going to the new world to build a home and raise a family.

Since both families were rather well-off there wasn't any problem financially. Mr. Kingsley sold most of his holdings in England and deposited a large amount of gold in a London bank. She, on the other hand, was given a large dowry. Some of the gold was used to transport her horses to the new world, and much was used to purchase property. They bought land in Virginia, built the Kingsley plantation and raised horses. From the first time I heard this story I was fascinated and wanted to learn more about our family's history, and about this strong willed female ancestor.

When we arrived in England we noticed the lack of young and middle-aged men. We saw mostly women, elderly men and little children. A whole generation had been wiped out. It was heart breaking to look into the faces of these women who had suffered so much loss. They had been robbed of the lives they had dreamed about. Most of them had lost members of their family. Yes, this bloody fight was over and they were grateful, but their generation had been deeply affected. It would take England a long time to recover.

We wondered how many breeding farms were still left in England after the war. On the first farms we visited the horses we saw were not up to Virginia breeding standards. We visited several more and in one not too far from London, we finally found and purchased our stallion. He was a beauty weighing about 1,300 pounds and standing a proud 16 hands high. He was full of spirit and we knew he would not be easy to transport to America, but we had to try. That's when we met Mick O'Leary, a horse trainer.

This would begin a new chapter in our lives. Mick was from Ireland, but stationed in England during the war. He was a true Irishman, full of energy, spunky, and witty. We liked him at once and hired him to stay with us and our horse until we reached Virginia. He was eager to come to America.

In fact, it was Mick who informed us about the stallion we had bought. "Well my darlin's, you've hired the right man! Now let me be a fillin' you in about this prize horse of yours. You see this breed is what is known as a thoroughbred. These fine animals were bred to have powerful lungs and strong legs for jumpin'. And I'm a tellin' ya' all these horses are traced back to three mighty famous stallions. Darley Arabian, Godolphin Barb and Byerly Turk. This is how it was in the late 1600's and early 1700's. The European breeders crossed their own horses with these three stallions to become thoroughbreds."

We appreciated the information. Now all we had to do was get the horse back to the States, then we would be able to fulfill Aunt Ginny's dream. We were pleased and confident that we had a great stallion.

Neither Charley nor I had saved much money during the war, so we did as I had been instructed by our father. I had carried the letter he had provided which would allow me to draw out some of the family money held in the English bank. The Kingsley name opened many doors to us in London, from the president of the bank to high society, all of which impressed us little. All we could think of was boarding ship in February, crossing the Atlantic, and arriving at the plantation in Virginia with this magnificent horse. It would be a fine homecoming after all!

CHAPTER NINE

Well, it didn't happen in February! We were detained another two months, but on a hazy April morning in 1919, we were assigned to the troop ship USS Dan Patch which was docked at Brest, France. We made our way slowly up the gangplank with hundreds of other soldiers and nurses. I pushed Charley up on deck, in a monster of a wheelchair. We could feel the damp air and smell the sea around us. We were all crowded together, but no one seemed to mind. We were homeward bound!

The one thing that pleased all of us was that the ship had good speed, and if we had fair weather we would dock in New York Harbor on time! There were a lot of healthy able-bodied men on board as well as a number of injured men. The most critical were left in Europe until they were able to travel home.

Each day, I got my exercise, pushing Charley around in that wooden monster of a wheelchair. I had to use all my strength to handle it. He enjoyed being able to be out on deck. His pride didn't get the best of him. In fact, I think he rather liked having me pushing him about.

Happy day! When we entered the New York Harbor every able-bodied person moved to the rail to get a view of the regal lady. I thought it might capsize the ship, or at least tilt it a little! When we saw the Statue of Liberty, there was silence at first and then a wild cheer went up. We were so glad to see our homeland again.

Charley sat with tears in his eyes and proceeded to say, "Sis, that lady standing on Liberty Island has welcomed hundreds of people since it was given to us by France. She stands for what we believe in, freedom for all people. Now that we have fought this Great War, there will be peace in our time."

"Yes, brother, let it be the last war."

As I stood gazing at the harbor I became aware of many little boats blasting their horns. There were hundreds of people waiting for our ship to dock. The warehouse windows were loaded with people leaning out waving and shouting. "Welcome Home!" Many on board the ship had loved ones waiting for them, but some of the others like us, would not have anyone to greet them.

We weren't upset that our family wouldn't be there. We were just eager to see the unloading of our prize stallion. After all the Army personnel left the ship, a few of us remained to see the animals unloaded. When they opened some lower doors, they let down a wide plank ramp, and out came the horses with their trainers. Each horse had a short, bright colored blanket covering from the base of the neck to the rump. Each animal held his head high and virtually pranced down the ramp. We spotted our stallion moving proudly with Mick O'Leary. Mick looked like he was leading the prize horse in the English Derby. There were a few mules in the group all tied together and making a lot of protest noises. They were just as stubborn as always, kicking up their heels and causing a fuss. I think it was the brightly colored uniformed band, playing tunes like, *When Johnny Comes Marching Home, Over There,* and other lively tunes that made the horses show off. And the mules…well, who knows what a mule is thinking?

We were excited to see Mick and our stallion. As soon as the animals were unloaded, Mick went off to find a boarding stable where our horse could stay a few days, because we had to wait a few days until a train with horse car was available. All we wanted was to go home and the quicker the better, but since we had to stay around a while we were glad to have Mick to take care of things. That left Charley and me free to see some of the city, especially the theater district, the place he would like to call home.

Before we left the ship, we became aware of a large banner stretched out at the end of the gangplank, but we were unable to see what it said until we were almost under it. What a surprise!

"Sis, do you see that? We are all invited to the Vanderbilt mansion in New York City for a lawn party, a picnic with entertainment!" This invitation was for all the men and women on the ship who had no family to welcome them home. That was us!

"Melinda Ann, I was in New York City before the war, and I saw the outside of this mansion. It was fenced-in and no one was allowed on the grounds. These people are rich. They own Fifth Avenue, from 51st Street to 58th Street. We might as well go see what it's all about." You can imagine our excitement!

But first, there was a parade! Before we went to the picnic, all the disabled men and their nurses were asked to ride in Ford motor car busses. We were taken to the center of the parade site. The able-bodied men marched proudly through the streets of the city. The ticker tape and confetti rained down from the buildings on both sides and into the eyes and mouths of the people. Some of the nurses joined the men in the parade. They marched with their heads held high. In our bus, we watched as the crowd went wild with shouts of, "Welcome home, welcome home!" Then the band began to play and the people joined in singing *Over There*. We were all happy to be home!

When we reached the Vanderbilt mansion we found the gates wide open with many soldiers wandering through the huge mansion and the grounds. They were amazed and awed by the size of the place. There were servants walking around with trays full of drinks and delicious food. Soon we came upon a buffet table that stretched at least a block long. It was filled with food of all kinds. I did not know I was so hungry until I smelled the meat cooking on an outdoor spit, and an enormous cast iron pot of red beans boiling away. Just like home! These people were prepared and we appreciated the "good eats," as one young country boy announced.

After a while, Charley was tired of me pushing him around in his wheelchair and I certainly was, so he suggested I take a walk while he sat in his chair reminiscing with some of the other men. I hung around awhile listening to their conversation.

"Say, buddy, how did you wind up in one of these chairs? Guess you're pretty lucky to still have both of your legs. I lost mine taking Vauquois Hill!" Well, that opened up a whole subject for Charley to explore. I'm sure he shared his experiences on the battlefield and off. He was a true storyteller and people loved hearing his vibrant voice. As the men listened to each other they smoked, chewed tobacco and spit in the brass cuspidors.

As I moved among the soldiers I stopped, smiled, and shared in their conversations. They spoke of the battles they had fought and won, of fallen comrades, and of course, the European women. They spoke of the wine of France and the girls they had left behind, but all agreed it was great to be in America and to be free!

Some of the women civilians were dressed in their war-time best, and the war nurses gathered around them and shared what had taken place while they were overseas. The New York women asked questions about France and how the women looked and dressed. They were curious about how those women had survived in the middle of a war.

After a time, I could not stand anymore talk of war and decided it was time to return to Charley, when a young woman approached me.

"Hi! You're Nurse Melinda Ann Kingsley, aren't you? I met your brother in the hospital in Nancy and I saw you there with him. I was to assist the surgeon who was going to remove his leg. I understand he kept his leg, thanks to you!"

"Yes, I'm Melinda Ann. I'm surprised you recognized me."

"That doctor never tired of telling your story. He was quite impressed with your belief in an old-fashioned procedure and admired your confidence and determination. Say, what are you planning to do now that the war is over? Are you going to continue your nursing career? Personally, I've had enough of nursing. I'm going home to find a decent man, get married and raise a bunch of kids. All I want to do is stay home for the rest of my life!"

"To tell you the truth, I haven't thought about it. I don't want to get married, that's for sure, and I certainly don't want to settle down and live in Virginia all my life. No! I want to travel first, and then perhaps take up nursing later. I like to help people and I want to learn more about nursing. I guess I'm just caught in this profession. I really like what I do. I hated that bloody war, but in peacetime I would be quite content working in a hospital."

The woman continued, "What do you think is going to happen to these men? So many of them came right off the farm and were sent overseas. Now that they've seen the big cities and the world, do you think they will be willing to go back to their old lives? I don't think so. Things are changing all around us and we are the new generation. While we were in Europe I heard about the terrible flu epidemic here. I guess they haven't had it easy during the war either. I'm not eager to return to my family because I got a letter saying my baby sister has died, and I know my parents are taking it pretty hard, so it is going to be rough when I get there. How about you? Did your family suffer any loss?"

"I don't know. I haven't received a letter from them in a long time." Then I thought about our mother and how weak she was when I left so it was possible she had sickened and died. Talking about this I became quite anxious to go home.

Then some officers called our attention to what was to happen next. It was 1:00 p.m. when we were all ushered to one of the lawn areas and asked to sit down because Mr. Vanderbilt wanted to speak to us. He came out looking rather handsome. With his booming voice he began to speak, "I'm proud to be an American and to open my home to all of you returning men and women. You did a great job over there and your country thanks you. Now for a surprise, those of you who wish go into the foyer of my home and proceed through the double doors into the ballroom. Please enjoy a dance given in your honor, and by the way, I have arranged with Florenz Ziegfeld to bring his beautiful showgirls to dance with you boys! Now go and enjoy yourselves!"

The able-bodied men rushed ahead of us, and the other men in wheelchairs and on crutch followed, as best they could. As we entered the large elegant ballroom, an orchestra was in place and playing. This event could not have been more disappointing to Charley. He looked very sad as he sat in his wheelchair, watching what he loved to do. He yearned to get up and dance with those lovely young ladies. They were beautifully dressed in long pastel evening gowns. They had no stage makeup on. They were fresh and natural looking, like girls attending a high school dance.

The enlisted men headed for the showgirls, but there were a few officers who asked the nurses to dance. I'm sure the ones who did felt a bit self-conscious in their nurse's uniforms. I was asked several times but declined. I decided it was hard enough for Charley to watch without me running off. So I remained by his side like many of the other nurses with their charges. Some men on crutches leaned against the side walls while others stood in the back of the ballroom captivated by the scene before us. There were many uniformed soldiers and women twirling around and around on the exquisite ballroom floor. It was fun seeing so many couples dancing to the music.

As I stood behind Charley's chair I watched in awe. A woman was walking around the back of the room, shaking hands and speaking to several of the soldiers. As she came closer we realized it was the famous Mary Pickford, a motion-picture actress who won fame as "America's Sweetheart." She smiled, took Charley's hand in hers, and thanked him for the service he had done for the country. When the music and the dancing stopped we heard Fanny Brice on stage telling jokes and acting like a big-mouth brat. Later she became famous for this act as Baby Snooks. She was very funny and made us all laugh.

When the dancing started again and an officer came by and told the men in the wheelchairs and crutches to follow him through the double doors. Mr. Vanderbilt had another announcement he wanted to make to the men who were unable to dance. I felt unhappy being asked to leave the beautiful ballroom and especially since the orchestra was playing, *Peg of My Heart*. Once outside in the foyer Mr. Vanderbilt stood on the first landing of the main staircase and delivered his second surprise.

"Ladies and Gentlemen, it is my pleasure to announce to you that you are invited to attend Barnum and Bailey's Greatest Show on Earth. Your buses are waiting!" For a moment we were speechless, but then a wild cheer went up. We applauded and whistled madly. It was all so unbelievable!

CHAPTER TEN

THE GREATEST SHOW ON EARTH

At the circus there were a number of volunteers waiting to guide us around the grounds and into the big top. There was a medium sized tent where the sideshows were performed. A man dressed in a white suit and white straw hat stood on a platform waving his cane and shouting at the top of his lungs. "Step right up, come see the show. See things that will amaze you! The Spider Lady, the Strong Man, the Tattooed Man, the Bearded Lady, and the Egyptian Dancer! Come one, come all!" Then he looked down at the children who were standing about watching and shooed them away.

I wasn't interested so I asked one of the volunteers to take Charley inside. The smell of popcorn was driving me nuts. I wondered how long it had been since I'd had real hot buttered popcorn. I followed my nose and soon came to a large red and gold popcorn machine where the vender was scooping up the fluffy white popped kernels. My mouth was watering for just a little taste. While I waited in line I looked at the big machine with its big red rimmed bicycle-type wheels and couldn't wait to get my popcorn.

Standing near the smaller tent were some open booths with men shouting for the folks milling around to come and play their game. "Toss the ball at the milk bottles, play the penny toss, shoot the tin ducks and win a prize." All the people were having fun and were in good spirits!

When the sideshows were over, the boys on crutches came out and then those in wheelchairs, talking, joking, smiling, and laughing. The main show was in the big top, and once inside we could really see how enormous the tent was with rope riggings everywhere. The mingled scents of cotton candy, hotdogs, popcorn, fresh hay, sawdust, and the sweat of several hundred people mingling together was overwhelming, but also exciting!

Our group was led to a platform in front of the center ring. There was a ramp where we could safely push the wheelchairs in place and those on crutches had no problem getting to the wooden folding chairs.

The performance began with "The Spectacle," starting with a dazzling parade of elephants, glamorous women in scanty glittering costumes, handsome men jugglers, fancy prancing horses, trapeze artists, and of course, the clowns.

Our seats were where we could see all three rings, so when the Ringmaster in his red cut-away coat with tails, black tie, and black riding pants with high shinning black boots stepped into the middle ring, we all shouted. He lifted his megaphone and looked our way. "Ladies and Gentlemen, welcome to the Greatest Show on Earth! The circus family wants to dedicate this performance to our gallant American troops. Welcome home, boys! Now let us stand and sing our beloved national anthem!"

All were on their feet applauding wildly. The circus band broke into a rousing rendition of *The Star Spangled Banner*. As we began to sing, a huge American flag was lowered from the ceiling. As I looked around I could see there wasn't one person who didn't sing with tears in their eyes and great pride in their hearts.

All three rings became alive with activity. Precision-trained horses galloped swiftly in one circle while standing riders leaped from one horse to another. In another bears danced on balls with their trainer's encouragement. In yet another a lion tamer put his head into the mouth of a big animal, and above all the trapeze high flyers did leaps and somersaults in the air, scaring us all.

My two favorite acts were: Lillian Leitzel, who performed her world-famous aerial stunt, and The Flying Wallendas. Miss Leitzel was pulled up close to the top of the tent on a trapeze swing, and standing on a small platform, inserted her right wrist into a rope sling, where she began to swing her body around and over as many times as possible. She broke her own record of 100 by doing 101 turns, as we all counted with the Ringmaster. When she returned to the floor she received a cape over her right shoulder and appeared to be in pain, but when her foot touched the floor she turned to the audience and raised her left arm and smiled while giving several majestic bows.

The Flying Wallendas performed without a net beneath them. They had developed a spectacular high wire act. The seven Wallendas stood on each other's shoulders in a 4-2-1 formation and proceeded to go from one side of the tent to the other. As they started across on the wire I held my breath and when they reached the other side everyone cheered.

Very few of us had ever seen a big circus like this and it was an experience I would never forget. Our group was the last to leave the big top. I noticed it was pretty quiet except for some of the circus carneys who had started sweeping up and getting ready for the next show. For our first day home it was a most exciting time. The busses took us back to the Vanderbilt mansion and then on to Grand Central Station. We were tired but happy. The time had come for us to say good-bye. Soon we would be boarding trains traveling to all parts of this glorious country of ours.

CHAPTER ELEVEN

We were at Grand Central Train Station in New York City with thousands of soldiers among regular passengers milling about. We waited upstairs for the trains to be made up. Charley was tired after standing up so long. He was using only his cane and now because there was no room for a wheelchair I put his duffle bag and my carrying case on the floor near one of the station entrances to make a place for us to rest. The station was teeming with people and you couldn't see past the person sitting or standing next to you. The heated building caused everyone to sweat and tempers to rise. Babies cried, people talked and yelled at each other.

When Mick O'Leary found us, he took us to the loading platform. He said the animal boxcars were loaded with mules and horses and were ready to be connected to our train going to Virginia. That's when we heard our stallion. He was alone in one of the cars because he was too high-spirited to share any space with another horse. He was kicking up his hindquarters and then trying to rear up to his full height protesting his confinement. Mick entered the side door of the boxcar because he was the only person who could get near the horse. He was so attached to the animal that he refused to leave him for fear someone might mistreat the stallion. Knowing how Mick worked with the horse made me think about how Aunt Ginny might deal with such an animal. She was excellent with horses, and had tamed a few wild ones in her time.

From New York it would take two days to reach Virginia. Some people stood in the aisle, and some sat three to a seat while others sat on the floor.

No one minded. Most passengers were soldiers and were content to suffer any discomfort just to get home.

Charley found us a seat where we could crowd in. "Charley, I want to go home just for a short visit, mostly to see Aunt Ginny's face when she realizes the horse is hers. I've no intention of remaining there. Mother and I don't get along and Birdie hates me. Then there are our brothers, Edward and Edwin. Who knows what they think."

"Sis, don't be silly. They'll all welcome you home with open arms. Of course, I don't know about Birdie, but I'm sure Mother wants to see her only daughter as much as she wants to see me. And Dad will be delighted to see you. I'm sure he is quite proud of you. And Aunt Ginny is going to be so surprised she'll probably hug you 'till you faint! As far as Edward and Edwin, well, I was never close to either one of them. But I do remember how they both relied on you when they were young."

"That's right, I was more like a mother to them than our mother. Say, how are you going to handle the situation about your leg? I know you're worried about how they are going to treat you. Look how strong you are now! Your injury will not ever keep you from anything you want to do. And besides, you don't plan to stay at the plantation anyway. Why should you care what they think?"

"Well, Sis, if I limp a little it should not embarrass the brave Kingsley family! They really don't know how close I came to losing my leg. I'm more worried about the grief I caused Mother and Father by running off the way I did. For years they had built up their hopes for me to take over the plantation. When I refused I know they were terribly disappointed."

"Charley, I hope by now our parents have forgiven you about the past."

Before we left France we had purchased a gift for mother and father, a lovely glass framed "Souvenir De France", bought in Paris after the War. It consisted of two exquisitely embroidered flags, American and French that waved proudly against a field of beautiful French lace which was surrounded by embroidered vines and ribbon roses. Other gifts for the family were a lovely music box for Birdie, a sturdy leather carrying case for Edward, the German helmet and an American flag from the casualty clearing station for Edwin, and a riding crop for Aunt Ginny. We were so excited about the gifts and could hardly wait to present them. We knew after Aunt Ginny saw her horse nothing would be more pleasing to her than a riding crop.

"Melinda Ann, I think you're right! I believe we did well in choosing the gifts we did for the family, but the greatest gift of all was the stallion. I know Father will approve even if we did have to get money out of the London bank. I've been imagining this family reunion all morning and wondering how Aunt Ginny will react. Sis, I know it's going to be a great surprise. Maybe it will breathe new life into the Kingsley Plantation. It could help the whole family start living again! It is possible that Aunt Ginny can reclaim the past by being the best horse breeder in Virginia.

"Yes, it's a dream for her, and knowing Aunt Ginny she might just be able to pull it off! I certainly hope so! Our Great-great-grandmother Felice would be proud if she were here to see it."

CHAPTER TWELVE

The next day the train continued to move through the country side; I sat quietly thinking. Then I heard a shout from the conductor. "Ladies and Gentleman, our next stop is Roanoke! Any of you boys who want to get off the train and march into the city with the Army Band, leave your bags on board and you can pick them up later. It's about time to detrain."

I was glad to be this close to home, about an hour from the train station! The city is located on the Roanoke River between the Blue Ridge and the Allegheny mountains. It's about 165 miles southwest of Richmond. About a mile from the station I looked out the window and read a sign, **Virginia and Tennessee Railroad Depot – Built 1882.**

"By golly, Sis, aren't you excited?

"Not really. The only reason I want to go home at all is to be with you and to see Aunt Ginny when we present her with the stallion. I want to see Father too. But I'm not eager to see Mother or Birdie. I'm sure their feelings toward me have not changed. Seeing the twins is all right but I seem to have drifted away from them since we got older."

Charley looked at me like he didn't quite understand my reluctance to be with the family but dismissed asking me any questions. As the train slowed to a stop he began.

"We need to get off the train. The conductor said they had received word that the streets are already lined with people waving flags and cheering. Melinda Ann, don't look at me like that. I'm as able-bodied as any of these men. Besides, I know our family will be there and I don't want to disappoint them. Come on, Sis, let's join the group!"

"Charley dear, you aren't really going to join them with your leg as sore as it has been, are you? I'm still your nurse and I do not advise it! It will be too difficult for you to walk that far!"

"Excuse me! You may be my sister and my nurse, but you're not in charge of me. I can make up my own mind. You see those men behind us? They are in worse shape than I am and they're going to march and I'm going to join them. I'm going to sling my cane over my shoulder like I'm carrying my rifle as a true son of Virginia. Come on Sis! You've been sitting long enough and you're stronger than most of us. This Virginia air will do you good!"

As we were preparing to leave the train one of the officers stood up and gave one last order. "Doughboys of the United States of America let us step off the train and form our ranks. Let's make the folks proud of us, so form your lines straight, men. Color Guards go up in front of the Army Band. Troops fall in behind. As we get to the edge of town the band will strike up, *Over There*. So all of you sing it loud and clear! You men and women are a credit to your country. Welcome home!" The men began to scramble, pulling on their uniform jackets, straightening their ties, wiping off their shoes, getting ready to detrain. Watching the men get off the train and form their lines made me so proud of our Virginia fighting men. Never had I been more proud of Charles Harley. He looked handsome in his uniform, standing tall, and marching with head held high and chest out. I noticed that so many of the soldiers who were suffering earlier now seemed to have forgotten their aches and pains. They all marched in step with renewed energy, and I was right in there with them. We marched into the station and saw the hundreds of people waiting for us, family, friends, and strangers.

Looking further ahead I spotted the whole Kingsley family cheering and waving their little American flags. As we got closer I saw Edward and Father joining our ranks and marching proudly beside us. The band played louder and the people sang and cheered, "Welcome home, welcome home!"

We were gathered into the arms of our family, Mother, Father, Aunt Ginny, Edward and Birdie surrounded us. There was no sign of Edwin, that scoundrel of a brother of ours. Where was he? Did I dare ask? I dismissed the thought from my mind and began greeting each one with a kiss and hug. All of them were eager to talk at once. Mother looked tired and was very pale. Father looked as strong and robust as ever. He was slapping Charley on the back with one arm and hugging me with the other. Aunt Ginny seemed pleased to see us too. I couldn't wait to tell her how much I loved her. I knew I had grown-up since I left home. She had tried to help me when I was growing up, but I didn't realize it at the time. I think she actually loved me, and just maybe even more than my own mother.

I made up my mind to not hold any hostile feeling toward Birdie or my mother. Time had passed and I was bringing Charles Harley home with me. I promised myself, I would let bygones be bygones. The past was the past and it was a new time. I was home in Virginia and that was all that mattered.

Seeing all the family gathered around us made me happy. Looking at each one I realized how much I really had missed them, no matter what our differences they were still my family.

Looking at Birdie closely I saw the she was down-right beautiful with her lovely olive complexion, sparkling brown eyes and her long brown hair twisted in a bun on the back of her neck. I noticed she wore a fashionable gray walking suit with a stylish hat. The gray suede boots added just the right touch to her outfit. I realized she wasn't at all behind the times. I did wonder what Mother thought about Birdie wearing modern fashions rather than designs of the late 1800's. Mother did not seem to notice – she was quiet.

Hearing a repeated car horn blaring I turned around and saw some man in a fancy new light blue Locomobile with stylish running boards. The man was trying to get our attention. When I looked closer at him, I saw it was Edwin. He was sitting in the driver's seat grinning like a Cheshire cat. The minute I recognized him I ran toward the car calling out. "Edwin! Edwin, what a surprise! You certainly got my attention. Now I know why you were not with the rest of the family. You've gotten yourself a fancy new car. Now level with me, who does this car really belong to, you or Father?"

I slid into the front seat beside him. "How in the world did you ever get Father to buy one of these contraptions? I know you didn't buy it and I'm sure Mother hates it. I'm certain she would have preferred a horse and carriage to this smelly noisy automobile. I really like these new machines, and the faster they go, the better I like it! One of these days I'm going to drive one myself!"

Edwin just smiled and let out a disapproving laugh. "That will never happen! Southern ladies will never drive a car. It's a man's job and not lady-like."

"Don't tell me that because when I was in France some of the best ambulance drivers were women and nobody seemed to notice."

I couldn't believe it. We had not been together more than five minutes and we were arguing, already. At that point Charley came toward us. As he came near the automobile, I noticed the slight limp, but if Edwin did he said nothing about it.

"Well, if it isn't my kid brother! How are you doing, Bud?"

Edwin ignored me, sat up straight in his seat and laughed.

"Hi, big brother! You do remember me, your exceptionally handsome younger brother, at your service, Sir!"

When the family converged on the car, Charley stood on the running board and began speaking. "It is time for our big surprise. All of you, except for Aunt Ginny, stay here and watch what happens. Come on Aunt Ginny, let's go up on the platform, I want to show you something. I believe I can hear him thrashing about trying to get out of the boxcar. Melinda Ann, ask Mick to bring the animal out so we can all see him."

I called out to Mick. "Mick, are you ready in there? Bring him out man, bring him out!" At that moment Mick slid the doors of the boxcar wide open and led the stallion outside and down the wide ramp. The family had held back, but when they saw the magnificent horse coming down the ramp they rushed forward. Aunt Ginny stood on the platform as Mick brought the stallion closer to her. She was almost face-to-face with the horse as Mick stood proudly holding the reins. Then, Charley and I stepped up on the platform and presented the horse to her.

We were so excited and happy! Charley was holding Aunt Ginny's arm and keeping her close to him for fear the horse would try to bolt or rear up. "Aunt Ginny, we believe this horse is the special animal that will make your dreams come true! He is full of spirit and hates to be confined, as you just heard. He's yours. We hope he will be the one to start the new line for The Kingsley Family Stables!

Aunt Ginny stared in disbelief and clearly didn't know what to say to us. Standing in the bright sunlight the stallion looked magnificent with his shinny sleek brown coat, and his long reddish-brown mane whipping in the wind. Holding his head high he looked like the champion he was.

We waited for our aunt to say something and when she did not, I couldn't stand it any longer. "Well, what do you think, isn't he a fine animal? Aunt Ginny, we hope you approve of our choice. He's somewhat wild, so please be careful."

Just as I said that the stallion reared up on his hind legs while his front legs pawed the air, scaring the people around us with his high pitched whinny and obvious disapproval of all the excitement going on around him. The automobile horns were blasting away, the Army band was playing loudly, and the people were yelling and milling around so it was no wonder the horse was upset. I knew we should have waited until things quieted down to unload the stallion, but we just couldn't wait any longer.
Seeing what was happening Charley yelled at Mick. "Get a better hold on him before he bolts! If he gets away we'll have a heck of a time getting him back!"

Mick was already holding the reins with all his strength and talking loudly in his Irish brogue to the horse, but it did nothing to calm the big fellow down. I was amazed at what happened next. Aunt Ginny approached the stallion quietly as she moved slowly toward him. I wondered what in the world she was thinking? She did not know this horse or what he was capable of doing. I yelled before I thought, "Aunt Ginny watch out!" Mick by this time, had gotten the horse's head down, and with his voice lowered he began stroking the animal on his slender neck. "Tick, tick – tick, tick – Come on big boy, calm down. It's old Mick here."

Showing no fear Aunt Ginny went down the steps and approached the stallion and he eyed her, pulling at the reins as she got closer. When she reached out and stroked his neck she spoke to him in soft gentle tones and almost whispered in his ear. He flicked his tail and reared part way up and, still watching her, he set his front hoofs down close beside her while he held his head high. When he saw Aunt Ginny wasn't afraid of him he cocked his head to one side and seemed to know she was a friend. Instead of rearing up again and pulling away from Mick he listened to Aunt Ginny, and as she stroked his neck he nuzzled her neck in return.

Watching Mick I could tell he was a bit amazed to see how she had gotten the horse's attention. Observing Aunt Ginny you could already see the devotion in her eyes for this animal. Mick beamed when he saw how the stallion and Aunt Ginny had regarded each other.

The grin on his face was one of merriment and it was quite evident he was attracted to Aunt Ginny the instant he became aware of her. I do believe if Aunt Ginny had had her riding clothes on she would have mounted that horse and rode him bareback all the way to the plantation.

"I really don't know what to say," Aunt Ginny stammered. "In my wildest dreams I never expected this. I have so many questions. Where did you purchase him, and does he have papers, where was he bred? Oh, I want to go home! I want to test him out on the track. Is he fast? Can he run? Is he a jumper? He looks like a champion. Oh, what are his blood lines? Yes, yes, I think he is a magnificent animal and perfect for breeding - my thanks to both of you!"

She asked so many questions we could not answer them all at once but there would be time when we got home. The rest of the family was surprised at our unusual gift. Everyone commented on it being so perfect and they agreed they had never seen Aunt Ginny so excited and happy.

Some people stood around watching our little drama, but when the excitement quieted down and the horse did not bolt, the people lost interest and shuffled away. The family must have been quite a sight as we piled into the automobile. Mother sat squeezed in between Edwin and Edward. Father climbed into the back seat and I sat on his lap next to Charley. Then Birdie got in the front seat and sat on Edward's lap. Aunt Ginny and Mick walked a ways behind the car leading the horse. Mick and Ginny were talking to each other nonstop and apparently getting along fine. Mick was in his traveling clothes and she was in a stylish tan colored walking suit wearing fancy suede high heeled shoes, which were surely not suitable for walking. Finally we convinced Aunt Ginny to get in the car so she sat in the back seat on Charley's lap. We were crowded but we were happy! After Aunt Ginny got into the car, Edwin directed Mick to a nearby horse stable where he could find proper transportation to the plantation for the stallion.

It would take us about an hour to get home but we didn't care because we were all talking at once and having a good time! Edwin was so proud of his driving ability and the fancy automobile that he had to show off and began acting like a tour guide. When we arrived at the turn leading to the Kingsley mansion he began. "All right folks, look this way as we enter the road leading to the Kingsley's humble abode. Observe the stately old oak trees and the smell of Virginia soil. There's no place like the good old South, a way of life that has been forgotten and lost by man, but not by our family. Observe the workers in the field. They are free men and women. We may pay the blacks lower wages than the whites, but that is the way things are done in the South."

He continued viciously. We don't allow them to drink from our public water fountains or eat in our local cafes or associate with white folks unless they are employed by them…but we let them fight for us and die for us. What I don't understand is, many black families have lost their sons in this terrible war and I believe they deserve equal rights with whites. They are just people like us and deserve every freedom we enjoy!"

Hearing his comments Father leaned forward and touched Edwin's shoulder. "Be quiet son. This is no time to talk politics. You'll upset your mother. We can have this kind of talk in the study after dinner when we are having our brandy and a smoke."

Edward piped up. "I don't agree – it's as good a time as any. The white man has always been superior and besides the blacks are used to hard work and their backs are stronger than ours, so why change things? We never owned slaves anyway so what does this kind of talk have to do with us?"

At this statement I thought Edwin was going to slug his twin brother and if Mother had not been seated between them, I am sure he would have. I knew how I felt on the matter. I'd seen black men wounded, and many had died as a result of their injuries. Their blood was as red as ours and their pain had been as great as any white man's I'd ever seen. These people had been loyal Americans and had fought gallantly, and as far as I was concerned all men were created equal. Birdie brought the whole subject to a halt. "This is supposed to be a happy day and I don't think it should be spoiled by this kind of talk."

As the house appeared in the distance, Edwin began again as our tour guide. "This is the famous Kingsley mansion, built in the late 1700's. It survived the Civil War and today stands as a monument to true Southern hospitality and traditions."

Now our mood turned from a serious vein to a lighter feeling, especially when we saw that the servants were waiting on the veranda and the front steps. They were joined by our neighbors and friends across the county.

Being on the plantation once again I realized it was one of the most beautiful and peaceful places I had ever seen. Although I had wanted to get away, I knew I'd missed being here more than I wanted to admit. Since the Civil War few changes had been made with the grounds and buildings. The mansion's four towering pillars and large veranda glistened white. The flower gardens and front lawn were exquisitely trimmed. The old weeping willow tree still stood at one corner of the house. It was there I had said farewell to my Grandmother Lilly, as she sat leaning against it. Another thing I remember about that day was seeing my mother and Aunt Ginny sitting on either side of her, holding each other's hands. It was a heartbreaking time for all of us, and it seems like it was only yesterday.

The old house welcomed Charley and me with its Southern charm as we were quickly ushered into the ballroom. What a pleasant surprise to be greeted with musicians playing, *When Johnny Comes Marching Home*. The music made everyone step lively as we moved from one group of friends to another. But we were starving so we moved as quickly as possible to the long buffet table where endless platters of food were temptingly arranged. There were serving people behind the buffet eager to fill our plates. Mother insisted that we wait until the dinner bell had been sounded.

In the center of this table sat the Kingsley glass punchbowl. Our name was etched on the silver rim and the bowl was painted with tiny delicate flowers on the outside. I was sure it contained some kind of liquor in a fruit punch. The bowl was a treasured object brought to this country from England by Great-great-grandmother Felice. I was told it had been presented to her on her wedding day.

I saw Mother inspecting the food table and the table decorations. Birdie was walking close behind her and watching every move she made. Mother turned to Birdie and asked, "Are all the arrangements for this evening taken care of? Let me know when all of our guests have arrived and I'll ring the dinner bell." The way she spoke sounded strange to me. Her voice had no feeling in it. It was dull sounding. Birdie knew I'd heard her. She looked at me, tilted her head in that haughty way of hers, and quickly left Mother and headed toward the kitchen. Mother just stood there looking bewildered as if trying to figure out what she was supposed to be doing.

Trying to be polite I turned to her, "Mother dear, everything is exquisitely beautiful. I know you arranged the flower decorations with particular care, and I appreciate it so much. It is good to be home!"

She was startled at what I said - as if trying to understand my words. Was she not hearing me or did she not quite comprehend? She stood looking at me like she was in a dazed condition - then she seemed to realize who she was talking to.

"Melinda Ann, I didn't do anything at all. Birdie wouldn't let me touch the table or the decorations. She is quite capable of seeing to all our needs. I don't do much of anything anymore."

Hearing this I knew Birdie must have taken control after I left and was managing the household. From the time I arrived at the train station, she had treated me a bit coolly but not with a lot of anger. She seemed to have mellowed some since I had been gone.

Keeping with southern tradition some of our guest had arrived earlier in the day. Most of the women would be changing into their evening flocks upstairs in one of the many bedrooms. I looked forward to wearing something different too.

Seeing we were not going to eat right away, I asked Mother if I could change my clothes and freshen up before we formally greeted our guests. She seemed confused but said. "No, I want everyone here to see you and your brother in your uniform. You may go to your room and freshen up while we change clothes but you stay in your uniform.

I didn't want to appear rude, but I felt tired and dirty from our long two day ride. I wanted a bath in the worse way! I wanted to slip into something more comfortable and more suited for a party. I didn't want to be quick about anything. I wanted to relax and take my time relishing being home. I went upstairs where I found a warm bath waiting. One of the servants had drawn a bath for me and it was delightful. Feeling clean once again I put on my uniform and didn't seem so bad. Sitting at the dresser I looked into the mirror as I brushed my hair and pulled it back into a bun…I didn't look too bad. The long brown curls were gone along with the large bow ribbon I once wore. I was now a grown mature woman.

My ankle-length dark blue shirt was wrinkled, but somehow my white long sleeved blouse had stayed clean. I pulled on my jacket and placed my nurses' cap squarely on the top of my head with great pride. I looked very much like the person my mother wanted to show off, trim and professional looking but not pretty and certainly no threat to any female present.

I knew I needed to hurry, but I wasn't looking forward to this ordeal and wished to put it off as long as possible. Considering myself in the mirror I was reminded of when I was working at the hospital in France. I'd been very capable and sure of myself then, but here it was different, I felt I was being controlled. Although I had been starving when we arrived my appetite had lessened and I just felt empty.

I had dreamed of being home, wearing a fine evening dress, attending a ball, and dancing throughout the night with some handsome gentleman! I did want to look pretty in a floor length gown, but to me that seemed impossible because I was so plain looking. I felt cheated, not because I wasn't pretty, but because I should have been allowed to wear an evening dress like the other ladies. If Mother wanted to show Charley and me off in our uniforms, so be it. When I thought about the whole situation realistically I knew it really didn't matter. I would wear my uniform because I was proud to be a nurse. And since Charley and I would both be wearing our uniforms it would make us both feel better.

Charley was upstairs and had been freshening up too. We walked down the hall to the top of the stairs. Meanwhile the rest of the family had changed into evening attire. We were all to make a grand entrance. I whispered to Charley, "Come on brother, its show time! Hold those shoulders back, stomach in, and your head high! Don't limp! We're on parade! Just look down on all of those folks looking up at us. I do believe we're being treated like royalty! What a laugh that is. I think Mother has always made too much of the role the Kingsley family plays in this community."

Hearing me say this Charley grabbed my arm, laughing slightly under his breath. "Sis, take my arm and down we go!"

Private Charles Harley and I, Army nurse Melinda Ann led the way slowly down the stairs looking quite military. Mother and Father were behind us as proud as peacocks in their best evening attire. They were followed by Aunt Ginny escorted by Edwin. I guess Mick had not been invited to the party. I suppose he was seen as hired help and not as a guest. I had to laugh when I thought of him being inside the house greeting our guests. He would have felt like a fish out of water.

When I looked over my shoulder I saw Aunt Ginny holding on to Edwin's arm as best she could. Aunt Ginny was smiling, laughing and talking more than I'd ever seen her. She was radiant that night. The funny thing was Edwin was almost skipping as he came down the stairs and Aunt Ginny was trying to keep up with him. He was grinning and flirting with all the eligible females in the crowd and the women loved it. He cut quite a figure in his handsome evening suit. All the young women seemed to be smitten by him even though to me he didn't look like the marrying kind at all.

Last coming down the stairs was Birdie escorted by Edward, and I will admit Edward and Birdie did make quite a striking couple. They were stately looking as they descended the long curved stairway. They could have stepped out of a picture book looking more like our ancestors than any of the rest of us. Edward was walking like a king, with his head held high and shoulders back, and beside him, Miss Birdie, clinging as close to his side as possible. It was obvious something was going on between them.

I often wondered why my twin brothers were so different. They are identical twins, handsome, jovial and friendly, but Edwin was always looking out for himself and cared little about what other people thought. At that moment, I wanted to grab him by his ear and send him spinning around like I used to do when we were children. I even considered a swift kick on his backside, but gave it up in the name of being a "Southern Lady". Edward was commanding and arrogant, but he was never out of control.

When we reached the bottom of the stairs the family moved through the crowd of well-wishers shaking hands and saying pleasantries. Looking around I noticed Mother and Aunt Ginny in their lovely modest gowns standing next to each other. Looking at them gave me the shivers, because they had never looked so much alike. Mother had applied some make-up so she was not as pale as she had been earlier. As I looked at them I couldn't help noticing that uneven smile of Aunt Ginny's. I wondered what had happened to her and I thought it was strange that I knew so little about my mother and Aunt Ginny's past. Neither one of them ever spoke much of their growing up years. They spoke of Great-grandmother Martha and Grandmother Lilly, but not about themselves.

CHAPTER THIRTEEN

It was shortly after midnight when our last guest left the homecoming party. All of us were eager to go to the stable and see Aunt Ginny's prize horse, so the family traipsed outside in the dark. The animal was storming about bucking and kicking in protest at being confined. He was causing such a fuss that even Mick was unable to quiet him. Soon we realized the stallion wasn't the only one who was agitated.

When Mick saw us, he came toward us with that bullish look of his. "I come here to America to see this great big country of yours, and I'm treated like a hired hand. Not that I be amindin' of course, but I would be obliged to taste some of that Virginia whiskey I've heard so much about!"

Well, Mick was a hired hand, but he was a true Irishman that liked his whiskey. He had been in England to purchase horses when he got caught in the war. He had proved to be a man who was loyal and trustworthy. I'd come to value Mick because he had integrity and he knew his job.

When Father heard Mick's remark he immediately came over to Mick. "Say, Mick, my man, let's you and me go into my study and have a drink or two while these people admire that big stomping horse."

Mick saw the invitation as one of trust and goodwill so he stepped up to Father. "Much obliged, Governor, I'd be honored to be sharin' in your company!" And off they went, arms draped over each other's shoulders like long lost friends. As they walked away, I really took a good look at Mick and thought he was about the same age as my Aunt Ginny. He looked to be about as tall as my father, reddish hair with graying temples, a close-cropped red beard with a touch of gray, and a bushy mustache. He had a freckled face with bright blue sparkling eyes. I noticed his shirt was about ready to pop open due to his bulging chest muscles. I knew if he could handle horses he had to be strong. He certainly loved animals. That's when it occurred to me that he and Aunt Ginny were a lot alike.

I've no idea how long Father shared his whiskey with Mick. The family had said their goodnights, so Charley and I left Aunt Ginny alone with her horse. Looking around as we left, I remember seeing that big horse nuzzling Aunt Ginny under her chin, as she fed him a lump of sugar. He was totally under her control. Now her dreams could come true and she could build the Kingsley stables up to where they had been before the Civil War. I was sure of it.

I could only imagine what it had been like when our Great-great-grandmother Felice originally began the Kingsley line of horses in the early 1800's before the war? And I couldn't help wondering how it would be in the future now under the direction of my Aunt Ginny and Mick O'Leary. Mick seemed right at home on the plantation. I was sure he would be a big part of my aunt's future plans.

When I climbed the stairs to my room I felt very tired and could hardly wait to fall into bed. I closed the door and slowly took off my uniform knowing it would be the last time I would be wearing it, and that made me sad. But I had to admit the thought of wearing regular clothes sounded pretty good to me.

I sat down at the dresser, combed out my hair and viewed myself in the mirror. It was true that I wasn't a beauty like the other women in my family, but I did have some good points. With my hair in a bun I did look older than my age, and that helped people take me seriously. My eyes are set wide apart with heavy lashes and full eyebrows. One good thing is that my nose fits my face, and my lips are wide and full showing my teeth when I smiled.

As a child I'd sat in front of my wardrobe mirror daydreaming endlessly of traveling, and being out in the world on my own. I had made up my mind that I would not be afraid of anybody or anything. I would push myself to the limits when I had to, but I was determined to not let life defeat me.

My old room had been changed, thanks to Birdie. The wardrobe closet had been moved and in its place was a modern dresser with a mirror hanging above it. I knew Birdie had been staying in this room because when I checked inside the wardrobe there were more clothes hanging there than I'd left. These were not fashions of the 1880's like Birdie used to wear, but elegant styles of modern dresses, skirts and blouses. Certainly Mother would not have approved of these clothes, but somehow they had been purchased. Since they were too small for me, I knew the clothes belonged to Birdie. I had learned overseas that I didn't need many clothes. Traveling as light as possible was necessary. I knew all my civilian clothes were dowdy and out of style, but that sort of thing didn't bother me. I would take care of the problem when the time came. If I traveled, a small bag would do nicely. I didn't need a big trunk which was so popular with most women.

When I finally dropped into bed I lay there looking up at the cream colored canopy hanging on the four-poster bed. Great-grandmother Martha's quilts and the feather pillows made me as comfortable as a queen. Turning my head I looked around the room. On either side of the bed there were low matching wood grained tables with porcelain lamps sitting on each one which Birdie had added. What once was my room had been rearranged by Birdie and I didn't like it.

I tried to fall asleep but my mind kept wandering. Aunt Ginny had been really nice to me, more like a friend this time. She was kind and actually seemed glad to see me. I couldn't help being amazed at the change in her. I knew she was resentful of Birdie taking over, yet she had never expressed any of her personal feelings to me. No, it was something else.

The next morning I planned to tell the family I was going to go west. I'd read someplace, "Go West young man, and go west". Well, what about us women? I wanted to forget the past, especially the war. I needed to find some peace of mind, and to rid myself of the awful pictures I carried in my head of the many dead and dying men I'd seen. I wanted the images to fade. I wondered if they ever would.

Mother had Birdie to take care of her, and Father had Edward to help him, and who knew, maybe Edwin would contribute somehow. I knew Aunt Ginny would continue to live in the little house on the property, and Mick would keep busy with the horses. So I felt free to leave. I had no intentions of remaining with my mother, or getting married, living the grand southern style and having children. The last thing in the world I wanted was a husband!

CHAPTER FOURTEEN

It was a glorious morning when I awakened. I jumped out of bed, dashed to the windows, opened the drapes and pulled up one of the sash windows. I breathed deeply of the sweet smell of the Virginia country air. There was nothing like it. My lungs filled and my mind was full of hope for the future. As the sun rose the horizon became shades of pink, silver, and gold. A multitude of small fluffy clouds lay above the rays of the sun making them stand out in the early morning sky.

The only sounds I heard were the morning birds and insects humming outside my window. There were no sounds of war, no suffering patients, and no smell of death. I'd awakened hungry to the aroma of fresh perked coffee and homemade biscuits. Now I would get a real American breakfast. There were times in France I thought I might never return, and I was convinced today would be a day to remember.

I looked out one of the upstairs back windows, and saw the family sitting on the veranda eating and enjoying the warm sunshine. When I started down the back stairs I heard Charley coming after me. I turned around and called to him. "Good morning, Sleepyhead."

"Aw heck, Sis, I was up earlier, but I couldn't stay awake so I went back to bed, but before I did I heard Aunt Ginny come into the kitchen for a cup of coffee. I do believe she spent the night in the stables. We brought her a real prize. I've never seen her so happy. I suspect meeting Mick O'Leary might have made the difference. Did you see the way they looked at each other?"

"Yes, they seemed to be pleased with each other."

"Charley, we both know there isn't any place for us here. I've decided to move on. It was just a matter of time. We just don't seem to fit in this family."

"We're just a couple of misfits for sure, Melinda Ann. I know my destiny is in the theatre and nowhere else, and yours is in the nursing profession."

"Yes, I do plan to go back into nursing. That's a passion that I'll never give up, but it'll have to wait until my head is clearer. I'd like to do some traveling, first."

"Did you hear someone walking around in the house last night? I heard footsteps going up and down the hall and stairs. I think it was Mother or maybe Birdie. I really do believe Mother is ill. Did you see how pale she was when we arrived?"

"Yes, Charley, I did notice. I even asked the servants about her and they said she had been sick ever since I left. The spells come over her right after breakfast and again after tea time in the afternoons. I plan to check her over and find out what the problem is. I am not a doctor, but I'd like to take a look at her."

"You know, Sis, Edward says Birdie is doing a fine job running the plantation, but Aunt Ginny has refused to help in anyway. She apparently has just hung around the stables and stayed pretty much to herself. I remember Aunt Ginny teaching us how to ride horses and play games. And I remember those family stories she used to tell us. Now I'm beginning to wonder how many of those stories are true."

"Me, too, I've wondered about our Grandmother Lilly, which brings me to my plan. I've decided to go out West to see some of the places where our grandmother traveled."

"Yes, I suppose that would be fun. And I also want to get away. Last evening Dad cornered me in the study and asked if I had thought of reconsidering my position here."

"What did you say to that?"

"I told him, no, and that I would be leaving soon."

As we went downstairs we were met by Father.

"Good morning, Father. It's good to be home and alive!"

Father beamed and stepped between us taking each of our arms and leading us down the stairs to the outside terrace. "Come my children, breakfast is waiting. Just smell that coffee!"

Mother had not been outside with the family, but appeared shortly after we got there. She came out looking healthy enough. The boys and Father stood up when she approached the table and then sat down when she took her seat. Southern traditions were still strong in our family.

Mother was the only one in the family who preferred hot tea to coffee. When I asked her why she said it was a habit she had acquired when she was a young girl in New Orleans. There it was again, the mention of New Orleans, but no more information. That was one place I did plan to visit.

If Mother had been ill in the night nothing was said about it. The minute she sat down she called for Birdie to bring her tea. Birdie swished in with a silver tray holding a delicate porcelain teapot, cup and saucer. Once Mother had her tea, she began, "Your father told me about your decision to leave the plantation. I don't agree with you, Charles Harley, but I've become resigned to accepting your choices. You are as strong-willed as your sister and she is impossible! After all I do realize you have been through a lot in the war and you have been wounded. You're a grown man and you want to make something of the rest of your life. It doesn't really matter anyway. Edward has proved himself capable around this plantation, and that's more than I can say for either you or your sister. Neither of you need to worry about us. You're free to go!"

I knew it! She was baiting him and hoping he would react or at least be jealous of Edward. But she was using the wrong tactic with Charley. I watched him as he looked at her. I could tell this bothered him, but he was not about to change his mind.

To relieve the tension in the air the family all started talking at once, while Birdie fluttered around taking care of everyone's needs like an overzealous hostess. She moved about Edward time and time again much too close to be proper. She was flirting with him and causing him to look rather embarrassed and I swear he was even blushing. Well, she was truly beautiful and she moved about the table like a delicate butterfly. Even Father noticed her and made some comment about how animated she was that morning.

I was disgusted with all the small talk and wanted to shut it out of my mind. While I finished my breakfast I lingered over coffee and read the newspaper. Charley interrupted, "Well, I guess this is as good a time as any. I know you all have noticed my limp and are wondering what happened when I was wounded. As well as I can remember it, I was in a truck being transported with some other soldiers when we were hit. When I came to, there was a man standing over me. I knew he was a medic but I was so stunned and in such pain I screamed at him to get me out from under what was left of the truck. I was desperate because I could not feel my leg. I was afraid it had been shot off. I thought the medic was just going to let me lye there and bleed to death. I couldn't crawl out by myself. I remember hearing the man tell me he and the other men were doing all they could to get me out.

"The man leaned over me and told me to take it easy and not to move because they had to jack one side of the truck up before they could pull me out. He said I was the only one who had survived the hit. All the other boys and the driver were blown to bits."

Hearing this Mother's hand came up to her mouth in horror as she let out a muffled gasp. The rest of the family put down whatever they were doing and gave Charley their full undivided attention and he continued.

"I must have passed out because the next thing I knew I woke up in a hospital in Nancy, France. Believe me, if it had not been for Sis, I would have lost my leg. By the time she found me in the annex of the hospital my leg was infected and gangrene had set in. The doctors were going to amputate my leg the next morning. I was terrified! To me that meant my life was over. My dreams would never come true. I would never be in the theatre."

Smiling at me Charley raised his voice. "It was her determination and the use of an outdated treatment, a mustard plaster which saved my leg. The doctor told me I would limp for a while but in time my leg would completely heal. I'm so grateful Melinda Ann found me when she did and that her treatment saved my leg."

Looking at Charley I was so proud of him. He wanted the family to know I had been there and the treatment I had used worked. I said nothing at that moment but I knew my family was glad of what I had done and that was good enough for me.

Edward and Edwin looked at each other and began asking Charley questions about the war which I had heard before so as he talked I remembered many episodes during those nursing days. It had been good to help all those wounded men and I was glad I was a nurse. Birdie, stopped moving about the table, and sat down to listen. She, like most women, asked about the women he saw, how they looked and if they were pretty which were a lot of foolish questions, as far as I was concerned.

When the conversation changed and Charley began talking about his theatrical experiences, before the war in New York and in England, I listened. "I have discovered the pulse of the theater business and I will not rest until I have achieved success on the stage, so I'll be leaving here soon." Then he stood up, bowed to Mother and turned to leave the table.

Mother stopped him because she had brought with her a stack of old newspapers she thought Charley and I might be interested in reading. I found an article in the back of one paper about the Women Suffragists and their imprisonment in November of 1917. I was appalled at what I read. The women had been arrested for picketing the Woodrow Wilson White House for the right to vote and were arrest for 'obstructing sidewalk traffic'! How insane can you get? The article ended with the fact that the women had been released after being in jail for over a month and nearly dying from neglect and hardly any food. Word had slipped out to their families, and soon the authorities were contacted. The last part of the article made me laugh. President Woodrow Wilson and his cronies actually tried to persuade a well-known psychiatrist to declare one of the women, Alice Paul, insane. It did not work because the doctor refused saying, "Alice Paul is a strong and brave woman, but that doesn't make her crazy." The best part of all was that the doctor admonished the men by saying. "Courage in women is often mistaken for insanity."

I wondered if Mother ever read the newspapers. "Mother, did you read those articles in the paper about the Suffragettes and their arrest?"

"Yes, I did! But I don't believe a word of it. Gentlemen of the police force would never treat poor defenseless women like that. It could not possibly be as bad as it sounds. I suspect the women got what was coming to them. After all, they should not have been out there obstructing the sidewalk traffic! Why in the world were they not home minding their own business and caring for their families? I really don't understand what is happening in this country. Everyone knows a woman's place is in the home. You had better not forget that young lady! You should be married by now and starting a family."

"No, thank you Mother, that is not for me. I'm not interested. And you're mistaken, those women did nothing wrong! If I'd been with them I think I would have done the same thing."

"Well, I am a Southern lady and I intend to always act like one. No, my dear, you would not have seen me wearing those tacky sashes across my chest and marching through the streets making a spectacle of myself. The people living around here would frown on that sort of behavior. I believe it's better for a woman to stay at home and hold her peace. That's something you have never learned to do."

"Mother, have you ever made a decision in your life on your own without someone telling you what to do, like Birdie? You have given the responsibility of running the household to her. Why didn't you ask that of your sister, Aunt Ginny? At least she is a Kingsley."

"As for Birdie you just leave her out of this. She has been a better daughter than you will ever be. Now, we're quite finished here! Birdie, Birdie, come and help me get to my room. I'm feeling faint."

Everyone else sitting at the table pretended they didn't hear any of our conversation. But I was so angry I yelled at Mother sarcastically. "By all means, Mother, let Birdie help you!"

Birdie burst open the double doors onto the veranda. "I think you have caused your Mother enough pain for one day. Why don't you leave this place and never come back? You have no idea what a strain she has been under since you and Charles Harley chose to leave her. You two are a pair of spoiled, ungrateful brats!"

"That's enough! Birdie, I'll leave when I'm ready so you might as well keep your mouth shut! Who do you think you are? Our family only took you in because you are our cousin, but you are not a Kingsley. If I did decide to stay here you would soon find out where your place is in this family!"

"Is that so? You think you know everything. Well, let me tell you, you're wrong! I certainly know more about the Kingsley family than you do, I know the truth!"

Charley in the meantime had sat down and was reading the newspaper clippings and ignoring us. When he became aware of our conversation he stood up without saying a word and went inside.

Mother was trembling and seemed very irritated. "Melinda Ann, I can't stand anymore of this squabbling. Birdie, you already have said too much. Both of you need to watch your tongues. I'll not hear any more of this. Now go on along Melinda Ann and leave us alone!"

I was furious at Birdie and wondered what she knew that I did not.

"No, Mother, I refuse to go until you tell me what she knows that I don't."

At that moment Mother crumpled up in a ball, clutching her stomach like she was having an attack. I rushed to her side but Birdie pushed me away.

"See what you've done! Get out of my way so I can take your mother to her room and put her to bed. It's none of your business what I know! Just leave and give us some peace around here. All she needs is a little rest."

"Wait a minute, Birdie. I have the right to look at my mother and you are not going to stop me. I think there is something terribly wrong with her and as a nurse I want to find out what." But Birdie stood between Mother and me. She turned around and helped Mother to her feet and guided her upstairs. I was shocked at how quick and strong Birdie was. It was apparent to me that Mother needed medical attention, but Birdie was set against it.

At first I suspected some kind of food poisoning, but I knew Mother had eaten like the rest of us except for her tea. Could it be the tea? No one served her, but Birdie. I knew I had to get to Mother when Birdie was busy elsewhere. I did not follow after them, but lingered at the table.

After that scene I became greatly concerned. What was wrong with Mother and what was Birdie hiding from me? Thinking back to the day Birdie arrived at the plantation, I could not remember seeing anyone leave her on our doorstep. My mother Tinny had told me once, that an old black woman, a servant of her mother Lilly had brought her here. She said the old woman told the child she was a cousin of the Kingsley family so they would take her in.

After Mother was safely tucked into her bed, Birdie returned. I couldn't help noticing she was dressed in a modern mid-calf skirt and a bright yellow blouse. She had not returned to wearing the pre-war costumes. Apparently she had not said all she wanted to say. She came at me with eyes flashing and her small, white gloved hands shaking. "Melinda Ann, I would be very pleased if you and your brother would get your things together and leave this plantation. Edward and I can manage quite well without either of you!"

"Birdie, there was a time when we were children that I thought you and I were friends, but now you've become sassy and down-right rude. You can't throw us out of our own house. When we leave it will be by our choice and not yours." She quickly turned and left in a huff. I knew I should be happy that she was content to stay and care for Mother, but I was curious.

During our clash, Edward and Edwin had paid no attention to us, and just lounged around drinking coffee and reading the newspaper. Mick and Aunt Ginny had left earlier after having their breakfast. Father was off somewhere and I supposed he was with Charley. I sat there looking into my lovely china cup with the black coffee steaming before me. I remembered the bent tin cup I drank out of while working at the hospital in France. That is when it came to me that I missed the daily challenges of being a nurse.

Just as I was about to relax I was surprised to see Mother coming outside again with Birdie following her. She looked pale, and disoriented.

"Mother, I'm glad you decided to come outside again. The fresh air will do you good." Birdie helped her get settled into one of the chairs, and then Birdie went to where the twins were sitting.

Turning around I couldn't believe my ears. Edwin made some lewd remark to Birdie which she answered with a look of disgust.

I said, "Edwin, what an inappropriate comment!"

"Gosh darn it, Sis, I didn't count on you being so crabby this morning. Edward, why don't you just tell her? He's sweet on Birdie Melinda Ann and always has been. He actually wants to marry her!"

Edwin had looked at his brother with disgust, and then, turning to Birdie, spoke to her. "Say Birdie, how about you and me takin' a walk? I'd be happy to show you a thing or two!" Birdie didn't say a word. She just looked at him with her go-to-blazes expression.

Father must have heard all this conversation because he came outside and spoke to Edwin. "Edwin, that's enough…leave your brother alone and stop irritating your sister. Then he turned to me. "I really think it would be best for you to leave, Melinda Ann. I can't stop you. You're free to go if you wish."

Hearing our Father say this, Mother, gasped for breath and let out a little cry. She tried to stand but was too weak so Birdie ran to assist her.

"Father, I appreciate your understanding and I'm grateful to you for so many things, especially sending me to nurses' training. Eventually I intend to take a position in some major hospital, but not right away. First, I want to travel and see some of this country. I plan to talk to Aunt Ginny to see if she remembers the route Grandmother Lilly took west. It should be fun to follow in her footsteps, and right now I need some diversion in my life."

"Actually, that's not a bad idea Melinda Ann. You have courage and determination. I want you to know I'm proud of you for what you did during the war, and especially for saving your brother's leg and nursing him back to health. As far as I'm concerned you have my permission to leave. You will be missed around here, but you need not worry. Birdie is more suited than anyone to be the mistress of the Kingsley mansion. Oh, and by-the-way Birdie, Melinda Ann, as a nurse most certainly has my permission to examine her mother if she wishes." Birdie looked like she had been slapped, but she didn't utter a word.

I was surprised, pleased, and a bit puzzled. Then Father continued. "Oh, yes, my dears, I've been talking with Charles Harley. He has made it clear that he is going east to follow his dream. I gave him my permission and he has already left. He told me to tell each of you good-bye and if you were ever in New York City to look him up. He said he can't stand good-byes!"

Hearing this, Mother let out a scream! "I can't believe it. Charles Harley has left without saying good-bye? He wouldn't do that to me! Harley dear, I don't understand what is happening with our children. Why does our beloved eldest son, Charles Harley want to break my heart? This is too much, I can't take it!"

Birdie took Mother's arm and led her toward the door. Mother stopped and turned around. "Birdie, take your hands off of me and stay where you are." As I watched my mother leave the room, by herself, with her shawl dragging on the floor, her gray-streaked hair partly on top of her head and the rest of it flowing down her back made my heart ache for her. She looked disheveled and frail.

Thinking about Charley leaving without saying goodbye to me made me a bit sad but also angry. I knew I would miss him more than anyone else. We had become good friends. We had depended on each other, and now he was gone without even a word to me. I felt there was nothing left for me at this place, so I turned to Edward. "Edward, will you drive me to the train station tomorrow morning?"

Edwin looked at Edward then at me. "Oh spit, Melinda Ann, Edward doesn't drive. He doesn't know how. I'm afraid he and the rest of the family would prefer to live out their days in the quiet more genteel time of the past. For crying out loud, we still have a horse and buggy ready to go on a moment's notice. This family just doesn't get it! Things are changing in this country. I'm not as dumb or worthless as some people think. Edward and I would have done a lot more growing-up had we been allowed to join the army. We sat it out because our parents said we were both needed at home! Maybe Edward was, but I certainly was not. I've decided I want a change, too!"

You could have heard a pin drop. Edwin never appeared to be serious about anything, but this time he was, and we all listened.

"I was playing cards the other night with some gents from New York City and they told me about big poker games that are taking place in the club-cars on most trains. I know I could win a bundle by riding the trains and playing poker, so I've decided to leave here, too! There is no future for me here. No, sir! Edward, you're the knowledgeable one in all the business matters, and I, on the other hand, am a carefree gambler at heart and always will be. The love of the game is in my blood!"

I was grateful Mother had retired to her room because that was the last thing she needed to hear. Birdie let out a sigh of relief and mumbled something under her breath. I think what I heard was, "It's about time. We don't need any of them!"

I was sorry Aunt Ginny was not here because she would have been surprised. I don't think she ever thought much of Edwin, but at that moment he was showing some character by standing up for himself. By golly, maybe he had some backbone after all.

As I rose from the table Edwin looked at me. "Another thing, Melinda Ann, please don't let Birdie get under your skin. She will never be independent like you. She will always lean on Father and Edward to lead and make decisions for her. She was born a southern lady and wants nothing more than that kind of life. She may look beautiful on the outside, and appear fragile like a butterfly, but underneath she is as tough as iron. You looked shocked when I told you about Edward and Birdie. Didn't you know? They've been sweethearts for years and just waiting to get permission to get married. Surely you can see how smitten they are with each other. It disgusts me, but I would not be surprised if they are wed soon.

Hearing this I was upset at the very thought of my younger brother marrying a cousin. In my mind that was unthinkable! After all, Birdie was my age and besides, one does not marry one's cousin. It just isn't done!

Edwin was gaining courage so he asked the final question. "Father, what do you think about my twin brother and Birdie? You must have known about their infatuation for a long time, haven't you? And I suppose you will give your consent sooner or later, won't you? They are both greedy and calculating. I'm fed up with them. The more I think about leaving the better I like the idea, and I'm not sure when I will return, maybe never."

Father was more upset than angry. "Edwin take that back. You can't be serious. You can't leave, too. It will be too much for your mother to bear. You are wrong about Birdie and Edward. I'm not aware of anything going on between them. They are more like brother and sister to each other and that's all. As far as Birdie is concerned, what I think about her or what I do on her account is my business. She's a fine girl, but as far as her marrying Edward, that has not crossed my mind. You Edwin have been a challenge to your mother and me, but I always thought you would grow-up and become a strong Virginia gentleman like your brother Edward, but I see that may never happen. Now as to your leaving, I probably will give you my permission, too. If you feel you have to leave you might as well get your things together. I love all of my children, but if you don't want to be here, I'm not going to make you stay."

Father looked so sad that my heart was aching for him. I could feel his pain. "Remember, my children, this is always your home. If you're planning to make it on your own, you'll find it is not easy. Don't say I didn't warn you. Of course, I'll always be here for financial help if you need it. If you let me know where you get settled, I'll send you an allowance."

He was letting us go, but still holding on to the financial purse strings to keep us connected. He knew we couldn't make it without his help and that would keep us dependent on him.

Then Father quickly turned to Birdie. "Birdie, I'm not sure what to say to you. I hope you have not been offended. I know you're fond of

Edward but I'm sure you have no intention of marrying him. You are most dear to my beloved Tinny, and I appreciate all you do for us. I hope your ungrateful cousins have not upset you too much."

"Oh, it's all right, Uncle Harley. It is just fine! Melinda Ann and I have never gotten along well and there's no reason why we should now. Edward and I can manage without help from anyone, even you. Your three other children are too selfish or too lazy to be of any help around here, so good riddance to all of them. And another thing, I'm appalled at how Charles Harley could have left without saying good-bye, especially to his mother."

That was a mistake. Birdie had said too much. She saw Father's look of disapproval and raised her voice. "Oh, don't look at me that way. I know all of you resent me and always have, but Uncle Harley you know I've been more like a daughter to you than your own. And Edward is worth more than all the rest of them put together. I know I belong here. And as far as being his wife, I've not considered the possibility."

Looking at Edwin and me she continued. "Your Grandmother Lilly told me something that I cannot tell you because I promised I would keep the secret and I will. When the time is right your parents or Aunt Ginny will tell you the truth, and until they do, you can think what you want of me because I really don't care!"

Well, I guess Birdie did have the last word because after her angry speech we all walked away. Father turned, went through the house and out to the front veranda to smoke his pipe. Edwin and I went upstairs leaving Edward and Birdie alone.

I was silent for a time because I couldn't help wondering what the big secret was, and why Birdie had promised our Grandmother Lilly she would not tell. As Edwin walked beside me he seemed angry and a bit surprised at what had happened.

"Since Dad has given us permission to leave I guess the only one who really wants us to leave is Birdie and just maybe Edward. So, Sis, we might as well pack our bags this evening and get out of here! To tell you the truth, I'm sick of being here and always taking second place to my brother just because he was born first. I hate being called the 'wayward son'. I will never follow in Edward's footsteps. I've always taken life less seriously than he has, but what of it? Who really cares?"

I replied, "Well, Edwin, maybe Charley had it right all along. "Follow your dream. Be an actor on the stage like him, or be a nurse like me and save the world or be a gambler like you and make your fortune. Just be the best you can be in whatever you choose to do."

"You're right! I'm going to do what I've wanted to do for a long time. Sis, I'm going to travel on the trains crossing this country, and maybe even get on a paddle wheeler on the great Mississippi where I can play cards anytime I want. I know I can make it on my own. I won't have to depend on Father any longer!"

As we continued to talk standing at the top of the stairs, I realized Father was approaching. I was sure he had overheard us.

"I heard that pretty little speech Edwin, but when you're losing at poker, and you probably will, you'll think differently. I want to see both of you in the library first thing in the morning. I have something to say to you. I will be the one driving you to the station. Did you really believe I would purchase an automobile and not learn how to drive it? I've been practicing when you were not around Edwin. I'm not some incapable old man, at least not yet."

Before we could say a word we saw Mother coming out of her room. "My dear Tinny, what are you doing out of your bed? I thought you were not feeling well and that you were going to stay in bed forever. I see you have changed your mind. That's good and since you're here, is there anything you want to say to Melinda Ann or Edwin before they leave in the morning? Yes, dear, they are both leaving the Kingsley plantation."

Mother stood looking at the three of us, wringing her hands as if she didn't understand a word. When she spoke, it was with a lot of emotion. "What started as a lovely day has long since turned sour. I don't understand any of this and I'm deeply wounded. What I'd planned for this family will now never come true. I expected that when each of you married, you would come here to live. I imagined we would celebrate holidays together and welcome the birth of grandchildren. I've tried to make each of you happy. I grew up in this house and I obeyed all the rules that you two seem to choose to disregard. I don't understand why you want to leave. . Oh, Harley darling, how could any of our children want to leave us? I never considered leaving the plantation or my mother Lilly. I held her hand when she died under the willow tree. I knew my place was here, and I will die here."

"Don't upset yourself, my dear, and we'll manage without them. Life will go on. Now you go back to bed and we'll speak of this later."

As Mother turned to leave she looked at me. "Melinda Ann, I don't care if you're a nurse, I will not allow you to examine me. I don't want you near me! These attacks come on because of a nervous stomach caused by all the unrest in this house. The sooner you leave the better!"

Saying this she called Birdie. "Birdie sweetheart, come here. I've had enough of this talk for one morning. Now I am truly ready to retire to my bed and weep for my lost children."

Apparently Birdie and Edward had come up the back stairs and had been waiting in Mother's sitting room. Birdie came swiftly toward Mother and took her by the arm and helped her to her room. Edward was shaking his head as he followed after the two women. He couldn't even say good-bye to us. Father watched them go and in his gentlemanly way he was calm and in total control.

"I'll expect to see you both in the library early in the morning. I want to leave this house before your mother gets up. She just isn't ready for all three of you leave the plantation." Saying this he left us.

I returned to my room and spent the rest of the day packing and gazing out the window. I was tired of hearing my mother trying to direct my life. I did not want to speak to anyone. I asked for my supper to be brought up to me on a tray. When I heard a knock on my door, I thought it was the maid, but instead it was Aunt Ginny. She asked if she could come in and talk for awhile. She had been told I was leaving the next day and wanted to tell me, 'good-bye.' At first we spoke of my return from the war, about Charley leaving and now Edwin. She said she wished she had been around when Edwin had made his speech. She was delighted he was going to get away from the plantation. When she asked me about my plans, I told her I wanted to go west, to follow some of the same roads her mother Lilly had traveled. She was guarded, but after a while she began to open up and share some of the stories and the places she had heard her mother speak about. This was the first time in years we had been together alone and really talked.

Once we got started talking we discussed the stagecoach roads and the railroad trains Grandmother Lilly might have taken. After conversing with Aunt Ginny, I had a pretty good idea where I was headed. I had a map marked with the towns and places my aunt remembered hearing about.

"Aunt Ginny, please, before you leave, tell me about the New Orleans property and why Father sold it. You were there when you were a young girl, weren't you? It will be the last place I plan to visit, but I would like to know where the house is located. Do you remember?"

When I asked her these questions she seemed to freeze up.

"Melinda Ann, I'm not sure I want to talk about New Orleans. I don't remember much about that time, but I can tell you the house is located somewhere in the French Quarter." She described the house and the grounds as best she could. Then all of a sudden she realized who she was talking to and the expression on her face changed. She stopped talking, hugged me, and quickly left my room. I packed my traveling bag and a small trunk which Aunt Ginny had insisted that I take, and I retired in anticipation of the next morning.

CHAPTER FIFTEEN

Dawn showed the promise of a beautiful day, with the sun breaking on the eastern horizon splashing brilliant shades of orange, red and gold. The sky was clear of clouds and the air crisp, but not cold. I loved the scent of the fresh morning air with the world waking all around me. The feeling of the new day brought with it hope and assurance.

As I walked slowly down the winding staircase it was perhaps for the last time. I looked at each of the paintings as I passed them. I felt like the entire Kingsley family, dating back to the beginning of the plantation, was watching me with each step I took. Their eyes were penetrating and accusing. It was as if they couldn't believe I would do such a thing, leave the home they had loved and had lived in for most of their lives. Was I ungrateful? No, I didn't think so because I knew I wasn't needed. I had experienced the world outside of Virginia and I wanted to find a life of my own.

At the base of the stairs, and on the wall directly behind the foyer, hung the two pictures that haunted me most, Grandmother Lilly and Grandfather Bart. Grandmother's gaze was sad and forlorn. She looked unhappy. I wondered what had been on her mind when her portrait had been painted. What were her secrets? Observing the painting of her helped me remember how much I'd loved her. I guess that's why I wanted to set out on my journey following in her footsteps.

Under each painting I saw a sparkling gold name plate that had been polished recently. I could read each of them quite clearly:

Lillian Benton-Kingsley 1865-1910

Bartholomew Stewart Hampton-Kingsley 1865-1909

Grandfather Bart looked haughty but handsome I must admit. They didn't look like a well-matched pair.

Breaking into my thoughts I heard Father calling me.

"Yes, Father I'm here, and Edwin is coming down the stairs as we speak. We are both packed and ready to leave."

"Thank you for being on time. Please join me in the library. I have a few things I want to discuss with you, as I did with Charles Harley yesterday. Please close the door. I do not want us to be disturbed."

He went behind his desk and sat down in his big brown leather chair, which made him look like a king. I felt like a peasant standing before an overlord. His expression was stern and sincere.

"Your mother wants you to believe this action of yours is causing her to be ill, but the truth is she will get over your leaving as long as she has Birdie to care for her. She has everything she desires right here. Her problem is that she envisioned model children who would do exactly as she wished, but God knows none of us is perfect, and most of us do just as we please."

Motioning us to sit down he continued. "I realize each of you have a dream of your own. Believe me I do understand. You see when I was a young man I was like my father and his father before him. We were farmers and never expected to be anything else. We wanted a decent piece of ground to plant and harvest. My family was poor and my father was happy just as long as he had a roof over his head. He wanted nothing more than to be left alone. He was content to make a good living for his family, but I wanted more. My dream was to become the manager or even an owner of a great plantation. I lived at home with my parents, and worked hard on a plot of ground that belonged to the Kingsley's. I was jealous of the Kingsley family, and yet I wanted to be part of just such a family. I didn't want to be like my father so when I had a chance, I chose to go away to school and get an education. When I returned home I found Tinny to be quite attractive so I asked permission to court her. Even though we fell in love I never dreamed she would accept me, but she did."

Father stopped talking and looked at each of us. "What I am about to tell you is very private. You must promise me, you will never let your mother know we had this conversation. We were married very young because she was already expecting a child. Oh, we knew it was wrong but as can happen we got caught up in our passion and couldn't help ourselves. I was so inexperienced I didn't realize how fast things could progress the first time you were with a girl, and neither did your mother. We were both totally unprepared, and too much in love to care at the time."

"Since Tinny was the daughter of Lilly and Bart Kingsley it made my chances of being an overseer possible. But don't get me wrong, I have always loved your mother even though she can be difficult at times. So a lot of this is my fault. I've always given her anything she wanted trying to make up for her being a mother at such an early age. Remember to never ask your mother about this, because over time she has convinced herself it didn't really happened. This is something I'm not proud of, but I feel you need to know about it. I don't want any of my children to make the same mistake. My advice is to abstain before you are married. Don't rush into marriage until you are sure you have the right partner".

I started to say something but Father raised his hand to let me know he had not finished. "When your Grandmother Lilly asked me to manage the plantation, and live in the Kingsley Mansion, I jumped at the chance. At that time your Great-grandmother Martha, was ill and in need of your mother's care. Bart and Lilly, and your Aunt Ginny, were in New Orleans at the time, leaving Mistress Martha alone, except for a few servants. The little house you children were born in was getting too small for four lively children. And since my parents were living with us then too it made the house even more crowded. Almost overnight I became the overseer of the Kingsley Plantation. I was master of the plantation and Tinny was mistress, which suited us both quite well."

"But there was a stipulation about living in the mansion, and your Grandmother Lilly had been quite adamant about this point. She told me I would have to drop my surname, Orchard, and take the name of Kingsley as my own. It was a tradition that went back several generations, anyone living here had to be known as a Kingsley. She was determined to carry on the name of her illustrious ancestors, just as your Great-grandmother Martha had done, so I agreed to her terms."

Clasping his hands, he paused, and cast his eyes down like he was embarrassed. "Your Grandfather Bart was the last true Kingsley. The rest of us are just interlopers, but don't tell your mother that. She doesn't want the rest of the world to know who we really are. She is too proud."

There was so much I wanted to ask him while I had the opportunity and he was being so hush-hush. I started to interrupt, but decided I'd better listen.

"Now let me tell you a little about the plantation. Edward and Felice Kingsley came to Virginia from England. I was told they sailed directly to Richmond and then traveled by stagecoach to Roanoke. They bought this property and built a small house and lived there for a while. Then they designed and built the mansion sometime before the War Between the States. I'm sure there is more to the story, but it was never disclosed to me and I am not sure if Martha even knew why the mansion was not destroyed by the Union soldiers. I've always wondered how the house survived when so many others did not."

He stopped, shook his head, and took a long look at Edwin and at me. "Now, I'm asking you to make me a promise, as your brother, Charles Harley, did yesterday morning. I want you to swear that you will never bring shame upon the name of the Virginia Kingsley's, as I did, and that you will never use our surname of Orchard. You are and will be known as part of the Kingsley family. Is that understood? I know what you're thinking. Yes, we are set in our traditions. We are a brave and proud bunch. We've gone through some bad times and some good times, and undoubtedly we will again, but neither of you should feel tied to this place. As your father, I am content to live here all of my days, but I want you to know I'm happy to see each of you follow your own heart's desire."

Well, that came as a shock to us! He really approved! As we sat before him our mouths were hanging open. "My dear Melinda Ann and Edwin, I wish you well on your travels, I want you to remember to send me a telegram whenever you get settled but I will send your allowances immediately. You must realize we have sufficient funds and I want to share it equally with my children."

Father left the room while Edwin and I composed ourselves. Edwin spoke first. "Sis, I don't get it. I've always thought Father was a weak man when it came to Mother, and that all she ever cared about was being wealthy. I had no idea how amenable he could be to our leaving. He wants us to carry on with our lives and if that means leaving here, so be it!"

"Edwin, I can't believe what we've just heard. Father has told us about things we didn't know about at all. But I believe he is trying to use the family fortune to control us."

"Melinda Ann, I know the old man better than you, and I agree. We don't know where we're going, but he does want to keep track of us. I don't want any of his money or even an allowance. I can make it on my own. Do you suppose he made Charley the same offer? I doubt that our brother would take any help from Father.

"Well Edwin, I do have a travel plan, but I'm not sure exactly where I'll be or for how long. But I'll have to admit if I get desperate for money. I won't be bashful about asking for it. And yes, I'm sure he made Charley the same offer. You know our father is very prideful. I can see Charley as an actor on the stage, and you playing poker sitting in some smoked filled club car, but dear brother, what happens when your luck runs out?

"Sis, that won't happen! I'm a good poker player, and I never cheat, but I win most of the time. Following the life of a gambler is exciting. I like dressing up in my best suit and putting on a show while I'm playing cards. I guess there is a little actor in me too! Just think of all those soldiers and business men, traveling on the trains with their pockets full of money. They are eager to play the game."

Hearing this I realized he was not a boy anymore. He was a man and if he won or lost he would do all right. As I looked at him I saw how handsome he was, and how appealing he must be to women. I only hoped this would not cause him problems in the future.

Father came into the room and urged us to move along for enough had been said. I was still surprised that he had taken us into his confidence. The servants had taken our bags to the automobile and Father seemed anxious to leave. I lingered in the entry hall. The real adventure of my life was about to begin and I was ready! Taking one last look at the staircase and the family portraits hanging there, I said my final farewell and turned to leave.

As we climbed into the automobile we were all quiet. I was eager to be leaving and I also pleased that Edwin was going with me. The thought of him remaining behind was absurd. For him to remain at the plantation would be a waste of his life. Some of my questions about the family had been answered by Aunt Ginny and more information than I ever expected had come from Father. Today he had treated me as a grown-up and not as a child. So it was as a grown-up I left my home resolved to be on my own and free of any family commitments.

Edwin leaned over to me and said, "Well, Sis, I guess we three are the black sheep of the family, Charley, you and me! We must be cut from the same cloth. Let's leave the plantation to Mother and Father, dear brother Edward and Birdie with no regrets and never look back."

CHAPTER SIXTEEN

Leaving the plantation had not been as hard as I'd expected. Indeed I didn't look back. The three of us rode in silence until we arrived in Norfolk. There, Father announced to us that he had been thinking, and decided that he might as well drive us on to Richmond where the railroad station was larger and on the main line. It didn't matter to us because we just wanted to get going. I think his purpose was to spend more time with us in the hope we might change our minds. I think he wanted us to follow our dreams, but at the same time wanted us to stay home.

Richmond is a beautiful city sitting on the James River about 125 miles west of the Atlantic Ocean. Father said we were about 100 miles south of Washington, D.C. As he drove us through the city we saw many fine homes surrounded by manicured flower gardens. Broad leafy green trees formed a canopy over the streets. But Edwin and I were not interested in the sights and sounds of Richmond.

Seeing that we were not impressed, Father drove on, but when we arrived at St. John's Church built in 1741 he stopped and spoke to us. "This is the oldest wooden building surviving in Virginia, and it is the place where Patrick Henry made his famous speech about colonial freedom in 1775. Then he proceeded to quote Mr. Henry. "Is life so dear or peace so sweet as to be purchased by the chains of slavery? Forbid it, Almighty God! I know not what course others may take, but as for me, give me liberty or give me death!" Father spoke those words with such feeling that we were again shocked. This was a side of our father we had never seen. Now, I knew those history books in our home library had not gone unread.

Edwin blurted out, "Father, we are going to leave Virginia. Will you please take us to the train station?"

The Richmond railroad station was considered large, because it served six railroads. We purchased our tickets, unloaded and checked our luggage, and found out which track our trains would be departing from. Edwin would be boarding a train headed north, and I would be going west.

I couldn't help wondering at the time, if I would ever see my family again, especially Edwin. I told myself not to worry. Edwin was a man and he should be out on his own. Since Edwin's train was to pull out first I went with him to say my good-byes.

Edwin was smiling and as excited as a school boy. He looked like a kid anticipating an adventure. He was very dashing in his tailored brown tweed suit and felt hat. I watched him as he boarded the train holding on to the guard poll and waving his hat at me. He carried a modest size leather satchel with a few toilet articles, and several new decks of playing cards tucked inside. The whistle blew and he was gone in a puff of steam.

Now it was my turn. As I walked slowly toward the train I reached into my pocket and my hand closed on the bills my Father had given me before we left the station. I wondered if he had done the same thing for Edwin. I had to admit I was going to miss Father.

When I found my seat I thought of Aunt Ginny, and how she had convinced me to take the large trunk even though I said I would not need it. I'd checked the trunk earlier laughing to myself, because it was almost empty. She had encouraged me to buy some stylish clothes as soon as there was a chance. This suggestion didn't seem important at the time, but later I did take her advice.

I was very hungry when I finally got settled into my seat, but I was too tired and emotional to pull out the food basket and eat. That would have to wait until later.

CHAPTER SEVENTEEN

The train was so full of people I didn't feel lonely, but rather excited at being on my own again. The route I would be taking started in Richmond, and proceeded west, from Richmond to Cincinnati, Ohio, on to Chicago, Illinois and then to St. Louis on the "Alton Limited", a fancy train I'd heard a lot about.

The station master had told me from St. Louis I would head to Pueblo, Colorado on the Missouri Pacific. There were so many different railroad companies. I didn't really care about the specific route. I just enjoyed riding on the train even though at times they seemed to move at a snail's pace.

I also learned that most of the long-distance passenger trains pulled a baggage car, three day coaches, six or eight sleeping cars, a dining car, and a lounge car – about fourteen cars in all. The seats were fairly comfortable and riding the train gave me a lot of time to relax. Several people sat down beside me and tried to engage in conversation. I listened patiently to them as I'd done as a nurse with the soldiers, but I found I wasn't interested. I tried to read newspapers, but when I did, usually fell asleep and dreamed.

When evening approached I began to realize I was hungry, but instead of eating out of my food basket I went to the dining car. I had supper, and found that dining on the train is an elegant experience! The tables were set with white linen cloths and large linen napkins. As I sat down, the dining car steward was at my side presenting a menu. The food sounded wonderful, and was not too expensive. I wanted to keep a close account of my cash, so I checked the prices of everything on the menu. I ordered: tenderloin steak at ninety cents; French peas, one dollar; mushrooms with béarnaise sauce for two dollars and a lettuce salad for thirty cents with a tea biscuit for ten cents. For drink I ordered a pot of Ceylon tea for sixteen cents. It was delicious and well presented. I ate alone.

After dinner I'd taken my time in the lounge car, so it was later than it should have been when I moved down the sleeping car aisle toward my berth. It was a rather spooky scene I saw. There were many pairs of shoes sitting in the aisle next to the bottom berths, waiting for the porter to pick them up for a shine before returning them in the morning. The empty shoes gave me the willies just thinking about the unknown people they belonged to. I wondered what their lives were like, where they were going and what their beliefs were. It didn't really matter of course, but my mind never seemed to stop asking questions.

In the mountains of West Virginia the tracks became very rough and the train was rocking from side to side. I had an embarrassing accident. Well, it wasn't really my fault – the train jerked and swayed while going around a curve, and I tumbled head long into the arms of the most handsome man I'd ever seen. He had wavy blonde hair and bright blue eyes with a definite twinkle. He was a total stranger to me, and here I was in his arms. Then I realized he was in his pajamas! If he had snapped down the aisle curtains to secure them for the night like he was supposed to do, this never would have happened.

At first he was startled, but I noticed he didn't release me very quickly and then I stammering, "Oh, pardon me, I'm so sorry! Please let me go!"

"Oh, don't be sorry. I enjoyed having a lovely woman fall into my arms! I don't mind it at all."

Hearing this I jerked myself out of his strong arms and jumped up off his berth for fear someone might see me in such a compromising situation. I ran to my berth. Each berth was partitioned off from the car corridor by heavy green baize curtains which made each one a comfortable private space for the passengers. I hopped inside mine and snapped the curtains shut! Feeling safe I placed my personal items and clothes in a little green net hammock which was hung in each berth for that purpose. I felt quite safe then and a bit excited about what had happened. Since I could not go to sleep I found there was ample room for me to curl up under the little lamp in the corner and read. I piled three pillows around me which made me feel quite comfortable. I didn't really know what to think about what had happened, but had to admit having a man's arms around me did feel good. The rest of the night, when I tried to close my eyes I saw his face, and when I did finally get to sleep I dreamt about him.

The next morning I awoke early, dressed quietly in the dark, and left my berth. I strolled through the dimly lit swaying cars being careful to keep my balance this time. I walked all the way to the last car with the open observation deck. I stood at the rail letting the wind blow through my long hair as I watched the rails flow off into the distance behind me with the wheels making that clickety-clack sound on the rails.

Before I went into the dining car I visited the small washroom and combed my hair into place. When I entered the dining car, there he was! He was sitting at a table looking straight at me and there was that twinkle again. The way he looked at me made my heart skip a beat, and my breathing become shallow. He stood up and I could see that he was tall. That wavy blonde hair was well groomed, and his bright blue eyes with the twinkle startled me. He was elegantly dressed in the best suit money could buy in that day. He reeked of wealth.

I quickly lowered my eyes and sat down at the nearest table with my back turned to him. But that didn't matter because I could see him coming toward me in the reflection of the train windows. He stopped at my table, leaned over and said. "Good morning, my dear, I do believe we have met before. May I join you for breakfast?" Well, what could I say? I could tell by his manner that he would not take "no" for an answer.

"Do I have a choice?" was my curt reply.

"A choice, I think not! Miss, I am delighted to meet you again this morning. Our first meeting was quite exhilarating." At that statement I'm sure I blushed because I was so embarrassed. He did not seem to notice, but proceeded to sit down, pick up a menu, and began to read.

I didn't know what to say, but I was determined he would not spoil my breakfast. It was my favorite meal of the day so I decided to order for myself, and this handsome intruder could do the same.

He introduced himself as James...something or other, which I didn't hear because I was so flustered I couldn't think straight. I wouldn't give him my name, because I really didn't want to have anything to do with him.

When the waiter came I ordered one pot of coffee, one poached egg, and an assortment of fruit. James "dandy," or whatever his name was, ordered the same thing, and when the check came he insisted on paying for my meal. I was floored and embarrassed and didn't know how to respond. When I looked at him I became flustered and acted like a silly school girl. My hands got clammy, and I was hot and cold all over. My brain was confused and my hands trembled. I knew I was being ridiculous so I kept trying to get control of myself. The last thing I wanted in life right now was to get interested in a man or have one interested in me.

When I stood up to leave, James was up and standing behind my chair pulling it out for me. He was quite the gentleman. Though I said nothing he addressed me properly. "I'm happy to have made your acquaintance, Miss what was your name? Perhaps, we will meet again."

Well, maybe that could happen, but my plan was to avoid him as much as possible. I was extremely nervous when I was around him, and now he had gone and spoiled my plans – he had awakened something in me that I didn't understand, a feeling that I'd never known before. That's when I decided I would never speak to him again.

I found traveling on the train more of an adventure than I'd expected. I was surprised, but I liked being catered to and looked after. One of the passengers told me the Santa Fe had added another unique status symbol for its passengers. The company had created a luggage sticker to advertise its owner's presence aboard any American named train. I thought that quite a novel idea.

I didn't see James again, so I put him out of my mind and by the time we reached Chicago I'd forgotten all about the handsome gentleman. Before we arrived in Chicago the conductor told us a little history about the city. All I previously knew of Chicago was the same story everyone knew, about the Great Chicago fire of 1871 and how it recovered and now is a modern city built on the ashes.

When the train finally pulled into the Chicago station I was grateful to get off. I decided to hail a taxi and have the driver give me a tour of the city. Not that I was that interested, but I just wanted to be driven around while I decided where I wanted stay overnight.

He drove me downtown passed Grant Park, and we entered the Loop, south of the Chicago River, in the famous central business district. We took the Congress Expressway to see what is known as the West Side. When he found out I was a nurse and had been overseas in the Great War, I got his attention. With quite a lot of excitement he told me there were several medical facilities on our route, and wondered if I would like to stop and see one. I wanted to get to a hotel before dark so I declined.

"Say, lady, I wanta' tell ya' this city ain't so bad, but the newspapers keep tellin' us we have a bad reputation for crime and violence. I can tell ya' what caused it all. You see it's because of prohibition. The government men put a ban on the sale of alcoholic beverages. And that's a bad thing, because men will always drink one way or another. Take me, I like a good cold beer once in a while, but you can't buy one legally. You have to go to the local bootlegger, and that ain't a good idea. Since September of 1917 we haven't been able to make any kind of liquor. No saloon can operate legally, of course, that don't mean there ain't places where you can get it. Oh heck, lady, I could take you to one of them places right now, if you want to go."

"No, thank you, mister, I'd just as soon drink a big glass of lemonade. Lemonade soothes the throat and is very satisfying!"

"That may be true for you lady, but give me a cold beer any day! Okay, okay! Back to our tour! Lake Michigan is on our left, and to our right are the tracks of the Illinois Central Railroad."

When he mentioned the railroad I immediately wanted to go to that station. Forget about staying overnight. The Illinois Central station is where I would buy my ticket for the famous Alton Limited to St. Louis. For the train, it would be just a daily run, but for me it was going to be a grand adventure.

You can imagine how surprised I was when I spotted James with a porter in tow coming to help me with my bags. I was shocked and overwhelmed to see him. He greeted me as an old friend and I became flustered again. I blurted out in almost hostile tones. "What are you doing here?'

"Well, when the train arrived in Chicago I decided to buy a ticket onto St. Louis. Isn't it a happy coincidence that we're on the same train?"

"I'm not so sure about that Mr. James, and I think you are following me around, and acting like we are long lost friends. And you don't have to help with my luggage. I can take care of myself! I don't even know you!"

Using an actor's bow, he addressed me. "Yes! We've never been properly introduced so allow me to introduce myself. My name is James…! The train whistle blasted and the noise of the depot drowned out his last word. It had happened again! I missed hearing his last name. What should I do?

Should I ask him to repeat it again or pretend I heard it? I've supposedly heard his last name twice now and I still don't have a clue what it is, but what does it matter, anyway? I decided to let it go.

"Mr. James, please don't make such a scene! You're embarrassing me. For heaven sakes be a gentleman! Okay, since we are boarding the same train I suppose we might as well be friends."

"Friends would be good, but I would like to become more than that to you. Now that I have found you or should I say you found me, I don't plan to let you go!"

This man was crazy! I had no idea who he really was and he certainly did not know me. More than friends - I doubted that.

At this point in our conversation, I was astonished to see my bags had been quickly loaded, and we had already boarded the train and were heading toward our seats. I could see I would not be able to avoid him, but this was getting a little out of hand. He did make me feel giddy when I was near him, and the touch of his hand made me feel faint. I admonished myself for having these feelings.

He reminded me of my brother Edwin, always testing the waters just to see how far he could get with a woman. But this Mr. James had the wrong woman for that and he would not seduce me. My mind was made up, to have no romantic entanglements until much later in my life. I had places to go and people to meet. So I made a plan to read the newspaper and not talk to him. I also would avoid looking at him, and then maybe he would get the idea that I wasn't interested.

I sat down with my eyes focused downward when he began to speak to me. "Melinda Ann, I know your name now. The conductor told me. I don't care how long it takes, you are going to look at me, and so you might as well stop playing this game. I want to see those beautiful eyes looking straight into mine. Oh, come on, look around you. I bought all the seats in the same row so I can have you to myself."

"Mr. James please, people are looking at us and they will hear you. Please lower your voice."

"I don't care! Ever since you fell into my arms I have been hopelessly attracted to you."

At this I jumped up and looked at him with eyes blazing. "Stop it, right now! You may be attracted to me, but I certainly am not interested in you!"

Just at that moment, the conductor came by and asked me if anything was wrong, and if this man was bothering me. I told him it was all right and that we were just having a little disagreement. I was sorry I hadn't asked the conductor for a seat in another car and considered getting off at the next stop. I just did not want this kind of complication in my life. But obviously he was interested in me so maybe I could be a little friendlier and perhaps by the time we reached St. Louis he would forget the whole thing. I hoped he would give up pursuing me and be on his way to San Francisco. Then I would be free of him, but suppose he was more serious than I thought? What then? "All right, James, I will talk to you and perhaps we can be civil to each other. But I do not want to hear anything about a romantic entanglement. We can be friends and nothing more!"

"Yes, my dear, I agree! That's a deal. I'll treat you like a sister. I'll be as your loving brother."

At that statement I couldn't help wondering which one of my brothers he would be like - Charley the perfect gentleman, or Edwin the ladies man, or maybe a combination of both. Well, what did it matter, because I'd made up my mind to not fight with my new 'friend'?

Secretly, I was somehow pleased that he actually found me attractive and wished to pursue me. I was acutely aware that this had never happened to me before, not in Europe or in Virginia. I knew I wasn't a beauty, but I was smart, or at least I thought so, and could control my feelings. It was true, having all this male attention was a new experience for me and I wasn't quite sure, but I think I liked it.

CHAPTER EIGHTEEN

After a while, I did get over feeling so overwhelmed in James' presence, and I found him to be very interesting. I learned he came from a wealthy San Francisco family and he let it be known to everyone on the train. He would spare no expense to get what he wanted and he thought that was perfectly normal. I was a bit embarrassed by his behavior, but I reminded myself it was just a chapter in my life and it would eventually come to an end. At least that was what I believed at the time.

Once in St. Louis, he suggested we tour the city and I agreed. We stored our luggage at the station and James engaged a taxi driver named Olen to drive us around the city. Olen was jolly and mistook us for newly-weds – which pleased James and irritated me. I kept my mouth shut and let the driver and James enjoy their illusion.

Olen began by saying, "St. Louis is on the west bank of the Mississippi River just south of its junction with the mighty Missouri River. It was here in the late 1850's that St. Louis became the main central port for all the Mississippi steamboats. Hearing this I was reminded of Virginia and the steamboats I had seen as a child, when the family saw the mighty river on a holiday.

Olen was quite the story teller. "Good old St. Louis really began to grow after the Civil War but that's a long story. We're going to go through Forest Park, and then we will end this tour at the Riverfront.

"Where would you two like to go now, to your hotel or how about getting some tickets to one of the old-time melodramas? They put on a show every night on one of those historical showboats."

Heavens! It was like being in Virginia. I'd always been fascinated with showboats and loved going on board, so I agreed and we went. The show was only fairly good, but the audience booed the villain and cheered the hero with great gusto. The evening meal was served during the show, and as I recall, the food was some kind of meat and boiled potatoes.

By the time the show was over it was way too late to go to the railroad station, according to James, so it presented quite a problem for me. Olen had waited for us and was now ready to take us to the hotel. I had not thought about what would happen after the show. We didn't have any luggage with us and we certainly didn't have reservations at a hotel. Besides, I wasn't going to spend the night with James. Olen, still thinking we were married, suggested a very expensive hotel in the best part of the city which suited James quite well, but I was perturbed. Who did James think he was? This was not the answer. He was not my husband and I would not allow myself to be compromised.

I would not go to a hotel with James, because it would be just like him to say we were married, and proceed to carry me over the thresh hold screaming all the way. No, Sir! That's when I blurted out.

"No! Mr. Olen Jones, don't take us to a hotel. Take us to the railroad station immediately. For heaven's sakes, we're not even married! I want to get out of St. Louis as soon as possible. I'm headed for Salt Lake City, and I'm not sure where he is going. We're just friends and nothing more!"

Now the taxi driver knew the truth, and he looked surprised. He really thought we were married and, in fact, when he dropped us off at the station, he told us what a handsome couple we made. I was aggravated, and James, holding my arm, laughed as I squirmed away from him.

I never dreamed traveling by train across the country could be so complicated. When we reached the ticket agent we found we would have to take the Missouri Pacific train to Pueblo, Colorado first, and from there hook up with the Rio Grande to Denver. Once in Pueblo it took us over night and part of the next day to get to Denver. James become sullen and withdrew from me when we purchased our tickets.

He told me he was not going to accompany me any farther than Denver, and from there he would head west. He said it was apparent that I had other things on my mind and was not interested in a serious arrangement while that was certainly true, I wasn't sure how I really felt about his decision to leave me alone.

Once on the train to Denver he ignored me and let me fend for myself. He said he had business in Denver and wished me well with my adventures. He was cold and indifferent for the rest on the trip. I knew I'd been right all along. He would not have respected me if I'd gone to the hotel with him.

And yes, part of me had wanted to go with him, but I was afraid and my convictions were too strong. My dream was to have a preacher waiting at the church and a ring on my finger before I slept with a man. I had not been promiscuous as a girl, and I would not bring shame on my family. Since it was an overnight run to Denver I purchased a space in a Pullman car and vowed to hole up in my berth as long as possible that night and into the next day. It didn't make any difference because I couldn't sleep anyway. I tossed and turned most of the night, then finally got up at the crack of dawn, and dressed as best I could in my berth.

I'd passed James going to the diner, and that was all. He tipped his hat and continued on his way. He did not speak a word to me, and acted as if I had hurt him deeply. Hurt him? I hardly knew him! I told myself it was better this way. We had had a good time while it lasted and now it had ended. That is what I had hoped would happen, but there also was a touch of sadness.

The scenery traveling through Colorado was lovely but my mind was preoccupied. I decided once I got to Denver, I would spend the day touring the city as I had at other stops. Then I would continue on to Salt Lake City to see what I could discover about my Grandmother Lilly's past. After all I was free to do what I pleased and go wherever I chose. I had not become involved with James or any other man and that was the way I wanted it!

CHAPTER NINETEEN

When we arrived at the Denver station, I saw James briefly. He came toward me dressed in a handsome tailored suit. He took off his hat, pulled my hand to his lips, gave a slight click of his heels, bowed, and told me he was happy to have met me, and hoped we might meet again someday. He held my hand longer than necessary and I was delighted at his touch. Had I made a mistake? I wanted to say something, anything, but I was speechless. He was so well built and good looking that I was again captivated, but the twinkle was gone. He dropped my hand and turned, leaving me standing on the platform with my luggage.

Watching him leave I considered chasing after him, but I remembered my vow. I didn't need a man now and maybe never would. As quickly as he had come into my life, he was swiftly gone and I was alone.

After securing a taxi I asked the driver Frank to take me around the city and not hurry, because once again I needed time to think. He suggested I sit back and relax, which I did. Since I'd not slept on the train I went to sleep about the time he was telling me that Denver was called The Mile High City. When I woke up he was talking about fishing in some place called South Platte River. When he mentioned fishing I thought of my three brothers going fishing with our father. I remembered my father and brothers sitting on the back veranda telling their many fish stories. It was fun to listen to them. I was always jealous because they spent more time with our father than I did.

I grew tired of his talking and asked Frank to take me to the railroad station. I'd seen enough of Denver. The ticket master advised me I would go to Cheyenne from Denver, which seemed out of the way, but he assured me it was the only way to get to Salt Lake City. The ride would be an overnight on the Union Pacific train. I didn't mind that at all. By now I was accustomed to sleeping on a train. That is, if I could sleep. My mind wandered and my thoughts kept returning to James. I wished I knew where he was and what sort of business he had in Denver. I knew it was none of my affair, but I was curious because he had never shared what kind of work he did.

Curiosity was one of my personality traits. Since I didn't get off the train in Cheyenne I asked the steward about the history of the city. He replied that the city is located at the foot of a natural ramp that leads up to the foothills of the Laramie Mountains. It is a rich agricultural land with a mix of livestock and commercial trading. When he said the pioneers thought it a fine country, I was reminded of my Great-grandfather and Great-grandmother Benton joining a wagon train headed for California. They came from Pennsylvania and had traveled the hard way.

I'd come a long way from my home in Virginia and I was amazed at how different the various landscapes had been, from the southern states to the western states. What a variety of scenery this country offered, from forested mountains to rolling hills, to the flat plains of Kansas, the sage prairies, to the high Rockies, and now the salt flats.

Once in the state of Utah the conductor spoke to the passengers about his home state like he was a tour guide. "Salt Lake City is located at the foot of the Wasatch Range of mountains. It is the biggest city in the state and it is the headquarters of the Mormon Church. It was the Mormon pioneers in 1848 who laid out the streets of the city with most running north and south or east and west." In Salt Lake City Capitol Hill was on the northern edge of the city instead in the center of town like Denver.

When I got off the train I chose a taxi driver who looked very much like my dad. He said his name was Peter Brown, a real gentleman who met me standing outside of his taxi. He put my trunk in the backseat with me and drove to a hotel. "Say, Mr. Brown, where are the salt flats, and would you mind taking me to them? Can you wait for me while I check in and drop off my luggage? I want to go to the salt flats, because my Great-grandfather Benton worked in one of the mines.

"Yes ma'am. I'll be happy to take you by the hotel first, but are you sure you want to go out there to the salt mines? The salt mines are fifteen miles to the northeast, and not the safest place for a pretty young thing like you. I'll take you to them if you want, and yes, I'll wait at the hotel. I haven't had many customers so far today. Say, how about I show you some of the city on our way out of town, and maybe you would like to see the Mormon Temple with its six towering spires, and the Tabernacle which is open to the public. I think there is an organ recital there today. You might enjoy that but you can't go into the Temple unless you're a Mormon. Are you a Mormon, Miss?"

"No, but I would be interested in an organ recital. Please, stop at the tabernacle."

I was delighted to see the magnificent organ and to hear the lovely music. The organ was huge and they said it was one of the biggest in the country, if not the world. To demonstrate the acoustics a man stood at the pulpit and dropped a pin. You could hear it in the back of the Tabernacle! Also of interest was that the building was put together with wooden pegs, and that the beautiful stained glass-windows had been brought in by covered wagon.

While we were driving around the taxi driver took me to Temple Square where we saw two monuments, one of Brigham Young, the founder of the church, and the other, The Sea Gull monument, erected by the pioneers who wanted to honor the gulls that devoured crop-destroying crickets in the summer of 1884.

After this little tour I asked Mr. Brown to take me to the public library. I wanted to find out if there were any records of salt mines going back to the 1800's. I hoped to find information about a Catholic Chapel carved out of salt, deep in one of the mines. It probably was an old abandoned mine by now, and chances are no one would even remember it. When I talked to the librarian, she informed me that salt was mined much like coal. Shafts were sunk in the ground, and wooden platform elevators were installed. However, in my Great-grandfather Benton's time they would have entered the shaft by riding a barrel lowered and hauled up by ropes. The librarian had few records, and could tell me little about past operations.

"Well, ma'am, did you have any luck? "No it was a waste of time."

"If you want I could take you to one of the mines where some of the men might be able to help you." That sounded good to me. When we arrived at the mine there was a lot of activity with men and trucks moving about. I sent Mr. Brown back to the city to give me time to look around and ask some questions. He agreed to return around sundown, and pick me up where he had dropped me off.

I began walking around one area and was puzzled that no one seemed interested in my presence. Even though I was dressed in my traveling clothes and looked out of place, not one man approached me. Not far away was a small wooden building that looked like a work shed. Without knocking I ventured inside and saw two men, both sitting at a huge wooden desk busy with some paperwork. One man looked up at me.

"Ma'am, could we help you? Are you looking for someone, a husband or a friend?"

"No, I'm not looking for anyone. I just want to talk to someone who is in charge and knows some history about these mines. You see I want to find a special mine that my Great-grandfather worked in around 1870. I was told that he carved a Catholic Chapel out of salt in one of the mines. Have you ever heard of that or know which mine it is?"

Both of the men shook their heads, said nothing more and went back to their work. I was persistent however, and continued asking questions. Finally they both gave me a blank stare, and that was the end of our conversation.

How rude! But I was undaunted. If they knew nothing, I would have to try talking to some of the other men. The shed was located near a huge cave which I assumed, was the opening of a working salt mine. I left the shed and walked a short way into the cave. I asked several men if they had ever heard of such a chapel, and if so did they know where it was. None of the men were helpful so I sat down on a nearby bench wondering what to do next. In a few minutes an older gentlemen came and sat down beside me. I asked him if he had ever heard of a master sculptor named Benton who had been in these parts during the 1870's.

I saw him come alert but he didn't say a word he just walked away. I realized, I had been asking about a Catholic Chapel, and suppose these Mormons didn't like that. Then it dawned on me that maybe the chapel no longer existed. That would be why no one knew of it.

It was early afternoon and finding nothing of interest to occupy my mind I decided to walk around, but not too far away from the work shed. I didn't want to get lost as the light was changing on the salt fields. Looking off in the distance I saw what appeared to be ponds which were really salt pools glittering with a multitude of colors, and some looked dirty in shades of blackish-brown. I stood fascinated at what lay before me and continued walking further and further away from the shed. I'd told Mr. Brown I would meet him at the shed by sunset so I quickly turned around, planning to retrace my steps, but I had wondered too far and I was completely lost.

As I turned I almost ran into a man who looked to be about 60 years old flashing a big warm smile and looking quite friendly. He spoke, "Young Lady, are you the woman who is looking for the Catholic Chapel? It's not around here, but I know the location. If you care to go with me, I'll show you where it is. The men in my family have been working these mines for decades and I'm quite familiar with all of them. The mine you're speaking of is a legend among the older miners. The young ones don't even believe it exists, but I do. May I ask how you know about it, and why you want to see it? Not many folks venture out this far just to see salt mines."

"My great-grandfather was the man who sculpted the chapel and I would like to see his work with my own eyes and prove to myself and my family that it truly exists."

"Okay, I understand. I'll take you there for a price. You must swear you will not tell anyone where it is or what you saw. Do you agree?"

"Yes, of course. I promise."

It did occur to me I might be in danger, but he looked harmless so I agreed to go with him. I was a bit uneasy, but I decided since I'd come this far I wasn't going to turn back. He asked me to follow him. We approached one large mound and standing at the entrance of that salt mine stood a young man. He was nice looking, but seemed uneasy at my being there. He spoke to the older man in hushed tones. I couldn't hear much of what he said, but I did hear him call the man, Father Powell.

What? I couldn't believe what I'd heard, a Catholic priest out here — what for? Of course, it was logical he would know of the chapel and that's why he had offered to take me to it.

"Yes, miss, I'm a Catholic priest and I come out here quite often to worship in the chapel. It's a place I can be alone and pray. I have loved it since I was a child. May I ask what your name is?"

"Yes, Father Powell, I'm Melinda Ann Kingsley from Virginia and I'm pleased to meet you."

"Well, Miss Kingsley, people haven't asked about this chapel and the mine for years. It has been my family's secret for as long as I can remember. This young man's name is Paul. He and his father work the mines. Paul is studying to become a Catholic priest and often comes out here with me. I think you will be quite safe with us, in case you were worried."

"This particular mine, you want to see, has been closed to the public for years. A group of salt miners convinced the owners that the mine was unstable and needed to be closed. As I understand it, they closed it in order to protect the mine and the chapel it contains. The secret had been successfully kept until you appeared here today asking questions. We are lucky because the men you spoke to are our friends and also sworn to secrecy."

"Father Powell, as I told you my great-grandfather was the sculptor of the chapel. His name was Earl Benton, and he was from Philadelphia. He came out west on a wagon train with his wife Grace and their daughter, my Grandmother Lilly. I've heard stories about him all of my life and I've always wanted to come here and see his work for myself. I want you to take me down into that mine and I want to see the chapel. Is that asking too much?"

"No not really."

"Now we understand and applaud you for your courage, but we must warn you that getting down there will be a challenge. We still use the big barrel your great-grandfather probably used to descend the shaft. If you're not afraid to put your life in our hands we will take you down there, but you must swear to not tell another living soul. The chapel is our secret. Will you swear by all that is Holy?"

"Yes, of course! And as far as my being afraid, I don't think so. I'm a former nurse in the United States Army Nurses Corps who was stationed in France during the war. I feel like I've been to hell and back from that experience, so gentlemen, going down a mine shaft in a barrel will not bother me in the least. Come on. Let's get going!"

I eyed the barrel before getting into it and it looked like a large old ancient bark bucket, scraped and splintered. The three of us stepped into the barrel through a small door which Paul latched shut. Father Powell untied the free rope of a block and tackle pulley system. The barrel was suspended from the moving pulley. As he played out the ragged looking rope through the moving pulley, the barrel lowered into the mine shaft. The stationary pulley was fixed to a crude wood A-frame at the top of the shaft. Each pulley contained three large steel wheels which the ragged rope passed over and around. As Father Powell played out free rope I began to notice how old and worn the rope was. I even saw broken strands in some places! Then it occurred to me – there were three persons in the barrel instead of the usual two. I wondered – would the worn rope hold three?

It was dark except for the miner's hats we wore, with the small carbide lights burning brightly and making the sides of the salt shaft shift with our shadows. There we were the three of us tightly packed in the barrel closer than I would have liked and I kept thinking about that old worn rope.

We had almost reach the floor of the cave when one of the old and rotten ropes snapped and we went crashing to the bottom. The barrel flipped and turned, tossing all three of us to the floor, or so I thought. I lay still with the breath knocked out of me, but as far as I could tell I was unhurt. I lay there, taking stock of the situation and wondering what to do next. Both Paul and Father Powell's hats had been knocked off their heads and now lay a small distance from where I'd fallen. Paul was across the shaft. I could see that he was shaken up and was probably bruised but otherwise did not seem hurt.

He began to stir, pulled himself up and reached for his miner's hat. When he became aware of me, he wanted to know if I was all right. He looked at the barrel and saw that it had lodged itself into one side of the old timbers and looked very unstable. He was afraid the barrel might swing back out so he asked me to move into the traverse tunnel to the right. But before I did, I realized Father Powell was not with us. We both looked around puzzled and then at the same time looked above our heads and there he was hanging upside down, with one foot caught in a loop of the free rope. He was unconscious having apparently hit his head in the free fall. He was bleeding a great deal from a scalp wound. The blood was flowing down his face and he looked terrible. He was suspended just far enough out of our reach to make it impossible for either one of us to get him down.

"You say you're a nurse? If you are I've got a plan, and you look pretty strong and agile. Father definitely needs some medical attention and we need to get him down. If you can climb up on my back, and get in a standing position on my shoulders, I think you can manage to cut him loose. Take your shoes off and let's give it a try. Are you ready?"

I kicked off my shoes, Paul knelt down, and I proceeded to climb on his back. He slowly stood up and had me to hold on to his hands while I raised myself up. I found my footing on his muscled shoulders, stretched to my full height, and found myself able to reach the entangled foot. Getting this close to Father Powell I could see he was slowly coming around. I was afraid that when he realized his precarious position he would react instinctively, jerk hard and fall straight down hitting his head again, and maybe breaking an arm, leg, or even his neck.

I put one hand on his ankle while I pulled the small pocket knife Paul had given me out of my waist band. As I tried to cut the rope I spoke softly to Father Powell telling him what had happened. He did react suddenly and surprised me by wrenching the knife out of my hand. Then like a trapeze artist he lifted himself up grabbed the rope with his other hand, and proceeded to cut himself loose. He dropped to the floor of the shaft with ease, as I tumbled down Paul's back. Father Powell's forehead was covered with blood that streamed down his face and into his eyes.

We stood looking at each other trying to make sure we weren't seriously hurt. I knew the scalp wound needed attention. "Father Powell, you're bleeding and I need to apply pressure to your forehead. Seeing the small dainty hanky I pulled out he laughed, reached into his pocket and pulled out a man's large white handkerchief. When I pressed it to his forehead it still didn't stop the bleeding. I reached down, raised my skirt and tore off the bottom ruffle of my under slip. Both men looked at me a bit surprised, but I needed a bandage and this was the only place I could get one. I ripped off a long piece and wound it around his head, applying pressure.

Paul spoke up first. "Now we have a more pressing issue. How are we going to get out of here?"

I replied, "I understand that's going to be a problem, but since we've come this far I would like to go on and see the chapel, first." They looked at me like I was crazy or that I didn't understand the gravity of our situation.

"You're still not afraid to go on after what just happened?"

"No Father! I'm not sure how we will get out, but I can't turn back now that we are here. If you know where the chapel is, I want to see it!"

"All right young lady, follow me, but watch your step in this dim light."

Father Powell had forgotten his forehead by now, and his scalp had stopped bleeding. None of us seemed to be the worse for wear, but although no one mentioned it all of us were concerned about how we were going to get out of the mine.

Father Powell led the way as we moved slowly deeper into the gray-white tunnel. We came to an opening covered with a heavy canvas curtain, old and crinkled with age. The opening was about five feet high and four feet wide.

Father Powell asked Paul to raise the curtain, and instructed me to stoop over and go underneath the canvas. Now we were in an even darker place, but as our eyes adjusted we saw an arched door covered with burlap. As we entered this door I was surprised to see light filtering down to us through deep light shafts to the surface. The light was being reflected by large mirrors. According to Father Powell my Great-grandfather Benton had used the same principles that the ancient Egyptians had used in the pyramids.

I realized that now we were in the chapel walking down the center isle toward the altar. As Father Powell lit candles along the way the walls began to sparkle as the light touched the salt figures. It was breathtaking to see. The altar was carved with a beautiful religious scene of angels hovering over the holy family.

Grandmother Lilly had described this place to me, as she had remembered it as a child. She said the whole chapel had an unearthly quality that words could not adequately express. It was inspiring! There in sculpted salt was the story, Joseph leading a small donkey which carried Mary and the infant Jesus, wrapped in her arms on their way to Egypt.

Paul lit the altar candles and as the flames shimmered the sculptured figures seemed to move. I was enchanted and awed by the experience. I stood there in wonder at how my great-grandfather had created such a beautiful work of art. I knew it was a shame that none of my family would ever see this quiet peaceful place. Father Powell knelt and thanked God for our safety, as he encouraged us to repeat The Lord's Prayer. Paul, being practical, said a prayer for God to help us find a safe way out of the mine. I said my own prayer as I let my eyes linger on each salt figure and imagined my Grandmother Lilly kneeling with her mother. Had she felt the same admiration I was feeling? I was sure she had. We had been in the chapel for about twenty minutes when we extinguished the candles and left.

As we reluctantly retraced our steps to the mouth of the tunnel we discussed how we could get out of the mine. It was getting late and none of us relished the idea of spending the night in a salt mine.

The experience we had shared had brought us together like old friends and we trusted each other. Now assessing our situation Father Powell began moving around and touching the walls like he was looking for something. Paul and I watched and waited for some explanation. Finally he stopped and pointed to what he was looking for. It was an old wooden ladder which was covered with salt and dirt and was attached to the shaft wall. You could barely see it.

"Miss Kingsley, can you handle heights, and how good are you at climbing? This ladder will not hold me or Paul, but you are small enough so it will probably hold your weight. We need you to give it a try. What do you say?"

"Oh I'm not afraid of heights and I've climbed a number of trees in my day, but what I don't understand is how will I be able to find the rungs on that old ladder? They all look buried to me."

"Let me show you! You will have to take the knife and cut out each rung as you move toward the top of the shaft. Here, I'll show you how it's done." He carved out the first four feet himself, then turned to me and gave me the knife saying, "If you want to get out of here, you will have to dig. It is a long way to the top, but you can do it."

I didn't really have a choice. I began my slow ascent, being careful not to look down. I strained to see the hidden rungs as I cut away the salt and dirt. When each rung was where I could hold or stand on it, I'd place my hand and foot in the cuts moving slowly upward. After about fifteen to twenty-five feet of this I was crying to myself. My hands felt like raw meat from the salt flying in the air and the roughness of the wood. I was tempted to give up, but I knew those two men were depending on me to get help. I wore one of the miner's caps with the yellowish light projecting on the wall. I was also aware of the two tiny lights below me. Sweat dripped down into my eyes and my hair was straggling out of the knotted bun.

I'd taken my shoes off, in order to get a better feel of the rungs as I climbed. However, that may have been a mistake because my feet began to cramp as I put my weight on each successive rung. I could barely see my feet because of my long skirt. I was also wearing a white blouse plus my torn under slip and my one-piece jersey. My stockings were sagging and in general I was having difficulty with all the material wrapped around my legs.

This was ridiculous. I reached down and unbuttoned my skirt. Then I carefully stepped out of it and let the skirt fall. Next my slip came off. Now, I was in a camisole, blouse and jersey pants, and long hose, but I didn't care because I was able to move better. I wasn't sure what Father Powell or Paul thought when they saw the garments come floating down to them but I didn't care. I could move more freely. As the clothes landed I heard the men cheering me on and applauding my female ingenuity.

As I neared the top, I found that some of the rungs had been removed or had rotted out which slowed my progress and made my footing less sure. But I was not going to give up. I just prayed I would not fall to my death. Within a few more feet I finally reached the top of the shaft where the remaining ropes dangled from the fixed pulley on the A-frame timbers at the top of the shaft. .

I crawled out and looked at the scene around me. All was quiet and I became aware of headlights coming in my direction. It was the driver I'd engaged earlier in the day. When the taxi came to a stop Peter jumped out and called to me, "Lady, where have you been? It is way past sundown, and I've been waiting around at that office like you said. But I got worried about you wandering around out here all alone and I decided I'd better look for you. I don't think you should have come out here in the first place. It's none of my business, but this is no place for a woman!"

When he got a good look at me he really became alarmed at what he saw. "Dear God, young woman, what has happened to you? Were you attacked? You look awful and you're only half dressed!"

I guess I was quite a sight from his point of view. I certainly was not the pristine young woman he had driven here earlier. I was a disheveled mess, and it was true I was only half dressed. There I was with a miner's cap, with a dirty face, red-raw looking hands, hair half pinned up with the other half straggling down, no skirt or slip, just my jersey pants and sagging stockings with holes in them. I was dirty, wet with sweat, and my bare feet were cold.

Before I could answer him he reached into the taxi, pulled out a blanket and threw it at me. "Wrap yourself up girl before you catch cold, and then you can tell me what happened."

I caught my breath, wrapped up in the blanket and replied, "Peter, there was an accident! The rope on the pulley system broke. Two men are still stranded in the mineshaft. We have to get help!" He grasped the situation quickly and started the car. Before I got in the taxi I ran to the top of the mine shaft and yelled down to Father Powell and Paul. "I made it to the top. That taxi driver is here and we're going to get help. Just hold on! We'll be back soon, I promise!" Once I was safe in the taxi Peter turned the car around and we headed for town.

We stopped at the main office but found it shut down as we expected. We drove the fifteen miles to town hoping to find some help. There were several men standing on one street corner, and after we told them our story they agreed to help. Some came with us and the others went for ropes and machinery to help bring Father Powell and Paul to the surface. As it turned out it was a relatively easy procedure. A second pulley system was rigged with a platform securely attached and then lowered into the shaft. Father Powell and Paul were soon standing outside of the mine, tired, and happy to be out in the fresh air. I'd not been able to stay in the taxi as instructed. When I saw them I ran to each one and hugged them long and hard still wrapped in my blanket. I whispered in each of their ears that I'd not mentioned the chapel to anyone.

They were both pleased and grinning from ear to ear as they told the other men what I'd done, cutting each rung out of the dirt and salt deposit. The men were quite impressed and applauded my efforts. Thank heaven they didn't ask any questions about the mine or why we were down there. Father Powell spoke to them. "Well, boys, this little gal told me her Great-grandfather worked in one of these old mines in the 1870's, and she wanted to see the conditions he may have worked under. This is one of the older abandoned mines with the barrel drop, and I thought she would enjoy it…well, as it turned out three of us were too much weight for that old rope and we all got tossed around. It was a good thing she was with us though because she is the best little nurse I ever did see."

Then he pointed to his head, pulled off the bloody bandage which looked like a limp piece of cloth soaked in blood. Then it occurred to him that he was standing there holding my skirt and slip over his arm, and I was still wrapped in a blanket. He handed me my things, and I don't know why I did it, but I dropped the blanket, placed my slip and skirt over my head pulling them down with the men looking on. They cheered, turned around and left. I was shocked at myself, but then Father Powell gave me a hug and said I was a smart little gal and they were happy to have met me. With an unmistaken wink that made me blush, Paul added that he was happy to have had such a wild adventure with me. We all laughed and thanked God we were able to get out of the mine alive.

Again I promised that I would not tell anyone about the chapel for fear it would be destroyed. My lips were sealed. Here was a family secret that could not be shared with anyone. I knew the secret of the salt mine chapel would be safe with me, and that Father Powell and Paul would continue to worship in the little chapel with its salt crystal walls for years to come. That pleased me. It would be something to think about in the future. Peter picked up the blanket, opened the car door and I got in.

"Well, that was exciting. Now what are you planning for tomorrow and can I be of service?"

"As a matter of fact, I would like to visit the local library to see if there are any records of wagon trains that traveled West about the time my great-grandparents were here. I wonder if anyone knows the story of a lost wagon train that was destroyed during a flash flood. There could be some record of it."

"All right you're on. Be ready about ten o'clock. I'll pick you up in front of your hotel. But don't go wondering off by yourself again. I might not be able to find you next time."

It all went as planned but I was disappointed with the information at the public library. I found out that some wagon trains had taken a Northern Route and others a Southern Route. Since I had no idea of the route or the name of the wagon master, the wagon train could not be identified so it was a dead end. Also there was not specific record of a train being lost in a flood.

I was far from being discouraged. I'd located and seen my great-grandfather's sculpture work in the salt mine for a brief time. Now in following Grandmother Lilly's footsteps west, it was time to find my way to Carson City, Nevada. The ticket master at the railroad station said I would have to take a train to Reno, Nevada first and from there take the Virginia and Truckee Line to Carson City, Nevada.

• 101 •

CHAPTER TWENTY

The day I left Salt Lake City it was clear and warm. As I stood on the platform waiting for my train, I was astounded at the landscape around me. The early pioneers of the Mormon Church had transformed this valley into a true paradise. I could smell native desert plants mingling with the scent of fruit trees.

Once I boarded the train, the ride was uneventful with the landscape changing little. I was entertained by the activity of the passengers. Those who were older moved slowly down the aisle grumbling about the young families with the uncontrolled children. The young parents trailed behind their children encouraging them to be quiet and to walk and not run. Then there were the people who sat down next to me trying to start a conversation. I knew it was rude, but I ignored them. I know they meant well, but I wasn't interested in speaking to anyone. As I listened to the clickety-clack of the train wheels I leaned my head back and thought about Reno, Nevada. I had heard it was a small city that thought of itself as big, a place where well known people visited, and according to the conductor, Reno was still a fairly wild town. That didn't matter to me. .

I had to face it. I missed James and his attentions more than I wanted to admit. I wondered what would have happened if I'd gone to the hotel with him. Would he have cared about me after that or would I have become just a passing fancy to him? Was marriage really not for me? Did I intend to stay single the rest of my life? Probably not, but that would have to come later. Right now I was on a quest re-tracing my Grandmother Lilly's travels. But, I still couldn't help day dreaming about James.

As I gazed out the window I felt I was being hypnotized by the rhythm of the moving train. I marveled at how long and hard it had been for a covered wagon to cross this endless stretches of sage flat land at twenty miles a day.

All I wanted was to get to Reno and this trip to be over. I had my supper, instructed the porter to make up my berth and retired early.

The next morning when the train pulled into the Reno station I quickly got off and went directly to the ticket office. I bought a ticket and boarded the train for Carson City. That's when I noticed a gentleman that I thought I'd seen on the train from Salt Lake City to Reno. Now here he was on the same train with me again. I don't know why I even noticed him except he looked like a city dweller and not a westerner.

Aunt Ginny had told me that in Grandmother Lilly's time Carson City had been a wide-open town with a small number of businesses, just a few houses scattered here and there, two churches, a livery stable, saloons, and a general store. I wanted to see where Lilly had lived as a young girl. I couldn't help wondering what changes had taken place since she had wandered into town. As the story goes a flash flood had caught their wagon train unprotected, and destroyed it, taking her mother's life and leaving teenage Lilly alone.

She found a home in Ruby's Parlor House not as a working girl but as a cook and housekeeper. I hoped I could find the place. I had no idea whether any of the women who had worked there were in Carson City or even still living.

I checked my luggage and walked to the St. Charles Hotel. As I wandered down the main street, the city looked pretty much as I'd imagined. It was set among rolling hills with many tall green pine trees gracing the streets. I did my usual thing in a new city and hired a taxi to take me around. The driver, Wally, took me to the oldest part of town, where several buildings of the late 1800's still stood. I decided to walk around on the boardwalk and explore the small shops. As I moved in and around the shops one sign caught my eye. It read: **"Old Fashion Treats – by Peaches"**

That name was familiar to me. Hadn't grandmother mentioned a good friend of hers named Peaches who was one of the girls who worked in Ruby's Parlor House?

I walked in to find myself in a gift shop and behind it a backroom with small wrought iron tables and chairs. The tables were covered with white Battenberg lace table cloths each with fresh flowers arranged in delicate china teapots. The decor was very Victorian and I'm sure very appealing to most women.

As I looked around at exquisite gifts and confections a lovely young woman approached me. She was about my age and height. Her cornflower blue eyes sparkled with delight. She had an old-fashion charm but was dressed in modern clothes. She wore a mid-calf length skirt, and a straight shirtwaist blouse.

"Could I help you, Ma'am?" Since I wasn't interested in buying any jams, jellies, dried fruits or nuts she was a bit puzzled. "No, but I would like you to answer a question for me."

"I would be happy to, if I can."

"If you have lived in Carson City most of your life, can you tell me something about the woman who owns this shop? Is her name Peaches? The reason I'm asking is that my Grandmother Lilly once lived here and she had a dear friend named Peaches."

"Yes, I've lived here all of my life, and Peaches is my grandmother. After Grandfather Charley died my mother, Ariel, and I managed the store. You must be Lilly Benton's granddaughter! I've heard numerous stories about your grandmother. What is your name, where did you come from, and how long are you staying in town? You must meet my grandmother! She is a living legend, now. Not that she likes being referred to as the town's oldest "working girl," but she accepts it gracefully with a sense of humor. Come on, I'll take you to meet her. She grabbed her jacket and hat, and had one of the other women take over for her. The next thing I knew we were in her car, a 1912 Franklin Runabout with one of those Renault hoods. "My name is Lillian Brandy, but most folks call me Brandy, so why don't you?"

"I'm pleased to know you, Brandy. My name is Melinda Ann and I'm very excited to be going to see your grandmother.

"Well, I need to warn you that my grandmother is quite old and feeble now. No one knows for sure how old she is. She never has told me or anyone else for that matter."

As she drove back through town we passed the train station and crossed the railroad tracks. Then she suddenly turned to me.

"Say, would you like to drive by the old parlor house? It isn't far from my grandmother's home and we have plenty of time before dark. I'd like for you to see it before you have to leave."

It felt like we were old friends. The quiet residential streets were covered overhead by long branches growing from old trees which provided welcome shade. We pulled up in front of a large two story house with a picket fence enclosing the front yard. At the side of the house was a trellis fence covered with morning glories. The house was white with gray trim and a wrap-around porch which the men were painting. A stack of white wicker tables and chairs sat on the front lawn along with a variety of hanging flower baskets.

Before we got out of the car, Brandy pointed to a sign hanging on a decorative pole standing in the front yard. The sign read, "Miss Harriett Hamilton's School for Young Ladies".

"Grandmother Peaches thinks it is quite funny that it is now a school for young ladies. She has often remarked that Miss Ruby's dream was for the house to become exactly that. Isn't that a scream?"

"Melinda Ann, would you like to go inside? I can introduce you to Miss Hamilton."

"Would I? Of course, I'd love it!"

Brandy pulled into the driveway.

"I'm sure Miss Hamilton will be pleased to meet you. You see she is aware that the house has had an illustrious past history because of the stories the old timers tell. Meeting you and hearing about your Grandmother Lilly will be a treat for her. Some people around here have not totally forgotten the house's more sordid past and recognize it as part of their history…now they are rather proud that it is a respected school for girls."

CHAPTER TWENTY-ONE

As we walked through the lattice arbor, which covered the rock path leading to the back of the house, we were met by Miss Hamilton. She looked to be in her forties. She wore a modest gray jumper which hung to her ankles, much like the one I had on. Her hair was light brown, pulled tightly to the top of her head and secured in a bun. She wore no jewelry except for a watch pin which hung from a ribbon pinned to one strap of her jumper.

Brandy quickly introduced me to Miss Hamilton.

"I'm happy to make your acquaintance, Miss Kingsley. I hope you girls don't mind coming in the back door since the front porch has just been painted."

"Not at all Miss Hamilton, I want you to show my friend around the house if it's not too much trouble. You see, her Grandmother Lilly once worked for Miss Ruby as the housekeeper and cook."

That's when Miss Hamilton's eyes opened with a startled look.

"Of course, we will start here in the kitchen. We have made some improvements over the years."

As we entered the all-white kitchen with its scrubbed linoleum floor I could feel the warmth of the gas stove. The sign on the front of the stove proudly stated, St. Clair Stoves Ranges. It was quite a modern appliance and it even had a *Robertshaw Automaticook* dial. The aroma of fresh baked cookies filled the room. There was a true feeling of hominess in the house. Standing nearby was a white refrigerator shaped like a rectangular box with a large door in front and on the top a foot of coil tubing about as high as a hat box. I wondered how this room looked when my grandmother saw it for the first time.

"The dining area is the most active room in the house. We eat all of our meals here and the students do their homework at the table. Now, Brandy and Melinda Ann, this is my favorite room, the parlor."

The parlor was a surprise with its elegant pieces of period furniture. There were two Empire-style tub-shaped chairs and a matching set of settees with button backs and upholstered seats. The upholstery was a gray green color with pink and white roses. There was an upright piano in one corner and some book shelves along one wall. It seemed a bit fancy for a girls' school, so I mentioned this to Miss Hamilton.

"My dear, every young lady needs to be trained in good manners and proper etiquette. They should learn how to set a table and be gracious hostesses, don't you agree?"

I couldn't resist. "Yes, of course, but formal etiquette is not necessarily the focal point of a woman's life. You know, modern women are already beginning to join men in the work place, although they are paid less. Will your young women be able to adapt to today's world?"

"The old values will never change as I see it. It is my job to see that traditions are kept, so in addition to teaching the girls the basic academic fundamentals of reading, writing, and arithmetic, I also teach them how to be ladies."

When we were finally on our way to Peaches I saw a few Victorian houses and some pre-war bungalows. Brandy slowed down and there, behind a picket fence, tucked behind some cotton wood trees, sat a lovely old Victorian house with a wrap-around front porch. It was growing dark so I could not see the color or details of the house.

Electric lights were burning brightly through tall slender glass windows that seemed to invite us inside. At the front door, Brandy called out to her grandmother and she knocked loudly on the door. An old woman, almost as wide as she was tall, answered the door. She took one look and invited us to come inside.

The minute I looked at her I knew it was Peaches. Her hair was white as snow and her cheeks full and rosy. Despite her wrinkles she was still pretty. She was a jolly old woman with a twinkle in her eyes that let us know she was still full of life.

When Brandy introduced me as Lilly Benton's granddaughter, she rushed over and hugged me.

I had questions for her, but it was she who started asking questions of me. She wanted to know all she could about my family when Lilly had gotten married and to whom, and where she had lived all these years, and most of all if she was still alive. I answered all her questions, and when she was satisfied she began telling us stories about Lilly and the days they spent together at Ruby's.

"Why, darlin', living in Ruby's house was a great adventure. Working there I learned a great deal about life and people. It was your grandmother who helped me change my way of life. None of us ever dreamed Lilly was so smart. She was such a cute little thing, and innocent as a lamb when she came to us. We all loved listening to Lilly tell her stories, and having her read the Bible to us. Miss Ruby thought we all needed religion, and I suppose we did. My life changed when one of my regulars asked Miss Ruby, for my hand in marriage. Can you imagine?"

We were intrigued and wanted to hear more so she told us of her wedding day in a little church with Ruby and all the girls present, much to the displeasure of some of the regular church members. After a good chuckle, she settled down and with a tear told us of the death of Jamie, her first child.

"But now, Melinda Ann, tell me more about your grandmother. I didn't hear from Lilly after she and Myrna left Carson City, but I did read about Miss Laurie and her singing career in America and Europe."

I was enchanted by this woman and was soon calling her Grandma Peaches, because she insisted and it seemed appropriate. I felt as though I was home, that I belonged. When we should have been leaving she offered us a light evening meal, and of course, we were hungry so we stayed and had a wonderful time. When I told Grandma Peaches I was staying at the St. Charles Hotel she would have none of it, and promptly sent Brandy to the hotel to pick up my luggage.

The guest bed room was a lovely Victorian room with tall Lace - covered windows looking out toward the front lawn. I crawled into bed, said my prayers, and fell asleep thinking of Grandmother Lilly.

CHAPTER TWENTY-TWO

The next morning standing on the platform waiting for the train I saw that man again. He was getting ready to board the same train I was, the Southern Pacific, called the Overland Limited to San Francisco. He never looked directly at me, but somehow I felt he was watching me.

Before I left Carson City I'd wired my father for money. I wasn't worried because I felt sure he would send me any amount I needed. My funds were depleted. I needed a good deal of cash, for hotels, meals, and most especially for a new wardrobe, which I was convinced was a must. Besides if there were any chance I would meet James again, I wanted to look my best.

James, James?...what was his last name. Oh dear God, I really didn't know. I didn't want to ask him a third time, because I was too proud. Now how was I going to find him in a city like San Francisco? It was a dilemma, but after all, he was not the reason I was going to San Francisco.

I knew that Grandmother Lilly had joined a troupe of players in Cripple Creek, and traveled a circuit which included San Francisco. She often spoke of a time when the company was booked into the Maguire's Opera House in San Francisco. With great sadness she reminisced of having missed the great Miss Sarah Bernhardt, who had been at that opera house the week before.

I intended to find Maguire's where my Grandmother said she had performed. I promised myself once there I would visit the entire theatre district and see if I could find any information about the shows that were advertised during the time my grandmother would have been there.

I tried to convince myself this was the reason I was going, but I knew the real reason was because my thoughts were increasingly on James and I knew San Francisco was where he was. I had to admit to myself that I was infatuated with him.

I wondered if he felt anything for me. I wanted to see him again, but then that old feeling would come over me that he was hiding something. But no matter what, I was determined to find him.

The Overland Limited was a costly, elegant train with all the latest equipment and I rode in the height of luxury. Passengers who could afford this train were well-dressed, well-mannered and reserved. I was concerned about my depleted of funds, but I knew my father would come through. I knew he would react quickly to the telegram I had sent him from Carson City. I felt sure an allowance would be sent immediately.

When the train pulled into the San Francisco station I was so excited I could hardly contain myself. I went to the telegraph office first, to pick up my money, but nothing was there, not even a message. I was a bit perplexed but still confident. I had addressed the telegram to Father and he should have received it by now. But Birdie! She always managed to answer the door when a telegram came. I could just see her opening it and then hiding it in her pocket. That would be just like her. Whatever had happened I had to have money, without it I would not survive in the big city.

Still relying on Father responding, I registered at the finest hotel in San Francisco just to keep up appearances. I explained to the hotel manager that I would be receiving funds soon, that my father was Mr. Harley Orchard-Kingsley, the owner of the famous Kingsley Plantation in Virginia. He frowned at me, but since I was from such an illustrious family he would trust me and wait a few days for me to receive the money. However if it did not arrive, I would be asked to leave.

Hearing this I became very concerned while it would probably be good for me to be on my own. I didn't have a job and was not really ready to go back to work. I thought I had plenty of money to finance the trip, but I'd not planned as well as I should have. I had to put those thoughts out of my mind. I went directly to my suite, after ordering a light supper to be served in my room.

I unpacked with the help of a hotel maid and I was shocked at how shabby my clothes really were for a young woman. I knew I should dress more stylishly, but it just wasn't that important to me. The truth was apparent when the maid asked, "Are these your clothes or your mother's?"

That proved it to me. I had to go shopping tomorrow morning! My plan was to find a shop that catered to San Francisco's elite and buy a complete wardrobe. But if I had no money, how could I do it? That's when an idea came to me. I went downstairs, marched right up to the manager of the hotel and told him my story, but he smiled and replied, "There is no problem, Miss Kingsley. In fact if you like, you may stay a month without any advance payment. And if you need emergency funds that also can be arranged." Well, that seemed a little strange, but I guessed my good name must have made him generous.

Just as I was turning to leave he stopped me. "Miss Kingsley, you have an envelope in your box that was delivered this afternoon."

It was addressed to me, but there was no return address or even a note inside. I assumed it was from my father because it was full of money. It would take care of me for quite some time. I told the manager I would be paying my bills and that I would need no advance from him. After removing a small amount from the envelope, I instructed the desk clerk to put the rest in the hotel safe. I retired to my room and slept like a baby the rest of the night.

The next morning I got up early, hungry for breakfast and went downstairs. In the hotel lobby there was a large group of women, of all ages, gathered for some type of a women's rally. I asked one of the women what they were doing there, and what type of convention they were attending. "Oh, you haven't heard? It is a rally for women who are interested in learning how our government really works and how to effectively use our recently acquired right to vote. They also intend to fight for better working conditions for women. It's all very exciting. You should join us!" Was I interested? Absolutely! Shopping could wait for another day. I was all for women's rights!

Most of the women were well-dressed and all had colored sashes hanging across their chests. At the end hung a round badge with their name and home state printed on it. I decided it would be fun, and the rally would be held in a large San Francisco Park. More and more women crowded into the lobby, and as they moved along toward the waiting trolley cars, I walked with them. Several of the leaders ushered us into small groups and told us to stay together throughout the day. Once in the park there were speakers and each group broke periodically for refreshments, instructions, and discussion.

As evening approached there were several tented areas in the park where we were invited to stop and eat. Cold lemonade, iced tea, chicken, beef, and roast pork sandwiches were offered by the influential women hostesses of the gathering.

When the trolley cars were ready to take the group back to the hotel, I didn't hear the clanging bell signaling us to return to the cars. I'd gotten separated from the girl who had befriended me and I ended up at the other end of the park. I was caught up in the moment and distracted by some poorly dressed people who were definitely not part of the women's group.

By the time I realized the group of women had gone, the trolley cars had left without me. Since I wasn't really part of the original group I was not missed. The policemen who had been standing around followed the trolley cars out of the park. They did not realize I was left behind. I was aware the police were there most of the day because this type of rally was unpopular with a great many people, especially the men, because of the women's rights movement.

Looking around, I became frightened. I was alone except for the group of bad-mannered people who were coming toward me. I knew I needed to get out of there, but as I made my move to run one woman who looked unkempt and dirty began to circle me. She stepped up in front of me.

"Whatch-ya-doin'out so late Dearie, and all alone?"

Another grabbed my pouch purse and began going through it. Then she turned it upside down and dumped the contents on the grass.

"Dang it, there ain't nothin' here but a bunch of brochures, a comb, a little bit of money, and some trinkets."

Saying this, she reached over and tore at my blouse ripping out one sleeve and spinning me around. I was so shocked that I didn't know what to do, or how to respond, but it made me mad. All I could think of was that they had not gotten much money, because it was locked up in the hotel safe.

Another aggressive woman pulled me forward and pinned my right arm behind my back. Then she reached up and pulled the hat pin out of my hat, which messed up my hair and caused the hat to fall to the ground. I tried to free myself from her but she was too strong for me.

"Get your dirty hands off of me and let me go!"

"Since you ain't got no money, and bein' a nice-looking girl, we'll take you to "Mother". She'll know what to do with you."

I began to get the picture. I'd heard of young women being pressed into living on the streets by just such a scheme. I began to relax and quit struggling but I was frantically trying to figure a way out of the situation.

"All right, let's go see this mother of yours," I yelled, "but let go of my arm!" The woman relaxed a bit and I immediately twisted out of her grasp, turned, and ran as fast as I could toward the streetlight at the entrance of the park, screaming all the way.

Running through the gate, I ran head long into a policeman who was coming into the park on a dead run. When the group of street women saw this, they dissolved into the shadows of the big trees. As the policeman took hold of my arms I was shaking so hard I thought my teeth would fall out. In a pleasant Irish accent he told me I was safe and nothing was going to happen to me. We walked out toward the bright lights of the city and there, as if waiting just for me, was a taxi. As I got in the driver said a nice gentleman had told him to wait for a woman who would soon be coming out of the park. His instructions were to take me to my hotel and not to charge me for the ride.

I was surprised to say the least, but also relieved. Who was this mysterious man and how did he know I was in the park in the first place? I really didn't care because all I could think of was getting to the hotel, taking a warm bath, eating a light supper and falling into my bed. My mind could sort it all out in the morning.

When I arrived at the hotel the lobby was deserted and quiet. I was glad no one was there because I was quite a sight. My hat was gone, my hair was falling down, my purse gone, my dress sleeve torn and one shoe was missing. I picked up my key hardly looking at the desk clerk, ran up the stairs as fast as I could, and went into my room.

When I turned on the lights, I was surprised to see a number of different sized packages wrapped in brown paper and several vases of flowers sitting around the room. I could not find a note or signature card saying who had sent them. I didn't know what to think. I decided it was too late to have supper so I stretched out on the bed exhausted fully-clothed and fell into a deep sleep.

When I awakened I thought about the previous evening and the frightening experience. As I was about to get up I heard the maid come into the room. She went over to the tall windows, pulled the drapes open letting daylight flow in. It was a misty, cloudy morning with the smell of rain in the air. But the weather would not dampen my spirits. I would go shopping and I would enjoy my day. But what of these packages, and how was I going to find James?

Perhaps I could hire a detective. Father would send me more money and he would understand. At least I hoped he would, but I didn't need to tell him why I needed the money. While all of these things were going through my mind, I became aware of the maid who was encouraging me to eat the delightful breakfast she had brought in. She said I'd ordered it. Well if I did, I certainly did not remember doing so. As I sat up and glanced in the mirror, I could see that I was still a mess, but the maid didn't seem to notice, she just fluffed the pillows behind my back and set the tray over my lap.

The tray had so many silver serving pieces sitting on it that I could hardly see the tray itself. A slender crystal vase held an exquisite single pink rose! I'd never had breakfast in bed except at the plantation when I was too sick to enjoy it. I looked for a card with the rose, but there was none. The maid said it was compliments of the hotel.

As I ate breakfast, the maid handed me a newspaper. On the front page was a picture of Mike O'Sullivan, the policeman who had come to my rescue. I had taken a sip of coffee and nearly spewed it from my mouth as I read over his picture, "Mysterious Woman Saved in the Park!" I was the woman! I had to laugh at thinking of myself as being mysterious. The article also included a statement that a gentleman was looking for this unknown woman and wished to contact me.

Who was it? It just had to be James. My search to find him might not be so hard after all. I was elated at the thought of seeing him again. I had to get moving. Then I thought of the packages and flowers. I almost tore the bed up and dumped the tray on the floor, but the maid restrained me. When I briefly explained my involvement with James, she was excited as I was. She helped me with my bath. I slipped on my undergarments and she fixed my hair. When I asked her who was paying her wages, she said it was on her work list that the hotel manager had ordered.

When I'd settled down, she brought me the packages, one at a time. I knew they were from James. They just had to be because he loved ladies in beautiful hats, fine jewelry, and smart looking gloves. We found a note in one package which read,

"To bring full justice to these gifts, please add the finishing touches, or whatever suits madams fancy at one of the ladies shops in San Francisco."

The note was not signed.

I turned to the maid and asked. "Which ladies' shops?"

She drew in her breath when she saw the names of the stores where some of the gifts had been purchased. "I think he loves you, ma'am. No need to contact that policeman because your gentleman friend knows where you are already!"

"Of course he does. Who else would go to so much trouble? It has to be James. But how does he know where I am? Oh, that would be easy! I'm staying at the most expensive hotel in the city. All the flowers and gifts must have come from him. Should I accept them? Am I crazy? It would certainly be unthinkable in Virginia, but things are different here. This is San Francisco! He loves me and I think I love him."

"Then I think you should keep the gifts."

"Yes! I'll keep the gifts and do the shopping. I want to look my best when I see him again. By the way can you tidy up for me, and if possible I would like for you to be my maid for the rest of my visit."

"Oh, Miss Kingsley, I thought you knew I've been engaged to be your maid as long as you're here."

"Who hired you?"

"I'm not at liberty to say ma'am."

I wasn't sure, but I suspected it was either my father or James. I carefully pinned my hat on and went to the lobby.

There were a few people at the desk and the staff was carrying on their duties. I ordered a taxi and told the driver to take me to the most elegant ladies' shop in the area. This was not like me to want to show off, but I was caught in the spirit of the moment. I wanted to please James. I knew he would prefer to see me in fashionable clothing.

To my surprise the shop was within walking distance from the hotel. When I entered the elegant ladies store, a lovely woman, obviously the manager came up to me and I introduced myself.

"Yes, yes, my dear, we have been expecting you. If there is anything you would like to see, we would be happy to show it to you. We have heard you were a nurse in the Great War. Well that is very commendable, but I must say, that outfit does not do you justice. Let us show you some beautiful clothes, outfits that will bring out the best in your appearance. You know my dear, clothes make the woman! We also have a beautician working in the shop next to ours. She has been notified to come here this afternoon. We really need to do something with your hair. You are much too lovely to pull your hair back in a bun and show that wide forehead. You'll see, when you step out of our shop, you will be a new woman. And you're not to worry about the cost. It has all been taken care of by that, handsome gentlemen, Mr. Sinclair."

"Do you mean James Sinclair?"

"Of course my dear, Mr. James Sinclair."

So that was his last name – Sinclair. At last I knew! But the name itself meant nothing to me.

Now what kind of a woman did she think I was? What must these sales women think of me, allowing a man to buy my clothes? It gave the impression I was a kept woman so I thought I'd better change their minds. "Oh yes, my husband to be must have let you know I was coming. Please show me the latest fashions. If I'm going to be part of San Francisco society I should have the best. As far as changing my hair, we'll see about that. A modern short cut is out of the question, but I might consider a more stylish set."

Watching these women move around me made me nervous. I was frustrated because I did not know where James was and when he would show himself. I supposed it would be when I was dressed according to his wishes.

I was told that the gentleman had given instructions that I should have all the gowns, dresses or suits that I wanted – and as many as I wanted.

When I thought about what he had done it made me angry. I had money of my own from my father, didn't I? It was my allowance! I could pay for all of the merchandise myself. Then I began to think, was I not good enough for James in my jumper and blouse? No I was not, I knew the answer. He had to doll me up, but for what? I guessed it was so I would fit in with his family and friends. But then I was much too carried away to think straight. When I thought about him I was confused and excited. If he wanted to buy me clothes or anything else I would accept.

I sat down on a lovely sofa in the elegant show room, and several models came out wearing a number of stylish outfits. The first creation was a Stein and Blaine, which was very popular in 1914. It was a cream colored tailored broadcloth suit, with a fitted hip-length jacket that had long inset sleeves and shaped fur-trimmed cuffs and collar. The fabric covered buttons fastened from one side of the high collar to the jacket hem, then down to the hem of the hobble skirt.

Before I could catch my breath, another sales lady brought in a matching hat – a large cream straw banded with black silk with the brim trimmed in the same fur as the jacket. It had a small single feather hanging down on one side. She said the ensemble could be finished with cotton gloves and black leather shoes with pointed toes and Louis heels. It was lovely, but not for me.

Seeing this did not please me the manager called for the next creation, a Bergdorf Goodman. It was reminiscent of the styles of 1916 just before the war. "No! I exclaimed I want an outfit that's in style right now!"

"Yes, Miss Kingsley, and we have just what you are looking for."

It was a Paquin, designed this year. Apparently the House of Paquin carried the latest styles. It would be perfect for my first meeting with James in his home town. I was so excited I had to try it on. It was an off-white dress trimmed in blue with a matching coat. The shawl collar, sleeve-cuffs, and hem of the over bodice were trimmed with black monkey fur. The three-quarter-length coat had inset sleeves with narrow turned-back cuffs, and open panel seams from below the bust line to the hem, held in place by a narrow button-down belt. I wondered if they had forgotten part of the skirt. It only came to mid-calf and seemed a bit daring to me. The hat was perfect, an off-white straw with a medium-wide brim and high crown with a pointed top. It was banded with a wide black silk ribbon. The sales ladies suggested I wear white stockings with black leather shoes that had an oblong buckle trim and edges piped in white, with pointed toes and Louis heels.

Once I had the whole outfit on I felt overdressed and daring. I could see my ankles! The woman looking back at me in the mirror was not the Melinda Ann I knew, but I was determined to become the woman I thought James wanted. Before I left the shop I'd purchased several ensembles, suits dresses and evening clothes, plus all the accessories - hats, shoes, and gloves. Also a few dresses, blouses and skirts for everyday wear and of course, I looked at the undergarments. My one-piece jersey was worn out, so I decided to try a waist-length pink chemise decorated with rows of vertical pin tucks and ribbons. I even bought a peach colored elasticized cotton corset, with light boning over the hips. And for good measure I added a number of cream-colored silk stockings and a dozen silk panties.

True to their word, the hair dresser came to the shop. She wanted to cut my hair. I'd made so many changes I wasn't willing to give up my hair as well. She proceeded to show me how to roll my hair up with a softer look around my face, so it gave the allusion that I had a short bob which was the style of the day. She also insisted that the new woman wore more make-up. This was difficult for me because I liked the old Melinda Ann look, which was plain, clean and healthy.

By the end of the day I was exhausted and decided to retire to my room, eat a light meal, and go straight to bed. I'd hoped to hear some word from James, but again I was disappointed. During the night a note was slipped under my door telling me a gentleman would call for me mid-morning. I was to be ready to pay a visit to some very important people.

I assumed it had to be James preparing me for some wonderful adventure. By the time the maid entered my room I was up and almost dressed. I had on that stylish Paquin outfit, and when I looked in the mirror it was a shock. I looked very much like a San Francisco socialite. I wasn't sure I liked that image, but I was sure James would approve.

CHAPTER TWENTY-THREE

When the knock came at the door, I was confused and wasn't sure what to do. Should I run to the door, throw myself into James' arms, hug and kiss him, or play it safe and walk to the door like a lady. I didn't have to worry about it long because the maid went to the door without my permission, and when she opened it I was speechless. Standing in the doorway was that mysterious man, the one I'd seen several times on the different trains. I didn't know his name, but I knew his face. Then it dawned on me, this man could be a detective. How could I've been so stupid? James probably had this man follow me from the time I left Denver! Through this man James knew every place I'd been.

Looking me straight in the eye this man took off his hat, but waited just outside the door to be invited in. I clutched the edge of a near-by table, very agitated. It was all making sense to me now. I'd been followed and spied upon. How dare James do this to me? This person had invaded my privacy! I was angry and wanted an explanation.

Before I thought, I yelled. "Enough is enough! You sir, have been following me! I want to know why and who hired you?"

My eyes must have been flashing because the man looked surprised at my anger and was about to retreat to the safety of the stairway, but I calmed down and asked him to come in.

"Ma'am, I was just doing my job. It was Mr. James Sinclair who hired me to keep an eye on you and that's what I've done. And Ma'am I'll tell you this if I hadn't been keeping tabs on you, you would have not had the money to pay your hotel bill. And you would not have been saved by that policeman at the park, and for that matter you would have not have been able to go shopping in that fancy lady's shop. It was Mr. Sinclair who had me watching you and provided all the money to take care of you. I think I'd be a little more grateful if I were you, Ma'am."

"Well, you're not me, and you can tell your employer I want to see him immediately."

"Yes, Ma'am, but he gave me instructions to take you to a place where he will be waiting, about an hour from here. The car is parked outside the hotel so if you are ready, we can go anytime!"

Oh, I was ready all right and eager to be on my way. Again, James had planned something without my knowledge. I was beginning to learn that that was just the way he was. James had to be in control.

The ride was pleasant and gave me some time to think. When we stopped at the baseball field I was unprepared. The driver asked me to get out of the car and wait until a gentleman came to get me. I didn't mind waiting but the outfit I was wearing was too stunning for a ballgame. It was getting warm so I looked for a place to sit down in a shady area. Across the way I saw a lovely large tree with a bench nearby. I turned toward the bench planning to sit down and get out of the sun, when out of the shadowed area walked James. My heart nearly stopped beating. I wanted to run to him, but my pride wouldn't let me. He moved toward me and seeing that I had hesitated he slowed his pace. I wanted to be angry with him, to scold him, to tell him he had his nerve having me followed by a detective. But I couldn't help myself. I began to run as fast as my new fancy shoes would allow. Seeing me start to run he smiled, threw his hat in the air, and crossed the green patch of grass with long deliberate strides. He lifted me off the ground and swung me around, and around.

"My dear girl, you are here at last and you look smashing, just the way I pictured you."

When he stood me on my feet I tried to catch my breath.

"I see the ladies fixed you up beautifully. I can't wait to show you off. I've come to the conclusion that I love you. Melinda Ann, I want you to be with me, always. We can't go into that now, but we'll talk about it later. I have two canvas chairs for us to sit on and watch the ballgame. I hope you don't mind. This is something I promised to do."

"Well, I'm glad to see you, too. I'm so happy you like the way I look… and yes, darn it, the ladies fixed me up. So glad you approve! You've decided you're in love with me and want to be with me always? Don't I have anything to say about this? If you're so happy to see me why are we meeting at a ball field? And thank you for being so thoughtful to bring those chairs along for our comfort, but what are we doing here?"

This was no way to propose to a woman, not at a ball field and not with so many people around. What was he thinking? Even though I was angry at him I was still relishing the thrill of being held in his arms. I tingled at the thought of his embrace, and by this time I'd forgotten how I was dressed. I was almost oblivious to all around me. When I looked at James my heart seemed to melt. He was quite handsome and I noticed that he too was a bit overdressed. But who cared?

We sat in our chairs, so close together I could reach out and touch him. I could feel his warm arm pressed up against mine. His body heat radiated through his clothes. I closed my eyes and imagined us together. I knew what a male body looked like. I'd seen many as a nurse, some scarred and disfigured for life, but here was James, a perfect specimen and one that attracted me almost beyond my endurance.

All of a sudden I came out of my reverie. What were we doing at a baseball field preparing to see a game? I was startled by the realization that I had not paid any attention to my surroundings because I'd been so obsessed with James. He had led me to the chair in front of a bleacher full of people. They had gathered to see the game.

I was grateful I'd brought my parasol along even though most women no longer carried them. A parasol can protect from the sun, as well as making a good weapon. I'd learned that from my episode in the park.

When the two teams began to warm up, two young boys, probably about eight and twelve, came running up to James. Before they could say a word, James, stood up and directed them to a spot on the side line of the field about ten feet away from me, making it impossible for me to understand what they were saying. When he and the boys had finished their conversation, James patted each boy on the shoulder and brought them over to meet me.

The young boys stood like little gentlemen, with their ball caps clutched in their left hands. Each one extended his right hand to politely shake hands with me. They were handsome lads with bright engaging smiles. Though I could see it took a lot of effort to stand still and talk to me, they did it. I'm sure they wanted to run back to their team and do what boys do best – play ball!

I learned the oldest boy's name was Alfred and the younger Bradley. When I asked James about them, he said he had promised their mother he would always support them in their school activities. Now they were attending a prestigious boy's school in the area. I thought it was nice of James to be supportive of his friend's children. I would look forward to meeting these people.

The game was dull at first but as it progressed it became more interesting. Soon things moved more rapidly. The young boys played their hearts out both in the field and when at bat. They were vocal at some of the umpire's decisions and cheered for their teammates. It was all part of the fun. It was obvious the boys were having a great time and the score was so close everybody including the spectators were worn out when the game was over. The boys were on opposing teams, but I couldn't help myself and cheered for both. When either of the boys were up to bat, I was on my feet urging him to hit the ball. A couple of times, I caught James looking at me, somewhat surprised. Seeing my unbridled excitement seemed to amuse him, and he winked at me more than once during the game.

Whenever I returned his gaze I became lost in his eyes. I knew I never wanted to be away from him again. I felt I belonged at his side. Oh, Lord, I had to think about that and what it meant. Marriage - and having some children perhaps two fine sons of our own like Alfred and Bradley. As I was lost in this thought the game came to an end. James gathered up our chairs. "Melinda Ann, why don't you go over to the club house at the end of the field? I'll put the chairs in the car and meet you there. I want to say good-bye to the boys. They have to go back to school.

I walked slowly to the small building basking in the feeling of being loved. I held my parasol over my head since the afternoon sun had burned off the morning fog. The day was indeed beautiful. I didn't go inside the building but stood on a small side porch entrance. It was really no more than a landing with several steps leading up to the door. As I stood, looking out over the grassy green area, I observed the stately trees that surrounded the ball field.

Suddenly I became aware of Alfred and Bradley racing toward me. Bradley had lost his cap to Alfred, who was chasing his younger brother, warning him to be quiet and to not tell. Bradley reached me before Alfred. He impulsively grabbed my hand and swung around behind me blurting out. "When you and my daddy get married my mother will be so happy, and we will all live together in the big house." Alfred swatted him and off they scampered, Bradley darting away across the green field with Alfred in hot pursuit.

What had that little boy said? Surely not what I thought I had heard. He must have said something else. Yet, I was sure I'd heard him correctly. And James had said that he had promised the boy's mother to support them in their activities. My God! That was it… That was the thing James had been hiding from me. He was married! Not only married, but the father of two sons! But if he was married, why in the world would he bring me to a ballgame to meet his boys? Why would Bradley speak of our getting married if they already had a mother? What must they think of their father bringing another woman to their game? And what would all those parents in the bleachers think of me? Now, I recalled how they had looked at me, whispering to each other. I'm the other woman! Oh, No! At that moment, I wanted to somehow disappear or run away. I was so horrified at these thoughts. It was so shocking I couldn't believe it.

James and the boys returned, and he very formally told them good-bye. "I'll see you boys at the holidays, Thanksgiving and then Christmas vacation." Alfred and Bradley bowed to him, shuffled their feet looking down and then shook his hand. Then Alfred poked Bradley in the back as a signal and they both came to, me with a smile. Each one said he was happy to have made my acquaintance and hoped to see me again. I wasn't sure how to respond, so I just smiled at them with longing in my eyes and heart. I thought, if only they were mine.

The car was parked down the road from the ballpark, and James and I walked in silence to where the driver sat patiently waiting. James opened the back door of the car and helped me inside. Then he went to the other side and slid in close beside me. I did not dare look at him, because I was confused.

Sensing I was distressed, he put his arm around me. "Something wrong, my dear? Was the game too much for you? I can tell you're upset. What's the matter?"

"The matter is you brought me out here without any warning, to meet your sons. And now I know what you have been hiding from me. You're married and you have two sons. I can't understand why you are putting me through this. Why did Bradley say, "When you and I get married, my mother will be happy?" I just don't understand! Do you have a wife or not? And what is this about our living together in the big house? It's time for you to be honest with me James. I can't put up with deceit, if that is what it is."

"Melinda Ann, you're just tired. What you need is a good dinner and a good night's sleep. Just relax. We can discuss all this later."

"No, James! We'll discuss it right now! You're dead right. I'm extremely upset!"

"I guess it was wrong of me to hide the fact that I have had a previous marriage and two sons, but I was afraid if I told you sooner, you wouldn't have anything to do with me. I wanted you to meet the boys first. No, I'm not married now. My wife died when Bradley was born and the boys have called my own mother 'Mother' since they were little. And as far as us living in my parents' home is concerned, that is something that can be discussed after we are married."

"James Sinclair, I have not said I will marry you. I'm disappointed with your deception and I'm not sure if I can trust you again. I need some time to think."

"You are kidding yourself, Melinda Ann you want me as much as I want you."

James suggested we go to my hotel and have dinner served in my room, which made me feel uneasy. He knew how I felt about him and he was not about to let time pass.

My desire to be with him was almost overpowering, and when I looked at him I saw the same longing in his eyes. We ordered dinner and by the time the waiter delivered it I was somewhat calmer. We ate, and to this day I can't remember what it was, but I do remember the wine and how it sparkled in our glasses. I drank more than I should. My defenses were down.

James drew me into the bedroom and before long my dress was discarded on the arm of a chair, my hat tossed on a table, my shoes and stockings were on the floor. There wasn't any need to slip into something else. My undergarments came off and fell to the floor. James was already undressed and had me on the bed before I could grasp what was happening. I wanted him to make love to me. I wanted to feel the warmth of his arms around me. There was no thought of changing my mind or stopping. The wine had had its effect on me and I was caught up with desire and passion. Though I was a virgin, I wasn't sure if James even noticed or cared if he had.

I do not remember falling asleep at his side. I just remember waking up and seeing that I was alone. I had nothing on and my head ached. My mind fought through the haze, and then it came to me - James! Where was he? Had I been played for a fool? My yearning body had betrayed my mind and had gotten me into a shameful situation. Had not my mother taught me? Never sleep with a man until you're married and have a ring on your finger. Well, I supposed I'd committed a grave sin and the frightening part was that I'd enjoyed it immensely…and wanted more!

Perhaps we could go to another hotel and register as man and wife. James would like that. We could go to the theatre, out dancing, or to one of those "speakeasies" I'd heard so much about. I decided that if I was going to be a wild girl, I was going to do it right - eat, drink and be merry! That would be the new me, the new Melinda Ann Kingsley.

My more sensible side said I should get up right then and leave town. I was still lying in bed thinking what to do when James entered without a knock. There he was, handsome and full of life, tossing off his clothes as he approached the bed. Without a stitch of clothing on he took one hungry look at me and climbed into bed. He kissed me while tossing me around playfully. He tickled my feet and ran his hands through my tangled long hair. He pulled me to him, kissed me passionately, and my body responded and before I knew it he was making love to me again.

I was in ecstasy! I forgot all about any resolve to leave San Francisco. My heart was in love and ruled over my head. I decided I would stay as long as he wanted me.

CHAPTER TWENTY-FOUR

It wasn't long before we were the gossip of the hotel, the rich Mr. James Sinclair and the lovely Miss Melinda Ann Kingsley. I'd promised my father I would not bring shame to the name, but here I was doing a pretty good job of it.

Once I realized that none of the money I'd received had come from my father, and that James had supplied it all through various sources, I became worried about what was happening at home. What really puzzled me was that I'd not received any kind of communication from my father, not a letter or a telegram.

Father must be ill! What was going on at the plantation? I'd wired several times and waited patiently for an answer, but none had come. I suspected it was somehow Birdie's fault. She always managed to answer the door when the mail or a telegram arrived by the carrier. I was convinced she read all the mail. I knew in my heart I should go home, but how could I leave James? Being aware that I couldn't stand to leave him right now, I decided to go back home at Thanksgiving.

After all, I was learning a whole new way of life in the big city. More importantly I was pleasing the man I loved. I was totally lost in his charms. I wasn't going to take any chance of losing him a second time. He was my future and he was all I wanted. I didn't care about anything else. Night after night he came to my room and we pleased each other.

Early in the month, and after a passionate night together, James reluctantly left me to make arrangements for a day of sight-seeing. I was to be ready to take a tour of his beloved city. It was always important to James how I dressed, so I chose a lovely tan walking suit with the collar and cuffs trimmed in brown mink, a stunning outfit and one of James' favorites. A matching hat complimented the suit.

James secured a luxurious touring car with an experienced driver to take us around the city. I was never so happy in my life as when he took my arm and led me down the main staircase of the St. Frances Hotel. I truly felt like a queen.

Once we were on our way we relaxed as we were driven through the most interesting parts of San Francisco. "Say, you folks are on your honeymoon, right?"

James smiled at the question. "You could say that."

"Well, welcome to my home town. The city was built on and around more than forty hills. Some of the steepest streets in the world are in the downtown area, near Nob Hill. This land was settled in 1776 and became a city in 1850. We are very proud of our cable car system. I'm sure you have noticed the cable cars seem to almost stand on end as they climb up or go down the steep streets. You need good brakes here!" Our driver was enthusiastic!

When we were on top of the hills we could see the sparkling blue water that nearly surrounds San Francisco, and gives the city a magnificent setting. The Pacific Ocean is to the west and the bay to the east.

"You know we had a terrible earthquake hit the city in April of 1906. Lots of folks died and the downtown was totally destroyed."

"I don't see any signs of it, now."

"No ma'am! By 1915 the town was rebuilt and all traces of that disaster had disappeared because San Francisco had to be ready to celebrate the opening of the Panama Canal. It was history in the making and we were going to benefit from its opening."

By mid-afternoon we were quite hungry and went to Fisherman's Wharf in the Embarcadero District to eat. There were a lot of small fishing boats jostling for a spot to moor near the city's most popular eating place. We found a delightful little restaurant near the water, and sat in a secluded corner. The specialty of the house was flounder smothered in a spicy sauce. We drank white wine and ate coarse bread with yellow cheese grated and baked inside. It was delicious! The ambience and service could not have been better.

We continued our tour with the lovely homes on Telegraph, Nob, and Russian Hills. These places had been chosen by the rich and famous because of their excellent views and convenience to the downtown area. We went by an old cemetery South of Mission Delores. We saw the graves of the early Mexican and American pioneers who settled the area and spent time reading the names on the tomb stones. This place was a reminder to me that life is short, and while we are living we should make the most of it. I also thought about the direction of my life and how I was living it. If I felt any guilt, it was then.

By dusk it was getting damp and chilly outside so we returned to the hotel. "Oh by the way, Melinda Ann, I have planned for us to go to the San Francisco Symphony Orchestra performance this evening. You'll love it. The financial manager, Mr. Alfred Hertz, is a friend of my mother. This fellow is doing a great job promoting the orchestra and she wants me to lend support by attending the concerts. Can you be ready about seven?"

Did I have a choice? It didn't seem like it to me but I wasn't really interested so I told him I had a headache and needed to rest after such a full day. I was surprised that he did not object.

"That is quite all right, my dear. I'll see if mother can go with me. I had wanted you to meet her but that can happen another time."

That was casual enough. I was a little miffed that he didn't seem to mind that I wanted to rest. He didn't insist that I go, but simply planned to arrange for someone else to accompany him – his mother. That was a bit upsetting, but at least it was his mother and not another woman. Besides, I wasn't ready to meet his mother. I wasn't ready to handle that situation.

The next morning James came into the bedroom, walked over to the windows, pulled opened the heavy drapes and greeted me. "Good morning, Sleepy-Head."

I was still asleep! My teeth had not been brushed and my hair was a mess…but he came to the side of the bed, bent over and kissed me on the lips. Then he pulled me up, stood me on my feet, and pushed me toward the bathroom.

"We're going to have some fun today. I'm going to take you to Chinatown. You'll have a good time." James was so abrupt!

I wasn't so sure, but he was right! I'd never seen such a place. People were milling around the narrow streets, some pushing and shoving as they went. James hired a rickshaw so we moved easily through the mass of people. As we passed the brightly decorated shops the odor of unusual food made us hungry. The street venders were everywhere selling their goods, from fresh food in carts to live fish in barrels. The faces of the people were strange to me. Their skin tones were various shades of yellow. Their dark slanted eyes made them exotic looking. I wanted to go into every store we passed, but James would not stop until we came to The Dragon Shop, where he went in alone. I sat in the rickshaw gawking at everything. Looking closely through the plate glass window, I saw it was packed with many bright colored Oriental clothes, boxes of herbs, and various size jars of preserved animal parts. It was not a place I wanted to go into, but I could see James knew his way around. Surprisingly he spoke enough Chinese to get him where he wanted to go.

When he came out of the store he had a package wrapped in newspaper under his arm. He handed it to me. "It's for you, but don't open it now. I've bought you something to wear later." I tore a little hole in the newsprint, peaked in, and saw it was something made of silk, red in color.

When we arrived at the hotel he suggested we have a light supper in my suite. I could open my package then. Of course, when I saw his gift I was delighted. It was a red silk dressing gown trimmed in gold thread with a dragon design on the back. The color was right anyway. Wasn't red associated with ladies of the evening? "This is going to be a special evening, my dear, so enjoy one of those bubble baths you like so well and powder up." When I got out of that four-legged monster of a tub, I smelled as sweet as blooming magnolias. James insisted that I wear the new dressing gown so I did. I pushed my curly hair down on my forehead and stuck a ribbon comb on one side which gave me a very provocative look. A feathered fan, which I planned to tease and entice James with, completed the ensemble.

It was a crazy evening and one never to be forgotten. When our dinner was brought into the room we put the bedspread on the floor, making a pallet. James asked the waiter to put the silver-serving dishes on top of it. The waiter must have thought we were foolish, wanting to eat sitting on the floor when we had a perfectly good table in the room. James gave the man a handsome tip and off he went without a word.

When we were both seated on the floor I found my gown would not stay shut, which made the whole evening more daring and exciting. I kept squirming around to get comfortable as we ate, but it became obvious that James was interested in more than eating food. Soon the ribbon comb came out, and my hair cascaded down my back. Before long we were rolling on the floor between the silver dishes and bottles of plum wine. I was delirious with pleasure.

Before we fell asleep, we were on our sides cuddled close together - like spoons.

CHAPTER TWENTY-FIVE

Early the next morning James whispered in my ear, "Melinda Ann, I have another surprise for you. I'm going to take you to a place called the Jupiter Club. It's a famous speakeasy here in the city. I have friends there I'd like you to meet."

"Really, you have been in a speakeasy? I've read about those places being raided by the police. Is it safe for us to go to such an unsavory place? Of course, James, if you want me to go with you, you know I will."

As I said that, I thought - this is just what I don't need, to risk being arrested in a speakeasy with the charming Mr. James Sinclair, and the next day having our names splashed all over the newspapers. But the potential risk made it all the more exciting. And I could see myself walking into a glitzy nightclub in a stunning outfit - my emerald green short sheath dress with a sequin butterfly on the shoulder.

That evening we took a taxi from the hotel to San Francisco's Barbary Coast where the Jupiter Club was located. It was a waterfront stronghold of notorious activities that the city authorities had been trying to shut down for years, according to James. On our way I felt excited at the same time anxious.

When James informed the taxi driver where we wanted to go, he said he was obligated to tell us, "In 1913 the city's Board of Police Commissioners decreed that in that area of the city there would be no dancing permitted in any café, restaurant, or saloon where liquor was sold. On top of that, no women patrons or city employees were permitted in any saloon in the district. And I can tell you for sure, the police regularly hang around at the front door of the Jupiter Club urging people to stay away, and occasionally they pull a raid. Now that I've told you all this are you still sure you want to go there?"

"That is where we want to go and that is where you're taking us!"

"Yes, Sir, I'll do that and if you want I'll come back and pick you folks up. Just name the hour."

"Who knows? When they close the club down, I guess. And you don't need to be concerned about us. I know for a fact the police won't be raiding the club tonight."

"Melinda Ann, I want you to meet this great piano player, Jelly Roll Morton and his woman, Anita Gonzales. Jelly is a real jazz piano improviser and his girlfriend tends the bar. It's a wild little place."

"James, how can these places be operating because it seems to me Prohibition is the law of the country? Why don't the police close them all down?"

"Don't worry your pretty little head about things you don't understand. You are with me, aren't you? Remember, bars and clubs were legal before 1919 before Prohibition outlawed them. My dear innocent girl, don't you know men will never give up drinking and neither will some women."

Well, that was true! I knew two things about Virginians. They would never surrender their weapons or give up their liquor. But I was worried. The other thing the newspapers reported was that in many of these clubs the back rooms were used for gambling, as well as unlawful business activities. But of course it didn't matter what I thought. James was determined we were going to this place.

The Jupiter Club was located in the cellar of a building on Columbus Avenue, away from all the big action on Pacific Street. We went down a steep flight of metal steps to the door of the club. James spoke through a small mousetrap door to give a password and the name of a reliable person before they would let us in. It turned out that James had been there many times before. The room we entered was filled with smoke so thick you could only see a few feet in front of you. It was so dark my eyes had not adjusted and I was sure I would have fallen flat on my face had it not been for James clutching my upper arm.

The music was rowdy and loud, and yet at the same time intriguing, because of a sensual beat and rhythm. It was intoxicating.

We were led to a small table for two. The young woman serving us brought our drinks in coffee cups. I thought it strange and said so. I learned the reason was that if the club were raided it would look like people were drinking coffee, not liquor. In Virginia whiskey was king and it occurred to me that I'd never tasted gin in my life but I found it quite pleasant mixed with tonic water. Sipping slowly made the pleasure even better.

We sat at our table listening to Jelly Roll Morton play his kind of musical style. It was unique to him and him alone. I'd never heard such music. James told me the names of each tune Jelly played, starting with the Beale Street Blues, High Society, Jazz Me Blues, and a real crowd pleaser, the Maple Leaf Rag. When he spotted us, Jelly played James' favorite, the Original Jelly Blues. Some parts of the piece had a Spanish twinge or Tango-like rhythm and I loved it.

Though it supposedly was not allowed, couples still got up and danced. I was shocked by the undulation of the dancers moving in the most seductive ways. To me their dancing bordered on the obscene, but it was fascinating to watch. Before long I found myself in James' arms on the dance floor being maneuvered around. Me! Melinda Ann, the innocent unworldly Miss Kingsley from Virginia. As I gazed into James' eyes I forgot about being prim or proper and acted as wild as I thought he wanted me to be. I danced with a devil-may-care abandon and hung onto him until I embarrassed myself. When the music stopped I almost fell into my chair.

Looking up, I saw that Jelly Roll Morton was coming to our table. He pulled up a chair and chatted with James like I wasn't even there. Jelly was a sharp dresser and a very cocky man. Sometime later James told me Jelly's idea of wealth and impressing the ladies was to have a closet full of $100 suits.

What fascinated me most was the diamond he had in one of his front teeth. When he smiled, and the light hit his tooth it sparkled. James finally introduced me to Jelly and then Anita came to our table and I was introduced to her.

Jelly went back to the piano and asked for requests. James yelled out, "*Panama, Prohibition Blues* and the *Stop Rag*." Somebody else called out, "*The Yellow Dog Blues*," and cheers went up. This one was a favorite. In this piece you could almost hear a train chugging away. James said it was a song about a lover who skips town by rail, leaving his sweet innocent gal behind. The people applauded wildly.

Not long after our evening at the Jupiter Club, the manager of a competing club across the street informed the police there was dancing going on in the Jupiter. He was trying to get the place raided and in the end succeeded. After that, with the police making constant raids the Jupiter's business slowed considerably and by the end of September it was closed.

One morning, after we had been out on the town dancing and drinking the night before, I woke up fully dressed lying on my bed. I had no memory of what had taken place the night before. It was as though I'd been unconscious for hours. The maid had not come in and I was totally alone. I lay there afraid of what I might have done the past evening and wondered why James had not undressed me and put me to bed.

I lay there thinking about getting up. My mouth was dry and my head ached something awful. I heard a slight noise but wasn't sure what it was. I longed for a hot steaming bath. Then I heard it again. Something was being pushed under my door. I rose shakily and stumbled to the door. Looking down I saw an envelope. I opened the door and looked out but no one was there, so I gently closed the door, being careful not to make any noise. When I reached down I nearly fell over, but managed to pick up the letter and open it. The room was too dark so I had to open the drapes to read it. When I did I could have fainted. It was from James, and it was definitely not what I had expected. It read:

Dear Melinda Ann,

I am so sorry to have to leave you like this, but I must leave for a very important business trip. I had planned to tell you all about it last night, but you drank too much gin and passed out on me. I put you to bed just as you were, so as not to awaken you. You were sleeping like an angel, my precious girl. You must know how much I love you. I've certainly told you often enough lately but I don't understand the way you have changed since we arrived in San Francisco. You have become a wild and reckless young woman. Not that I love you

less, but I hope this is not a pattern you intend to keep. We can talk more about this later when I return sometime in October.

Until then my dear girl, all my love,

James

And just when in October, I'd like to know? And what was that about loving me less? I'd become wild and reckless? Yes, maybe that was true, but I thought that was what he wanted. Didn't he want a woman to be wined and dined and one who was free with her sexual favors with him? If he didn't like what I'd become, who did he think had introduced me to such a life? With him I had more money than I'd ever been used to, and clothes priced far beyond what I could afford. I was living like a queen in one of the most expensive hotels in San Francisco.

No! Most of this was his fault and the thought came that I was sorry I'd ever met him. I had not been that kind of woman, but had fallen so deeply in love that I couldn't think straight. I'd lost my self-control and then as a result my self-esteem. Not anymore! If he thought I was going to wait around this hotel until he decided to show up, he was mistaken. When he returned I would be gone! Anger had ended the headache and I headed for that hot bath.

I rang for the maid and with her help was soon dressed and my bags packed. When I was ready to leave, I checked at the main desk to see if any messages had been left for me. There was nothing. It had been a wonderful fling, but it was over!

Now, I knew what I had to do. Run! Get out of the city as fast as I could and never look back. I had completely forgotten what this trip was about. I'd started out to follow my grandmother's adventures and maybe unlock some of the family secrets so the next place for me to go was New Orleans.

It was time to get back on track. I would contact my father through his bank in Roanoke. I would explain my situation and find out directly why I hadn't heard from him.

When I thought of my father, I knew he would not in any way approve of the life I'd been living. How could I tell him and break his heart? I decided right then not to contact him and make it on my own somehow.

My mind was made up. I was finished with James. My wild adventures were over. I would get on with my life, and I vowed right then I would never fall in love again. I had loved one man and I had lost.

CHAPTER TWENTY-SIX

Once I was on board the Southern Pacific's Sunset Limited train and settled, I felt a huge relief, like a weight had been taken off my shoulders. I did not have to think anymore about James leaving me, because I had left him. I didn't have to have a man in my life. I could find a good job as a nurse and settle down to a humdrum life without love.

As the train continued east on the first day, I gazed out the window at the passing scenery and thought about New Orleans. I had seventy-three hours to figure out what I would do there. I was leaving the golden west and all that had happened there behind me. I would return to being the real me, adventuresome and independent! But the extravagant living was over. If I was careful I had enough money saved from James' generosity to last for some time.

I felt drawn to New Orleans – the place that held so much mystery in the Kingsley family history. Aunt Ginny had described the house once owned by the family and had given me directions on how to get there. The first day on the train passed slowly.

The evening of the second day I went to the diner and enjoyed a delicious chicken dinner. I retired after the meal and had a great night's sleep. I woke refreshed with a determination to continue retracing the steps of my Grandmother Lilly. By the third day I was bored with train travel. As we approached New Orleans I pulled myself together, put away the newspapers, straightened my traveling suit, and centered my hat on my forehead. I would enter this famous city as an attractive lady.

When the train pulled into the station it was too late to find the former Kingsley house in the French Quarter, so I hired a taxi to take me to a hotel. Most of them were full, because of a convention but the driver finally managed to find a nice quiet hotel for me. I was looking forward to a restful night away from the noisy, swaying train. But I had to keep pushing thoughts of James out of my mind.

The next morning I was excited about locating the house, and since I needed some exercise I decided to walk down Canal Street to the French Quarter. The small businesses along the way were interesting and window shopping was fun, but I was on a mission. The shops gave way to two story homes with balconies edged with decorative wrought iron grillwork.

When I reached the district that Aunt Ginny had described, I recognized the house at once. It was French architecture that included a courtyard with lots of wrought iron fencing. The tall arching windows were set in yellow stucco walls. As I walked around the place, I came to a gate and ventured inside. The patio was shady with a rock water fountain in the middle. The pathway wound around lovely flower beds, and closer up the house was bigger than I had imagined.

As I stood alone, taking it all in, I could imagine my Grandmother Lilly and her daughter, my Aunt Ginny walking in the cool of the evening in this same garden. As I turned to go to the front door and knock, a woman met me approaching from the side of the house. "Are you lost, young lady? If so, perhaps I can help you. My name is Mrs. Montgomery."

"No, ma'am, I'm not lost. I'm sorry if I seem to be intruding. You see, my grandparents, the Kingsley family of Virginia, once owned this house, and I am interested in its history. I know very little about this place and would like to go inside if that is possible."

"That name Kingsley is familiar to me, and in fact I have something I found that must belong to someone in your family. We are the new owners and don't know a lot about the history of this place, but you are most welcome to come in. Why don't you join me for a cup of tea? You'll have to excuse the mess. We are re-modeling part of the upstairs. Sometime in the past, a large bedroom was made into a library and sitting room. Now I want to make it into a bedroom again."

I was grateful for the invitation, since I'd skipped breakfast. We went to the back of the house, and entered into a small cozy kitchen. She motioned for me to sit down at a small round table. It was placed in front of a lovely curtained window that looked out over a flower garden. When the tea was steeped to perfection she brought out some delicious pastries. We got along right away and enjoyed each other's company. She kept inquiring about my family.

When she was satisfied who I was, she took me upstairs. As we entered the bedroom she walked over to the window seat and pointed to it. "This window seat was nailed shut and I wanted to use it for storage so we pried it open and that's where we found the diary. I believe it belongs to someone in your family named Ginny."

"Ginny – is my Aunt Ginny!"

I was mystified as to why Aunt Ginny would leave something as personal as a diary in a window seat, and even more why it had been nailed shut.

When Mrs. Montgomery handed the diary to me I noticed that it had been carefully wrapped in a floral embroidered dresser scarf. In the bottom of one corner were the initials, **LBK.** It must be a scarf my Grandmother Lilly had made.

Holding the diary in my hands was overwhelming, but then Mrs. Montgomery offered me this counsel. "When you read your aunt's diary, try to be understanding of what you find inside. I know it was a bit nosey of me, but you must understand I never expected to meet any of the Kingsley family, so I read portions of the diary. My heart aches for you because I know that what you're about to read may make you wish you had never read it. The diary may contain more information than you are ready to accept."

I wasn't sure what to say to her, but I knew I was going to read every word. I wanted to know more about this house and what had happened here.

Now I had a diary written by my aunt and nothing would make me consider not reading it. Little did I know what I was about to learn.

I thanked my hostess for a lovely afternoon and for the diary. I promised that I would be opened minded, when I read it. I said my farewells and left for the hotel. On the way I bought a few pieces of fruit, some cheese, and a loaf of French bread. I planned to spend the rest of the day reading and learning about my family.

Settled in my room, I read the first entry which was printed by a child. It was Ginny probably around the age of eight. It read:

This diary belongs to Ginny Kingsley

April 3

```
Dear Diary,

Today my mother married my new daddy, Bart
Kingsley. Now my name is Kingsley, too. I
don't like my mother marrying Bart. He is a
handsome man and my mother really is silly
about him. She made Tinny and me promise
we would not tell him of our past. For the
wedding she made me wear a cotton dress with
a slight train hanging on the back. I don't
like to get dressed up. The older women at
the wedding kept telling Tinny and me how
pretty we looked and how sweet we were. I
would have liked to put ants in their pants
and worms in their food. I don't like mother
giving most of her attention to Bart and not
to us. And that woman who is Bart's mother,
Martha, I don't like her either. She likes
Tinny better than me.

I was so upset after the wedding I ran away
to the barn and that's where Bart found me.
He cuddled me and held me so that I could
feel his heart beating. He patted me on my
fanny and whispered he loved me and would
never let anything bad happen to me. I guess
he is all right for a step-father, but I
won't call him father, and I won't call his
mother grandmother.

That's all for today,

Ginny
```

I had to chuckle. That sounded just like Aunt Ginny, and not so upsetting to me, but when I read the next entry on the 11th of May, I was shocked. It was sickening. This poor child was playing with her sister in the hay loft when Bart found them. Ginny's dress was dirty and torn. Bart had Tinny go inside and he would help Ginny with her dress. He kissed her on the mouth and proceeded to take off her petticoat and even her drawers. Ginny was sure her mother would not like what he was doing but Bart told her that since he was her new daddy that gave him the right to look her over. One thing led to another and soon he was fondling her all over and explaining that this would be their secret and she must not tell anyone. She had been taught she was not supposed to tell secrets.

Once I'd started reading I could not put the diary down. Bart Kingsley, my grandfather, was supposed to have been such a wonderful person and here he was mistreating his own stepdaughter. I was sick at my stomach and angry. How could a man treat a child like that?

On the 20th of June, Ginny again wrote. She was to meet him once a month in the barn so they could play their secret game. As I read further into the diary, the more upset I became. This went on for years without anyone suspecting. He never hurt her or went too far until a later entry when she and Bart were in New Orleans. The entry that distressed me most was one where she described their "wonderful time in New Orleans" when Bart had discharged the servants and they had played house together. The bastard told her he had loved her from the time he caught her in the barn playing hide and seek with her sister…and now that she was a full grown woman he was going to make love to her. He admitted he never really loved Grandmother Lilly and only married her because his mother, Martha, had insisted. What a ladies' man he must have been.

Why Aunt Ginny kept this secret to herself was a puzzle, until reading further I discovered she actually had fallen in love with the man and wanted him for herself. Her last entry was dated December 9, 1909.

On that day she and Bart were in the New Orleans house sleeping together. She wrote that she felt like a new bride. Bart had taken her to the opera, wined and dined her before returning to the house to make love to her. Oh yes, I knew that one…it had happened to me. She continued that she had asked him to divorce her mother Lilly, and marry her. He had only laughed and said that was impossible. That's when she got mad and had threatened to tell Lilly. She felt she had the right, because she was the one who could satisfy him and not her mother. Aunt Ginny was in love and was confused, and I could understand that also.

I couldn't help wondering if Lilly had ever found out. What would I have done in such circumstances? I don't know for sure, but if I had been my grandmother, I think I would have shot him, husband or not! Why do men do that to young innocent girls, and how many times do they get away with it?

I was innocent when I met James, but with him I knew what I was doing and I was old enough to make that choice. Ginny was only a child, and willing to please her new father any way she could.

When I had almost finished reading Ginny's diary I was surprised to find an entry written by Grandmother Lilly just a few days after Bart's death. It is perhaps the saddest letter of all and the one that disturbed me most.

> "Bart is dead and Ginny grieves for him...he not only destroyed my life, but also my daughter Ginny's. I hate both of them...
>
> ...I caught them in bed together...Ginny and I had a terrible fight...I kicked her out...she went to a saloon, got drunk, got into a fight, broke her jaw in a fight... Bart went after the man who had hit Ginny and he got shot...now Bart is dead.
>
> "Ginny and I are going home...I'm not sure how I'll explain Bart's death and Ginny's broken jaw, but somehow I will and the family will never know the truth. I plan to carry this terrible memory to the end of my days."
>
> Lilly Benton Kingsley

I sat in my hotel room holding the diary in my hands and was not sure what I should do with such a personal item - destroy it perhaps or keep it and return it to Aunt Ginny. No, it was a dead issue from the past and I would not ever read it again or even talk about it to anyone other than

Aunt Ginny. My Grandmother had wanted the diary to be sealed away forever so I decided to abide by her wishes. I would burn it!

No wonder my mother Tinny always stood up for Aunt Ginny and told me to keep my mouth shut about her. She must have known all along but kept that secret to herself. It occurred to me what silly creatures we women are when we are in love with a man. Our defenses are down, and men take advantage of that weakness.

I looked at the clock and it was not very late. I was hungry I needed to escape from the sordid thoughts swirling in my mind. I had read in the newspaper that Jelly Roll Morton was in New Orleans on a limited engagement, so I called a taxi to take me to a club to forget about the diary and my family.

That club should have been the last place I wanted to go, but heavens, who was I trying to kid? I missed James and the nightlife. I had to admit it was fun while it lasted but, right now I was in a hateful mood. I needed a gin and tonic.

The taxi driver was concerned about me being alone.

"Ma'am, may I suggest an escort for the evening? I know a nice gentleman who would be happy to show you the nightlife of New Orleans. You want me to get him?"

"No thank you, I don't want anything to do with men. I like being alone, so drive on."

"Yes ma'am. I know where Jelly is. It's a small club and the people there are so crammed together no one will know you're alone." It was true. None of the people inside seemed to care or even notice I was there. That suited me fine. I was shown to a small table out of the way and close to a dark corner. Instead of gin I ordered one of the new soda drinks and settled in for the evening.

Jelly Roll wasn't alone. He had his jazz band playing with him. They played one of my favorites, *"After You've Gone,"* and it fit my mood perfectly. After a few more slow tunes they really got going with *"Alabama Jubilee,"* *"Alexander's Ragtime Band,"* *"Castle House Rag,"* *"Darktown Strutter's Ball,"* and the really wild *"Twelfth Street Rag."* They improvised and sometimes I lost the tune. Around two a.m. they stopped, but that didn't please the customers. They wanted one more and they shouted for the band to end the evening with, *"Waitin' for the Robert E. Lee."*

I was a lady and in perfect control of myself when I left the club. I stepped out in front of the building and the taxi driver I'd hired earlier had come back to get me. I thanked him and gave him a good tip.

The next morning I was not hung over as I always was with James. I was better off without him, and now what I'd learned about Aunt Ginny made me want to swear off men forever.

It was a beautiful day so I wandered around the city, and saw some of the best and worst parts. I felt drawn back to the French Quarter where the house was but did not go. Instead, I visited the tall, gray-spire Cathedral of St. Louis. There I knelt before the holy altar and prayed my heart out. It seemed I had failed in love and had learned more than I really wanted to know about my family.

I left the church and walked until I was worn out. That evening I decided to go out for dinner at one of those famous New Orleans restaurants. Getting dressed was always a big hassle for me. I had learned to be stylish and never casual when I left a hotel. Walking out the front door, I was greeted with the warm evening atmosphere of the city. I hailed a taxi and climbed inside. When I stepped into the taxi I was astounded to see JAMES! Yes James!

"James, what are you doing here? You didn't like the woman I had become and left me flat in San Francisco for some kind of business trip. How did you find me here I'd like to know."

James smiled, "Just be, patient and I'll tell you."

He grabbed me hard and pulled me close to him, smothering me with kisses and whispering in my ear. "My dear girl, you tell me why you left San Francisco. I told you I would return in October. Why couldn't you have waited? What made you bolt out of town?"

When I didn't respond, he pushed me away. He looked into my eyes and could see something was terribly wrong. Lifting my face in his hands he kissed me gently on the lips. "Tell me, dear one, what has happened to make you look so sad and unhappy?"

Because of having him near me again so unexpectedly, I was stunned and simply could not reply. I was at a loss for words. I'd given him up, but here he was. I started to cry and threw myself into his arms. For me to act like this was ridiculous, but once again I was out of control.

"Melinda Ann, please get a hold of yourself and tell me where you were headed!"

"Out, I was just going out! I'm hungry and I want to eat and I don't know how you found me! Can't you understand?"

"We are not going anywhere until you tell me what's wrong. We are going back to the hotel where we can sit down calmly and talk over whatever it was that made you leave San Francisco, if it takes all night. You can change into something more comfortable, get relaxed, and calm yourself down. I want to know why you left when you knew you are the only woman for me."

Changing clothes…relax…calm down…! I knew what that meant, but I wasn't about to let myself be fooled. I was determined that I would not go to bed with James ever again!

"James, I would not have left if you hadn't written such a harsh letter. What was so important that you had to leave me in the middle of the night?"

"I went to a business meeting fully expecting to have to leave the city but when I arrived I was informed the trip had been cancelled. I headed right back to the hotel and found you had checked out. The clerk was hesitant to tell me where you had gone, but when I insisted he said you had mentioned something about New Orleans. I went to the railroad station and took the Sunset Express the next morning. I arrived a day later than you. The first day I wasn't able to locate you, but I remembered you talking about the French Quarter and describing the house that had belonged to your family. I found the house and met Mrs. Montgomery. She told me that you had been there and remembered the name of the hotel where you were staying. I had planned to come here and find you this evening, when I saw you coming out of the hotel, I told my taxi driver to go and pick you up."

"I was going out because I needed time to think and did not want to stay in the room. I wanted to go out. James, could we please go somewhere and eat? In that letter you left you called me wild and reckless. I thought that was the way you wanted me to be!" "I realize now that was wrong and I apologize. I know some of the reason for your leaving was my fault. Melinda Ann, as far as your behavior in San Francisco is concerned, I think I contributed to it. I wanted to show you the city during the daytime and under the lights at night. It was exciting for me to expose you to all of those new places and people but I never expected you to go wild on me. I suppose that is what you believed I wanted. But you don't understand I want you to marry me."

CHAPTER TWENTY-SEVEN

It was going to be interesting to see James' reaction when I told him I was going to Danville, Virginia. I didn't answer him last night. He says he wants me to marry him. He even promised to come and get me this morning.

I was waiting at the curb with my luggage when he showed up. James looked dismayed. "Where are you off to now? You haven't given me an answer."

"I haven't made up my mind. I'm off to Virginia to see the place where my mother was born. If you want to join me that is up to you."

"Hold on! Of course I'm coming with you!"

Then he turned to the taxi driver. "Take me back to the hotel. I want to pick up a few things."

James looked impatient and I could almost hear what he was thinking— more darn family business.

"You should know why I'm going there. I told you already! I plan to look up the couple who helped my Grandmother Lilly when she gave birth to my mother Tinny and Aunt Ginny. She had been abandoned by her husband, and I want to know why. Maybe I will find out someday if I ask enough questions."

"I don't really care about your Grandmother Lilly or why her husband abandoned her! I just want you to get this obsession with your family out of your system. The quicker we go where you want to go, the sooner you will answer me. I advise you not to put me off too long. I'm an impatient man."

"James Sinclair, I didn't ask you to follow me." I halfway didn't expect to see him at the train but he came and soon we were on our way.

All across the South we saw the handsome mansions that had been reconstructed since the Civil War.

The next morning we were rolling through the hills of North Caroline and I knew Danville was right across the border.

We hired a taxi in Danville and drove out into the country. We saw a lovely lush green valley where my grandmother had described it. The farm house and barn was not old and dilapidated as I had thought they might be. The fields of grass stretching out before us were ready to be cut and bailed. Good looking stock roamed the pastures. I was hopeful that Theresa and some of her family still lived on the farm.

As we drove up a gravel road I could see the barn where I was sure my mother had been born. When I knocked at the house a women come to the door dressed in a simple housedress. She was tall with gray hair tied up in a bun.

"My name is Melinda Ann Kingsley, Lilly Benton was my grandmother. Are you Theresa? We're your parents Sarah and Martin Bell?

"Yes, I am Theresa and those are my parent's names. Please come in! I've heard a lot about your grandmother. She was the woman who gave birth to twin girls in our barn! That was a day to remember!"

"That is what I came to see you about. I have some questions to ask you about that day."

We sat down and she excused herself to the kitchen, when she returned she carried a tray with three glasses and a big pitcher of ice cold lemonade. James took the drink and wiped his forehead with his handkerchief. I could see he was not going to be content so I suggested we walk out to the barn.

On the way Theresa and I shared stories about the day my mother and aunt were born.

"It was after a rain storm when my pa saw the barn door was open. He checked it and that is when he found Lilly up in the hayloft about ready to deliver a baby. And the surprise was that there were two babies."

"Did you see the birth?"

"No, I was too young, but I did get to gather the supplies my ma needed to deliver a baby. I was very excited and I was full of questions about the lady in the barn. When we brought her down from the hayloft and put her to bed she named the babies. The first one was Virginia because she had been born in Virginia and Tiffany because they had been born under a tin roof. Sounded kind of strange to me but that didn't last long. We soon shortened their names to Ginny and Tinny. When Lilly recovered she moved to Danville and set up her seamstress shop

"Did her husband ever come back or get in touch with Lilly?"

Theresa shook her head. "Your grandmother didn't want to talk about him and we never saw him. She did tell us he was a gambler and not a good person. That was before the flood destroyed her house. When we went there and asked about Lilly and the girls, a man said he had heard Lilly and the two girls had been rescued by some rich Virginian. And that's the last time we heard about them."

"Why did you or your family never contact my grandmother? She was puzzled about that, but assumed you did not want anything to do with her once she was married."

"Oh no Melinda Ann, that is not the reason. We all loved Lilly and the girls. I am ashamed of why we did not contact her. You see, we read in the newspaper that Lilly had married Mr. Bartholomew S. Kingsley but we had not been invited to her wedding. We believed she did not want to see us."

"Not long after that Mr. Kingsley came to see us. He said his mother Martha did not want us to contact Lilly ever again. She was afraid Lilly's past would spoil the Kingsley name. He offered to pay off our mortgage and send me to a women's college back East. I wanted to further my education and my parents wanted to keep their property so we agreed."

Here was another secret out in the open. Great-grandmother Martha and her son had bribed the Bell family to save their precious name.

"Theresa, I understand. That was a good reason but I'm sorry it happened. I believe my grandmother would have enjoyed hearing from you. But you must not blame yourself. What is past is past." She had a lot of questions and we talked the rest of the afternoon.

James was ready to jump out of his skin and was up moving about the room like a restless lion. When we drove down the road leading from the house, I looked back and realized how different it looked from the Kingsley Mansion. I knew, then, it was time to go home. Home to where my roots were. When we were on the train again James began asking questions about the Virginia Mansion.

"I'm eager to meet your family, especially this Birdie character and, the mysterious Aunt Ginny." He seemed interested in what I'd uncovered about my family. Yet he told me in no uncertain terms, I was wrong to read Ginny's diary in the first place. Diaries were private and personal and none of my business.

He seemed drained by the day's activities and wanted me to stop my research, saying enough was enough. "After all you have done, Melinda Ann, I hope you have learned your lesson and will stop prying into other folks' private lives. Live for today and forget all this nonsense. It is time for you to go home, face your family, marry me, and get on with your life. Just remember, you will never have to work again. Once we are married you will take your place at my side in San Francisco."

I heard him, but I would not accept that he was right. I believed that I had the right to find out on my own what no one in my family would tell me. I was angry at his comment about me not working anymore, but I was sure once we were married he would come around to my point of view. I was born to be a nurse and getting married should not prevent me from being one. All I knew was that I was going home with the man I planned to marry. I suppose I was too much in love to see what different goals James and I had. I didn't want to recognize this.

CHAPTER TWENTY-EIGHT

I visualized, in my mind, what a surprise it would be when I told my family I was getting married. I could just hear them. Melinda Ann has finally found a man and is going to settle down!

Then James became quite serious, "Melinda Ann, why don't we just forget about going to Virginia and head to San Francisco. We'll have a big wedding and reception there. My mother will arrange everything. You won't have to worry your head about anything. If we did go to my home you could forget about your family secrets. You don't owe them anything. Besides, didn't Birdie tell you, you were not needed there anyway?"

Listening to this, I became angry. "James, don't you understand how important it is for me to be married in my own home, in the presence of my friends and family? I want to be married at the plantation and not anywhere else. To be honest, I want to show my family and all those ancestors how well I've done and the woman I've become. And I want my father to give me away in his proud elegant manner. And I would like all of my brothers to be there. I'm so proud of you, Mr. James W. Sinclair. I want to let them know you want me to be your wife. I can't do that by running away. Surely you can see how important this is to me." James dropped the whole matter.

When we arrived at the Danville railroad station we purchased our tickets to Lynchburg, Virginia on the Southern Railway. From Lynchburg we would go to Roanoke, and once there, buy a car. We would arrive at the Kingsley Mansion in style and elegance.

I will admit, I'd been careless in letting the family know where I was, but after not hearing from them, I assumed they didn't care what was happening in my life. I was sure nothing much had changed since I'd left. I knew Charley was somewhere in New York City. I had no idea where Edwin was. I made up my mind that seeing my father, mother, Edward and Aunt Ginny would be enough for me. And Birdie - I didn't care about seeing her but I did wonder how she would take the news that I was getting married.

Riding on the train was pleasant for James but not for me. Once we were settled James, and not me, began to plan for our future. "Melinda Ann, I think we should go to Europe for our honeymoon. We will go to England and perhaps to Ireland and Scotland if you like. I have friends in England and I know they would be pleased to entertain us. We could definitely get caught up in all their social engagements. And we could go over to France where I have a number of friends in high places."

"Just hold on there, James. I've something to say about this. I'm amazed at your disregard for my wishes. You know high society does not interest me in the least. I've longed to go to Scotland for years, because I would love to see where my Great-great-grandmother Felice came from originally. I'm sure I have cousins still living there. I want to look them up and see if anyone has any knowledge of Felice Stewart Cornwall who married Edward Philip Kingsley of England. And as far as going to France, I'm not interested. This is my honeymoon, too, you know!"

He glared at me, "Why in the hell do you care about those people anyway? And what good does it do to go looking for more information about your family. This is supposed to be a fun, relaxing trip with only our pleasure to be considered. I'm surprised at you. Haven't you learned more about the Kingsley family than you need to know?"

"James, that's up to me to decide and it has nothing to do with you. You don't understand! I've heard the stories about Edward Kingsley going to Scotland and there engaging in a battle. While he was there he was wounded. Somehow he met Felice and they fell in love. They were married and returned to England. In England, she and Edward bought a small cottage which included several acres of land. On that property they had enough land to breed horses, but neither really wanted to live in England. They had a great desire to go to America, find some property, build a house, and raise a family.

"Both sets of their parents were rather well off. As a wedding present her parents gave Felice a great deal of property and money which she deposited in an English bank. Felice left her parents, as well as her brother, behind in Scotland. Believe me, if we do go to Scotland I intend to visit my cousins. If you don't want to do that you can darn well go to France or elsewhere, and I'll catch up with you, later."

"Damn it, Melinda Ann, you're as stubborn as a mule. I'm doing all this for you. Why can't you just go where I want to go?" Then he laughed! "If you are going to be my wife, you will have to honor and obey."

That did it, honor and obey. "Obey? Just what does that mean James?"

"Oh, you know! You are to do what your husband tells you to do!"

"Wait a minute. That works both ways!"

"All right, we are not getting anywhere with this conversation. I can see I'm upsetting you, Melinda Ann, so let's just forget about our honeymoon until later."

I couldn't explain my feelings to him. Something drove me to all of these places - always feeling there was something more I needed to know about my family. Would I give up? The answer was, no I would not! We both fell silent for the remaining ride on the train.

When we arrived in Roanoke it was a pleasant day, but there was no one to welcome us, as there had been to welcome Charley and me after the war. We were on our own so we went to the automobile sales emporium and James bought a fancy new car. He didn't care about the expense as long as we traveled in style. I was surprised, but pleased. We would drive up in high fashion, not only with our up-to-date clothes, but with the latest model Oldsmobile. I was going home, not as a failure but as a wealthy woman in my own right. I did not need the plantation or anyone in my family to succeed in life, and I certainly did not need any of my father's money.

I gave James the directions and soon we were driving up the old familiar road to the Kingsley plantation. I noticed the lovely arch of tree limbs hanging over our heads as we moved toward the house. It was all so quiet that I felt we were the only people alive. There were no workers in the fields. As we approached the house, I saw a black wreath tied with a large black bow hanging on the stark white front door.

"Oh my God, what has happened? Who has died, and why wasn't I notified? I should have been here!"

Without thinking, I started to open my door and jump out when James yelled at me. "Wait until I stop the car!"

When he came to a stop, we were in front of the house. I jumped out, ran to the front door and banged on it, but no one answered. I pushed it open and found the house to be very still and quiet. I ran around yelling for my mother, father, or anyone in the house. No one answered me. I threw open the parlor door. Birdie was sitting in a dejected manner holding some letters and a few telegrams in her lap. She jumped up when I came into the room. She looked shocked. "Melinda Ann, what are you doing here? Your father died a week ago and was buried in the family plot.

"Birdie, why in the devil, didn't you contact me? What did he die of? I'm a nurse! I could have helped!"

"No you couldn't have helped. He was well one day and dead the next. You've made it clear that you don't care about what happens to this family. Why should I have contacted you?"

I am sure Father would have wanted me to know. You did give him my telegrams, didn't you?"

"He never knew you tried to reach him. What is done is done, and I can't change that now."

"Birdie, where is mother and who else is here? I'm going up to her room right now."

"Your mother is in her room but it won't do you any good to see her. She has been in some kind of trance since your father died. She doesn't want to eat and she wanders around her room mumbling to herself. She doesn't know anyone except me, but do as you like. As far as your brothers are concerned, I was able to contact Charles Harley in New York and he arrived home yesterday. Edwin came swinging back home several weeks ago. He said he was on a losing streak and needed funds, that good-for-nothing brother of yours! He was down to his last dollar when he came home, but when Mr. Harley died I think it sobered him up. He offered to stick around for a while and help Edward with the funeral arrangements."

"Birdie, I don't care what you say. I'm going to see my mother right now. You seem to forget. I am a nurse and I am going to check on her. You stopped me once, but you won't this time! I'm sorry I was not here for my father's funeral, but it was your fault that I wasn't. If I'd known he was sick, I would have come home immediately."

When I entered Mother's room, she was walking around aimlessly and twisting a piece of ribbon in her hands. She was a pitiful site. I put my arms around her and gently led her to bed. Mother smelled of sweat and looked neglected. Her hair was an oily mess. She had not bathed in a week or more. She was disoriented and I suspected she was drugged. I turned on Birdie. "What have you been giving her? What kind of medication is she taking?"

"You haven't been here. You haven't been taking care of her. I have! Now you come home acting like you're the mistress. The lawyer will be here in a few days to read your father's Will and then you're in for a surprise. My dear adopted sister, you and your brothers will finally know the truth!"

"What truth?" She ignored me. I wanted to slap her but instead she quickly turned and headed down the stairs with me following her. As we entered the parlor James was waiting for us. I calmed myself down.

"Birdie, I want you to meet my husband-to-be, Mr. James Sinclair."

She looked up into his handsome face and fluttered those long eyelashes of hers, saying, "Why, Mr. Sinclair, I'm delighted to meet you. It is a pleasure having you here. You are most welcome."

Why that little tart was openly flirting with my fiancée. "Birdie, stop it right now. James doesn't know you, but I do. You don't have to worry. We are not planning to live in Virginia, but if you push me, I might just change my mind."

I wasn't going to change my mind, but I wanted to make her think I might. Of course, the plantation would be passed on to my father's heirs: Aunt Ginny and mother.

"Melinda Ann, I don't care where you live. In a few days, you're going to learn a big secret of the Kingsley's, the one I've wanted to tell you many times!"

I stood there looking at her, wanting to slap her hard on both cheeks this time. I knew she was up to something and I suspected Mother was being drugged by her. I would meet with my brothers as soon as I could get them together. I knew Edward would not listen. He was too infatuated with Birdie to pay any attention to me, and he would not believe it anyway. But I had to make the other two aware of what was happening.

CHAPTER TWENTY-NINE

That evening I gathered my brothers in the parlor.

"Charles Harley, Edward and Edwin this is, Mr. James Sinclair, my fiancé from San Francisco."

Charley reached out and shook James' hand with a look of 'I'm impressed.' Edward was cordial and polite, and Edwin was over eager asking questions about the poker game action in San Francisco.

Mother had been brought in earlier and now sat in her favorite chair calm and quiet. She had been bathed, dressed in a lovely pale green gown, her hair was combed, and she smelled like flowers. Birdie knew better than not to have Mother looking her best. I had tried to help get her ready but she had pushed me away saying it was no longer my responsibility.

Charles Harley, as the head of the family, poured all of us a small glass of sherry to enjoy before dinner was served.

We all sat down except James. He knelt down at mother's knees and took her hands in his and patted them tenderly. He told her his name, but she didn't seem to comprehend who he was nor did she seem interested.

In swished Birdie in her up-to-date evening gown. Things have changed. She did not look like a Southern bell any longer but a modern dressed lady. She really believed in dressing for dinner. Looking around the room she grasped the situation. "Oh, I hope I'm not intruding, I see you're having a family conference. I do hope I'm not interrupting. Should I remain, Edward, or should I leave." She looked ravishing and I'm sure all the men noticed.

"Please remain, my dear. It's a pleasure having you join us. Sit down beside me and have a class of sherry."

What made the evening bearable was when Aunt Ginny and Mick O'Leary arrived for dinner. They were surprised to see me and both were pleased to meet James. Aunt Ginny assumed Birdie had contacted me at the death of my father and had wondered why I hadn't come sooner.

Aunt Ginny learned that James liked horses and was quite the equestrian. James, Mick, and Ginny sat together at the other end of the table and their conversation was about horses. Birdie chattered endlessly. I sat by Mother, trying to help her eat, putting her fork in her hand, and wiping her mouth with her napkin. It was very sad.

I observed my mother more closely. I hadn't had a chance to discuss her condition with my brothers, but I intended to do so. In the short time I was there, I realized her mind was wandering.

First chance I had the next day, I gathered my brothers, Aunt Ginny, and Mick in the garden, so as not to be overheard by Birdie. I also included James because he was going to be part of the family. It was there I told them what I suspected. At first they didn't believe me and Edward became livid.

"Melinda Ann, you may be a nurse, but Birdie loves our mother, and she would never harm her. Do you hate Birdie that much, to accuse her of poisoning our mother? Do you really think she is putting poison in her tea?

That's not possible. You're just jealous of her. You always have been and you always will be."

James spoke up, "It seems to me all of you should listen to Melinda Ann. She is a certified nurse who has been trained in evaluating sick people. My advice to you is to take your mother to the hospital or call in a doctor. Have him examine your mother and see what he says."

They agreed and decided we would take Mother to the hospital in Roanoke to get a diagnosis, and that satisfied me. If Birdie was giving mother something she was being very careful. And it was true she loved Mother but at the same time Birdie wanted complete control of the household. I'd observed her fixing mother's trays and not once did I see anything unusual. Was it possible that Mother was just becoming senile? She was confused and had memory loss. I would not accept that as the answer. I needed my mother to be strong so I tried to blame Birdie.

The next day we all piled into two cars and took mother to see our family doctor. Edward told Birdie she needed to remain behind in case the family lawyer arrived. Since she was most eager to hear what he had to say she was most willing to be left behind. The doctor ran some test and checked Mother out. "You know your mother is way too thin, and her color is not good. I suspect she has been ingesting something like small doses of arsenic and for how long I don't know. How she is getting it? You'll have to find that out for yourselves. It is a white powder used to kill rats and insects – it is has no taste. I am going to have to report this to the authorities.

We were all stunned. It had to be Birdie but where was she getting it and why would she do such a thing? Then it came to me. Maybe it wasn't Birdie, maybe it was Mother doing it to herself. She had been wearing a big ring that opened like a locket. It was supposed to hold a small amount of smelling salts' which she sniffed quite often. Why? I asked myself.

Where would she get the poison? I remember on her dresser she had a powder box but the contents were not flesh color but pure white. I had seen white powder like that in the gardener's shed. It was used to kill rats.

When I explained what I suspected the boys, Aunt Ginny, Mick and even James agreed. We had to check out Mother's powder box and take it away from her. The doctor said if our suspicions were true he would not contact the authorities. In her condition she seemed to not hear us or even care what we were discussing. The doctor said it was just a matter of time before her body gave out. She would need constant care. We agreed to send word to him as soon as we looked at her powder box and removed it from her room.

On the way home we were all silent. Once there Birdie insisted on putting Mother to bed. I took the powder box off of Mother's dresser and brought it downstairs with the ring. It was as we expected. I had Edward tell Birdie what we had learned. She was horrified and blamed herself for not realizing what the problem was. Seeing her break down and cry made me realize she was not as tough as I had always thought. It proved to me she really did care for Mother. Why she didn't like me and why she kept her secret from me all these year became very clear the next day.

The family lawyer arrived, unannounced. We all gathered in the parlor. Mother sat in her chair looking dazed and Birdie perched on the sofa next to Edward, who held her hand. Charley stood near the fireplace looking like the serious actor he was. Edwin sat sprawled in Father's favorite chair. Looking at Edwin, I was sure he was contemplating what he would do with his inheritance. To him it was all about hard cash.

On another sofa sat Aunt Ginny and Mick, unmoved by the proceedings. They both looked wonderful and Aunt Ginny was never so calm. James and I sat together on a small settee. Numerous times he had tried to take my hand, trying to give me support. I was too nervous to be still, wondering what my father had bequeathed to each of us in his Last Will and Testament. I wanted the proceedings to be over so we could get on with our lives.

The lawyer sat by the fireplace in a large arm chair, dressed in his black somber suit, white shirt, and black tie. I wondered if he knew something we did not know. The reading of the will began.

> "I, Harley Orchard-Kingsley, being of sound mind do hereby attest to the fact that I am the soul owner of the Kingsley estate, and do direct that my executor settle all debts owed at my death, including the cost of my burial, before distribution of the estate.
>
> I further attest that my beloved wife, Tiffany (Tinny) is ill and unable to serve as my representative; therefore I designate my eldest son, Charles Harley, as my Executor. One half of my estate shall belong to my wife with the provision that she may live on the estate for the rest of her life.
>
> I hereby direct my Executor to distribute my estate as follows:
>
> To my sister-in-law, Virginia (Ginny) Coleman-O'Leary I leave that portion of my estate that includes the stables, the small family house, and the lands pertaining there to, to be described here and after.
>
> To my eldest son, Charles Harley, because he has shown no desire to work the land or be

master of the plantation, I hereby bequeath the sum of money in the amount of, $145,000.

To my daughter, Melinda Ann, I bequeath the Orchard-Kingsley holdings in England near the town of Leeds, plus the sum of $45,000.

To my son, Edward Maxwell, I bequeath the Kingsley Mansion and the grounds surrounding it except for the inheritance mentioned above.

To my youngest son, Edwin Earl, I bequeath the coffee plantation near the foot of the Ngong Hills, in Africa, plus the sum of money $45,000.

To the illegitimate daughter of Bart Kingsley, Birdie Mae Kingsley, in appreciation of all she has done for this family, I bequeath the sum of money, $25,000.

The remainder of the estate shall be devoted to the continuing care of my wife, Tiffany Kingsley.

Signed this day, April 4th 1919
By Harley Orchard-Kingsley
Witnessed by, Mr. Melvin Clark,
President of the Roanoke Bank and Trust

That was the big secret! Birdie was Bart's daughter! She sat there looking at us smugly as if to say I told you so. We absorb the shock silently.

CHAPTER THIRTY

We were all in agreement that what our father had done, for each of us, was fair. We decided to celebrate. The family gathered in the parlor to toast our father and each other.

It was Aunt Ginny who spoke up first. "I would like to make an announcement. Mick and I were married shortly after he came here with the stallion. Your father gave his consent. He knew we were in love and encouraged us to go into Roanoke and get married. We were married by the Justice of the Peace.

"Well said, my darlin'! Mick grinned. I know you've all had some surprises lately, but I'm a'thinkin' a good stout drink of whiskey instead of this tasteless sherry would benefit us all." We laughed and raised our glasses in a toast.

While the other members of the family visited, I went over to Aunt Ginny. "In New Orleans I found your diary and I confess I read it."

"Well, I'm sorry about that but it is all in the past. Please don't discuss it with anyone else."

"I won't but I think you can fill in the puzzle as to who was Birdie's mother. Who *was* her mother?"

"I'm sorry Melinda Ann I can't answer that question and it is best you leave it alone.

"I promise you I will never tell anyone about your diary, but I can't stop asking questions"

At that point Edward spoke up. "Now everyone, I want to announce Birdie's and my engagement. We will be married soon. This is the day I've been waiting for. We will be Master and Mistress of the Kingsley Mansion, what we both have always wanted."

About this time, James rose to his full height, cleared his throat, looked at each person, and slowly began to speak. "Meeting all of you has been quite an experience and one I shall never forget. I want to announce to you that Melinda Ann and I are engaged and want to be married here. I would like each of you to put down your differences and help me and Melinda Ann prepare for our wedding. She has dreamed of getting married in this house. Can we count on you?"

Everyone cheered, even Birdie. I thought she would be upset and resentful but she wasn't. She even offered to plan the affair if James would take care of the expenses, to which he agreed.

I thought of my father and hoped he would understand we were not being disrespectful in our going on with our plans.

After the toasting was over, Charley and Edwin had their arms around each other's shoulders and congratulated themselves on being bachelors and men of the world. Charley gave a brief recitation from one of his recent performances having to do with the pitfalls of marriage. We all laughed!

Edwin, not to be out done, offered to get a card game started. All this time Mother sat not saying a word, or hardly moving in her chair. Birdie assisted Mother out of the room.

Aunt Ginny and I went into another part of the house and talked about what had transpired during the day. We also shared my wedding plans. We talked for several hours. When I mentioned that, James and I were planning to go to England, Ireland, and Scotland for our honeymoon she was pleased, but not too interested. She stated, "I've never wanted to travel because I've always been content to stay put after my experience in New Orleans."

When I retired that night I was full of anticipation for the days to come. How exciting and fulfilling it would be to be married in my own home. I could hear the men playing cards into the wee hours, while we women slept, at last finding a peaceful calm had settled over the Kingsley Plantation family.

CHAPTER THIRTY-ONE

Birdie surprised us all. In the days to come she blossomed and fluttered under James' spell. Whatever he asked her to do she was willing. She was a proud woman and wanted nothing more than to please such a charming man. I, on the other hand, joined them with some apprehension. They both were having a grand time, and I was angry at the way they both tried to take over my wedding plans. Thank goodness Aunt Ginny was right beside me encouraging Birdie not to over-step her authority. She would remind her, "After all, Birdie, this is Melinda Ann's wedding. You are not the mistress here yet." This statement would cause Birdie to walk away in a huff.

James had this idea that I should be happy to have so much help, especially Birdie's. That was what worried me. She had decided our wedding would be the talk of the county. I don't know what she hoped to gain from the experience, maybe to be accepted by Roanoke's Southern Women's Society, or to prove her ability to plan the biggest gala of the year.

The day I was ready to tell Birdie to back off and leave the wedding plans to me, no matter what James wanted, I was notified by the hospital staff that there was another flu outbreak. I was needed in Roanoke so I temporarily dropped my wedding planning. Birdie and James had already made most of the arrangements, so I decided to let them continue.

When it came time to purchase my wedding gown, James did not understand why he would have no say. It was Aunt Ginny who helped me shop for the perfect dress. Birdie was not welcome, and my mother was too ill. The dress I found was perfect, white fluffy chiffon fitted with one side off the shoulder of the bodice, with a shear chiffon elbow-length cape. The skirt was three-quarter length with fitted pieces of white, chiffon wrapped at an angle around the skirt, making it seem to float as I walked. The veil was white chiffon fitted on the head to one side with a dainty spray of orange blossoms. And no matter how James pleaded to see it, I would not let him. Being old-fashioned, I believed it was bad luck for the groom to see the bride's dress before the wedding.

The day Aunt Ginny and I came home from shopping, I was in an unusually happy mood when guess what happened? We were sitting in the parlor enjoying a cup of tea. Birdie came prancing into the room carrying Mother's wedding dress, which was beautiful because it had been carefully wrapped and stored. It was the same dress Great-grandmother Martha had worn. She carried it in her arms. "It's too bad you're too big to wear your mother's dress. It's much prettier than yours I'm sure! If you'll just wait here a moment, I'll show you how it looks on me. It's going to be my wedding dress. Don't you think it's proper for me to wear it?"

I really didn't believe she would try it on and then proceed to show the dress to us, but she did. A short time later she came parading into the parlor. The dress was cream in color, but other than that it looked fine, like Birdie had stepped out of the 1830's! She didn't fool me. She was showing off her small figure and fluttering around like a butterfly.

As she was dancing around the room James happened to come in and he admired her in the dress…he flattered her till she blushed and fluttered her eyelashes. "Mr. James, do you really like this dress? It was Mistress Tinny's, and it fits me perfectly. Isn't it beautiful? It's too bad Melinda Ann can't wear it, but then she's a lot heavier than I am.

Ouch that smarted! Well, I wasn't all that big, but I was taller and had broader shoulders than Birdie. What did I expect from her? James found me attractive and that is all that mattered.

We were disappointed that none of James' family would be coming to our wedding. His mother had told us such a trip across the country would be too much for her. Besides, this was the social season and she didn't wish to give it up. It would also be too hard on the boys to miss school. She reminded us, in her letter, she would arrange for a church wedding and reception when we returned to San Francisco. What was wrong with her thinking? Did she think our wedding would not be legal or final in Virginia?

"I will admit, James, I'm disappointed that your family chooses not to come. I would like to have introduced your mother and sons to the Kingsley family."

"Melinda Ann, that is just the way my mother is. Her social life and her friends are more important to her than anything…and I guess that includes me. Of course, our wedding will be legal, but my mother doesn't feel you are married unless you have the ceremony in a church. Let's not let this spoil our wedding."

It wasn't worth arguing about with James so I dropped the whole matter.

CHAPTER THIRTY-TWO

On my wedding day I stood in my mother's bedroom in front of the gold framed full length mirror and gazed at my reflection. I was surprised when I saw myself. Never had I thought I was beautiful, but at that moment I was radiant, very calm, and most sure of myself.

As I looked in the mirror I saw my mother's reflection behind me. She sat in her chair staring out the window. She never looked my way or even acknowledged I was in the room with her. I wanted her to get up, come over to me, and speak to me. I wanted her to tell me how I looked and what it was like on her wedding day. I wanted her to help me dress and adjust my veil, but it didn't happen. She was so mentally far away from me and the family that we elected to leave her in her room. During the ceremony one of her dearest friends watched over her. It broke my heart to see my mother like this. I wanted to shake her awake. Yet that was not possible.

It occurred to me that neither of my parents would witness my marriage. Charley would give me away, but it would not be the same. I had always dreamed that my father would give me away. When I should have been smiling and laughing I was crying, and I was all alone.

As I wiped the tears away, Charley entered the room. "Can I be of help, little sister? Let me place your veil on your pretty head, and tell you what a lovely bride you are. Come now and let me escort you, one more time, down the grand staircase." Sweet Charley understood.

Before we left the top landing I looked once again at the portrait of Great-great-grandmother Felice. It had always been there, and seeing her seemed to give me confidence to strike out on this new adventure in my life.

Charley walked straight and tall beside me with no hint of a limp. He proudly held my arm as we walked down the stairs. When the preacher asked who would give me away, my dear brother said, "Her family, and I." And when the preacher asked if there was any cause that James and I should not be married, not a sound was heard, but in my heart I felt uneasy and I could not understand why.

As I turned my head and looked at James I felt only love for him as he placed the ring on my finger and we said our vows. It was done at last. We were man and wife.

After the wedding and the reception was over, I saw resentment in Birdie's eyes when she looked at me. Why was she angry? She had done all she could to make it a grand occasion, but now that it was over she was not pleased.

A couple of days after our wedding she came to me when James was in town. "Melinda Ann, this is now Edward's and my house and I don't want you here any longer, so please inform Mr. James to make your plans and leave." I couldn't believe my ears, but so be it.

When I told James, he was sure I was mistaken. Birdie had always been so kind to him and willing to please that he doubted my word. Again it wasn't worth an argument so I dropped the subject, but I insisted we leave as soon as possible.

Charley left the day after the wedding, heading to New York. He asked us to stop by the theatre where he was currently in a production. He planned to leave us tickets at the box office. Since we would be leaving from New York Harbor, I was delighted at the prospect of seeing my older brother on the big stage.

Dear Edwin planned to return to New Orleans, but before he left we had a private conversation. "Sis, I've done some poking around on my own, not on purpose you understand, but quite by accident. A few months ago I was on a paddle-wheeler going down the mighty Mississippi. I was in a hot game of poker when the stranger I was playing with said I looked familiar. He was a very old man and he kept staring at me. "Boy, you remind me of someone I used to know, a long time ago. A man named Dick or was it Derrick? Yes, this Derrick fellow was known up and down the river as a fairly good gambler, but he couldn't keep his mouth shut. As I recall what happened, he was drunk one evening and during a poker game he offended another high roller. An argument began and the next thing we knew Derrick was lying dead at the feet of the other man. He was shot clean through the chest. The man claimed self-defense, but they never did find a gun on Derrick. Say, young man, could this man have been any kin of yours? You play poker a lot like him, and you sure do look like him."

"I didn't answer the man, but I'm sure the gambler who was killed was our grandfather. Melinda Ann, you always have wanted to know about our real grandfather. Well now you know. I was shocked to think I look so much like the man. And I will admit it was a rather sobering thought. A man can get killed playing poker, and I don't want history to repeat itself. That's why I came home. It's true I was low on funds and I was beginning to believe my luck had run out. But being back here for even a short time has let me know there is no place for me here. I'm going back to New Orleans with the money Father left me, and this time I'm going to invest in some kind of business, maybe a big paddle-wheeler. I've also been thinking about going to Africa. I will look over the property left to me and see if I want to stay there or not. I hear there is some money to be made in raising coffee down there. What do you think?"

"It's up to you. You're an adult. Go to wherever you want to. Africa sounds like a good idea. Just promise me you will keep in touch with us in San Francisco. I'm not surprised to hear about our grandfather. I learned some things about him when I went to Danville. His name was Derrick Coleman and he was no good, even if he was Grandmother Lilly's first husband." That was it. Derrick had been shot, and in my mind he deserved it.

Edwin, James and I left the plantation within the week. Edwin headed for New Orleans. We traveled from Roanoke to Lynchburg and from there to New York City on the Southern Railroad. When we reached New York we would board a mighty ship headed for Europe. We were excited and wondered what this adventure would be like. We would have time to really get to know each other and time to discuss our future.

CHAPTER THIRTY-THREE

Our ship the Mauretania, was our ship which was a masterpiece of British engineering. James informed me that the Mauretania was one of the fastest and largest ships ever built and was also one of the most luxurious afloat. He assured me I would find it a comfortable vessel. And as usual he filled my head with information which was of little interest to me. However, to a man it was an interesting bit of facts. Such as the specifications: The length: 790 feet, beam: 88 feet, tonnage: 31,938 gross tons, service speed: 25 knots, engines: steam turbines powering four propellers. And it carried 2,335 passengers.

I was being educated in all of this as we boarded the ship and we were directed to our first class spacious cabin. James was eager to get out of New York Harbor and be on our way to Europe. He envisioned, I'm sure, a quiet voyage as I did.

I had hoped and planned to go to the theatre to see Charley in his latest show, but James wanted us to cross the Atlantic on this ship so he booked passage. Unfortunately it left port a few days before Charley's opening night and I was disappointed. Again James seemed oblivious to my needs. I thought he was selfish, but he said he had his reasons.

Once on board the ship we headed to the Verandah Café, which was located on the upper part of the ship above the main deck. We were hungry for a meal where we would be able to experience a breeze from the ocean. The café was framed by three walls and the fourth wall was open to the fresh sea air. It gave us a time to relax before returning to our cabin.

I was worried about the fact that so many people believed this ship was unsinkable because of the watertight bulkhead doors. I remembered what had happened to the Titanic which had occurred ten years before in 1912 and they thought she was unsinkable, too. Anyway, since the Titanic sank the Mauretania was fitted with enough lifeboats for all on board. That gave me some peace of mind.

What interested me most about the history of this lovely ship was that during the war in August 1914, the captain was ordered to bring his ship to Halifax instead of New York City. She was called in for war service after being refitted for a troop ship. She shipped over 10,000 soldiers to Greece. When trooping was finished her hull was painted white with red crosses along the side. Before the war was over she had shipped almost 15,000 wounded soldiers home. The war duties of the Mauretania ended in 1919, when the last soldiers were finally shipped home.

Again the ship was refitted to her pre-war luxuriant status and once again carried passengers. She was slower due to her war time hard work managing to average slightly over 17 knots. We didn't care. James was sure in the future this ship would probably leave coal burning behind and welcome oil as her new means of energy.

After we had eaten a light meal, shared a bottle of wine, and enjoyed the sea breeze, we sat for a long time watching the ocean before us. During this time I was deep in thought, while James studied the waves and watched the seagulls.

My anger toward Birdie still threatened to steal my peace of mind. Who was she to send me away from my own home, even if I was planning to leave? Our parting had not been pleasant because she was so angry about all the work she had done to make my wedding perfect. She told me I was ungrateful and I suppose I was. Even if I had been pressed into duty, at the hospital in Roanoke, I was still upset. What annoyed me most was that James had gone along with her.

The other thing that worried me was the thought of her marrying my younger brother Edward. I was appalled by the idea. After all, she had watched over him since he was a small child, and she was older than he. I couldn't believe Edward would actually go through with the marriage. I was glad I would not be there to witness the event.

Aunt Ginny was against their wedding ever taking place and had told me so before James and I left. She had talked to both Edward and Birdie, but to no avail. Edward was blind to any of Birdie's faults. He only saw her as beautiful, caring, and strong. He knew he had loved her all of his life and she deserved to be mistress of the plantation.

What was he thinking? He wasn't a Kingsley. He was an Orchard! Of course, their children would be part Kingsley and that was what was important to Birdie. She knew whose child she was and that entitled Birdie to be the mistress of the plantation. She thought marriage to Edward would seal her fate. No one would dispute her word or authority as Mrs. Edward Kingsley, and she was probably right.

When James awakened from his nap and I came out of my wondering thoughts we returned to our lovely cabin. On our way we received a cablegram from Edward and Aunt Ginny. It read:

MR AND MRS JAMES SINCLAIR STOP
CONGRAATULATIONS AND BEST WISHES STOP
ENJOY SAFE JOURNEY STOP
LOVE YOUR FAMIY

When James opened our cabin door, the room was filled with baskets of flowers. There were gifts with cards from his family and friends. But all the flowers were from him. How he had managed it, I do not know. I felt so pleased and happy seeing so many expressions of love. He lifted me up and carried me over the threshold. I nestled my head under his chin and without a word he carried me to the turned down bed with its inviting coverlets and fluffed pillows. Champagne sat chilling in a silver bucket full of ice, a lovely platter of fruit and cheese sat on the small table near our bed, and on my pillow was a single red rose tied with a red ribbon. There was a card with a message:

To my beloved wife, Melinda Ann,
The girl of my dreams.
Love always, James

What a wonderful sentimental fool I had married. Our love making had always been exciting and wild. He didn't waste time with drinking or eating. He began to undress me like he was engaged in a race against time. He was somehow out of his clothes and had me undressed before I knew what was happening. He had waited too long to be denied. There was little preparation between us. We loved the feel of each other. He knew how to hold me, how to touch me, which threw me into wild passion. Once we had climaxed, James held me close, tickling my ear with his tongue, kissing me until I felt like a limp dishrag. I've never known such pleasure or completeness.

The next morning we were up as the dawn broke over the horizon with the great ocean stretched out around us. We dressed in our more casual clothing and lounged in deck chairs letting the warm sun sooth our tired bodies. Our every need was anticipated and granted sometimes before we even requested anything.

We would be dining at the Captains table with several other couples, two singles, a Professor from some prestigious college, and a recently widowed woman of great acclaim.

When it came time to go below and dress for dinner, James pulled me out of my day-dreaming and whisked me to our state room. He was in a delightfully playful mood. Walking down the narrow hall he patted my backside, laughed, and grinned that silly grin of his which reminded me a of a school boy. This look always melted my heart.

When we arrived a minute late for the evening meal, side glances and stifled snickers were heard not only by me, but by others as well. I think I must have blushed at such attention and James looked like he had just won the Kentucky Derby. He was downright glowing. Each of the gentlemen stood until we ladies were seated. How handsome they all looked in their evening attire and the ladies in their lovely gowns.

Sitting at that table I began to feel the men's dominance asserting itself. The gentlemen, and especially the medical professor, did all the talking and treated the women as if they were not present. I soon learned we were expected to listen and not intrude in their conversations. This did not set well with me and apparently not with the widow woman either. She was rather heavy set and tall, her brown hair graying at the temples. She wore an empire line, peach colored dress with a flowing cape draped around her shoulders. The coverlet had embroidery edge going up one side and down the other. When she opened her mouth and spoke she could be heard over the men. We had learned she had retired from the opera as a contralto.

Her speaking voice made all of us sit up and take notice. "Gentlemen if you please, I have something to say. My late husband, God rest his soul, was a man of the world much like each of you. He was well educated and well thought of by his peers. Yet he was born of a woman and as such he honored all women. He valued my opinion. So may I suggest the women present be encouraged to speak their minds and share their opinions as well?"

Most of the women were in stunned silence except me. I almost jumped up and gave her a round of applause, but instead I looked at the other women present. We all began to acknowledge her and proceeded to agree. It was time women were allowed to take part in meal time conversations. If the men did not like that arrangement they could retire to the smoker and have their private conversations later.

Once this was out in the open, she began discussing her travels around the world before the Great War. At first, the men looked perplexed. The Great Dame Loretta, our advocate, spoke up rather loudly and requested we all meet later in the ballroom where there was a piano. The captain has asked me to give a short evening performance.

I was thrilled and quickly accepted on our behalf, and James looked at me as if he could shoot me. Obviously he had other plans. He preferred another section of the ship where the people were less snobbish, but it didn't make any sense to me. Why would he look for third class entertainment when we could enjoy a performance by a true opera singer?

As much as James would have liked to seek out other less formal groups, he went along with the idea. After we had eaten our delicious meal we went into the ballroom, and gathered around the piano. Madam Loretta was standing there with her pianist ready. She began to sing and her rich voice filled the room, causing others to come in and join us. The waiters and the other help lingered nearby.

Madam Loretta turned out to be quite a delightful person. Not only did she sing opera, but also some of the modern tunes of the day. She could belt out a popular song as well as any night club performer. James was impressed, especially when she asked what we would like to hear. He called out a number of songs and she gladly obliged. It was a wonderful evening and late when we finally got to bed.

The next day broke clear and warm. We strolled on deck watching the ocean flow by the ship. It promised to be a rather pleasing day. We had a late breakfast and before lounging, we played a game of shuffle board.

We were beginning to relax and truly enjoy ourselves, when the Captain approached us with a stern expression on his face. He spoke to James first in hushed whispers, and then he looked at me. He said he had read, on the ship's manifesto, I was a professional nurse and wondered if I might join him below decks at the infirmary. Turning to James he said, "Mr. Sinclair, I am in need of your wife this morning. The ship's doctor tells me we may have a case of smallpox on board, and if so, it is a very serious problem."

Though he spoke softly I heard and was shocked because if it were smallpox the whole ship was at risk. Then he asked James if he had had the pox. James stammered, "Yes, I think I recall having a slight case." I told James there was really no such thing as a light case unless he had had chickenpox instead. I on the other hand had been around the disease and had never contracted it. I was one of the lucky ones. I was somehow immune and who knew why. I then became alarmed for James' safety, so I sent him to our cabin with instructions to wash his whole body and stay put. I would direct his food and drink to be carefully prepared and served to him. I was taking no chances. As I accompanied the Captain to the infirmary, I watched James going in the other direction toward our cabin. I'd convinced him, one case of smallpox on the ship would mean there would be others.

As we started to enter the infirmary, I told the Captain not to go in with me. He would be at risk, also. He listened and quickly turned on his heels. He said he and the crew would do whatever they could to prevent the spread of the disease.

When I entered, a middle aged man approached me wearing a long surgical gown, mask, and head covering. The doctor confirmed we were dealing with smallpox. Sure enough, when I was dressed properly, I found not only one person with symptoms but four, an entire family. The mother complained of a severe headache and backache. She was exhausted and had a pink raised rash on her skin. It had started on her chest and spread outwards. First there was mucus in the mouth and throat, then her face, forearms, trunk, and legs were covered with pox marks. We estimated she was in the eighth or ninth day because the rash had turned into pus-filled lesions that had become crusty. She had been vomiting and now had diarrhea. Her husband was in the early stages and both children were as bad, if not worse, than their mother. I knew they had to be cared for and isolated from the rest of the passengers. The incubation period for smallpox is approximately 12-14 days.

The ship's doctor and I knew prompt diagnosis was of the highest importance in combating smallpox. We needed to isolate the patients and search for persons who may have been in contact with the family. If the woman was in her last stages that meant she had been around countless others. We agreed we must alert the Captain first, who would tell the crew and then the passengers. Smallpox can cause a wide spread hysteria, so we needed to let all the people know we had the family isolated. Those who knew the family should present themselves immediately.

After this was announced, there was an uneasy feeling everywhere on the ship. All activities were stopped. The passengers were told to stay in their cabins. Only one person per family was allowed to come to the dining areas to pick up food twice a day. All precautions were carried out. However we saw several new cases a day for the remainder of the trip. The ship became a hospital ship once again. We had converted a secondary ballroom near the infirmary into an isolation area. By the time we reached our destination at Southampton, it was obvious we were in trouble. There were over hundreds of cases in various stages on board, so the port authorities quarantined the ship. We were not allowed to dock. We were told to stay in international waters, which we did. Supplies, which were greatly needed, were ferried out to us in small vessels but the crews never mingled. No one aboard, sick or well, was allowed to go to shore.

Before long it was clear the disease had swept through the entire ship. Most patients lived when their fever broke. It was terrible to watch the people in pain and a shock to see the pox marks that were left on all patients, some less than others. I never worked so hard in my life, but I wasn't alone. All doctors and nurses who were on board were pressed into service. There were several retired doctors, like the old Professor, who jumped right in and helped. Even Madam Loretta came to our need because she had had the pox as a child. We took turns caring for the sick, eating when possible, and sleeping at odd hours of the day. It all reminded me of the war and brought back my realization that nursing was a noble profession and a needed one. Those old feelings surfaced once again. I was happy doing my job.

There were not enough garments to keep all of us covered in white gowns and head coverings. The ship's seamstresses were called upon to sew a simple type of uniform out of the white sheets and table clothes on board. We had volunteers helping us who had had smallpox and lived through the experience.

The Mauretania was an enormous ship so I've no idea where they took the dead bodies. It was rumored they were buried at sea in the dead of night and I suppose that was best. More than once James had tried to get past the guard stationed near the ballroom to get a glimpse of me. I had told the guard not to let him pass. Yes, I knew he was worried and who wouldn't have been? His life was at stake and I wasn't about to let him be exposed. Finally, he stayed in our cabin and I sent word to him whenever possible.

We requested more doctors and nurses to be brought on ship to aid in the care of our patients. But that did not occur. When the last cases were being released we were informed the disease had arrived before us.

After forty days we were allowed to dock and advised to leave England as soon as possible. I could not leave because all available nurses and doctors were asked to go to London and help at the hospital to care for the sick. We transferred the well folks to another ship and they were taken to a port in France. James was among them. He protested our being separated again, but he had no choice. Our honeymoon voyage had turned out to be a nightmare for both of us.

CHAPTER THIRTY-FOUR

James planned to go to Paris. Later he would make arrangements to get back to London when it was safe to be with me. By the time James had arrived in Paris, I had found an inexpensive quaint rooming house near the hospital. I rented a second story flat. It was small but adequate. I spent most of my time at the hospital battling the terrible epidemic, so I was there very little. I was convinced I was doing a noble work and that James would be proud of me.

Within a month James was in London looking for me. I'd written him several letters to a prearranged address in Paris. First he went to the hospital and missed me. After that he went to the best hotel in town and booked a suite of rooms thinking he would take me back there.

After he was settled, he came looking for me at my rooming house. When he inquired about Mrs. James Sinclair, the man at the desk said I was not registered. Then James asked about a Melinda Ann Kingsley and yes, I was there. This threw James into a rage because I was still using my maiden name. He then demanded the key to my room and proceeded to bound up the one flight of stairs. The very idea that I was going by my maiden name caused him to doubt my loyalty.

I was at the hospital when he came to get me, but I was in an isolated area and could not be reached. Not knowing he was there, I went on with my duties. About dusk I left the hospital and walked slowly home, letting the moist London air clear away the smell of the hospital. The odor of death seemed to cling to my clothes. I sat on a small bench for a while watching the few people moving quickly through the streets. The scare of the pox was uppermost in their minds. In the small park near-by, the swings were empty and freely blowing in the wind. There were no children at play, which made the park a lonesome place. I shuddered as I stood up and walked passed it. By the time I arrived home, it was dark and the fog was thick, adding to my distress. I was too tired to think of eating. All that I could imagine doing was sleeping, the only way I could forget the day's activities and dream of my beloved James.

It was quite a shock when, the owner of the rooming house told me I'd had a visitor, a man who claimed to be my husband. He apologized for letting the man into my rooms, but he said the gentleman became quite angry and demanded the key.

I remember telling Henry it was all right. Yes, I was married, but hadn't given him my married name because I assumed it didn't matter as long as I paid my rent. In my excited state, I ran up the flight of stairs to my flat and flung open the door, expecting to throw myself into the arms of my beloved. Well, that was not the case at all. When I stepped into the room James' back was turned to me as he stood looking out a window in my flat.

He whirled around, "Melinda Ann, coming up the stairs I saw that man living below you. He looked out, called to me, thinking I was you. Do you think I am stupid? You and that gentlemen must find it quite cozy living so close together." I looked at him almost in shock. "What gentlemen? What are you talking about?"

"You dishonor me with such behavior, and to prove it, you were passing yourself off as a single woman. I inquired of the desk clerk, and he said he did not know a Mrs. James Sinclair. When I asked if he knew a Melinda Ann Kingsley, he told me, indeed, you were up on the second floor. And another thing, I am appalled at your living in such inferior accommodations. As my wife you need not live under such circumstances. It is a disgrace for you to live in such a dismal place."

All of this anger, because I'd not given my married name when I registered. "James, please calm down. You see it did not matter to me. This is a quaint old building which suits my needs, and besides it's close to the hospital. I spend my days working there, and I'm here very little. Can't you understand that? So this rooming house is good enough for me. And besides, James, even though I'm your wife, I do have the right to choose where I want to live, don't I?"

He could not contain his anger. "This rooming house may be good enough for you, but it is not for me. I want you out of this flat as soon as possible. I'll be damned if you're going to live here. Must I remind you that you are my wife, and as such you will do as I tell you! And the answer is no! You do not have the right to choose where you are going to live." Hearing his harsh words, I almost collapsed.

Then seeing all my distress, at being addressed in such a manner, James grabbed me hard, then he held me at arms length, looked me up and down. When he saw my disheveled appearance, he was horrified and exclaimed, "What have you done to yourself? You look like a worn out piece of trash, your hair is a mess, there is no blossom in your cheeks and you are as skinny as a rail." Then he pushed me away in disgust and exclaimed. "Melinda Ann, you are not the woman I married. You are a stranger to me. I'm not sure if I even know you anymore."

Tears were beginning to flow down my face. I was too tired to care or to think. I just wanted to collapse. When he saw my expression and how he had hurt me, he pulled me close, pressing my head gently into his chest. By this time I was crying so hard I could not stop. This wasn't like me. I'd always been strong. Why was I falling apart now? It was like someone had opened the flood gates. My tears were flowing and my sobs were those of a child. I'd worked so hard and tried to be brave, as I watched countless people die. Seeing James and the anger he exhibited, was more than I could handle. I remember fainting and the next thing I recall is waking in a silent room.

Moonlight streamed through a dirty window as I slowly came awake. I knew I was alone again. I found I was in my night gown and my hair had been brushed. I felt my face was damp, and at first I thought I must have gotten the pox. I stirred, and at once a figure rose from a chair nearby. It was James. He patted my shoulder and told me to go back to sleep. I'm not sure how many days I was in this condition, but he said it was over four. I remembered little except seeing James spooning soup into my mouth and making me drink fluids. All I wanted to do was sleep and forget.

When I awakened, I did not have a clue as to what had happened during that time. I was concerned about my job responsibility to the hospital. I knew I was supposed to be there, but I had not let them know

I was ill. To my amazement I learned James had sent word that I was seriously ill and would not be returning to the hospital ever again.

I will never forget how furious I was when he told me what he had done. I remembered little, slowly sitting up on the edge of the bed. I didn't scream at him or even yell. In a low voice I told him, "James, I'm not going to sit here and listen to what you've done while I was sleeping. You have gone too far this time. My job is important to me, and I'm not just going to up and quit because you say I have to. How dare you come here, accuse me of having an affair, and then have the nerve to tell me I can't live where I want to, and that I have to quit my job."

"Melinda Ann, you are pushing me too far! And whether you like it or not, we will leave this terrible place. Then we are going to take up where we left off as husband and wife! You seem to forget you are married to me! Now I am in charge, and we will leave London as soon as possible. Since the epidemic is coming to an end, you have no reason to stay. The hospital can get along just fine without you, and we can continue our honeymoon trip."

This tirade just caused me to freeze inside. I wondered how he dared to tell me to give up nursing and just become his wife. Did he consider me a piece of property he owned? What did that mean anyway?

I fretted for several days and finally I told James I was well enough to take a walk while he made the arrangements to leave his hotel. After he left I was so mad I went directly to the hospital and spoke with the director. I told him what had happened. He listened patiently and then abruptly told me there was nothing he could do because a woman's place was with her husband.

I tried to accept what he said with respect, but I thought my presence at the hospital was valued much more. And the next thing the director told me nearly knocked me off my feet. "You see, Mrs. Sinclair, your husband informed us that he was very wealthy. If we would release you from your job and never bother you again, he would donate a new wing to our hospital, an offer we can hardly reject. You yourself know how much a new wing is needed. Surely, you can see our position."

"Oh, I can see your position all right, and if you do meet with the board of directors they would surely vote to accept the donation and be very pleased to receive such a gift." And I thought, what was one nurse compared to a new hospital wing?

That same day several of my colleagues came to me, begging me to talk to my husband. I needed to explain to him what being a nurse meant to me. They also wanted the generous gift my husband had promised. They were as baffled as I was at his stand against my being a career nurse. Yes, I knew we were just newlyweds, and had not even completed our honeymoon trip, but this was a problem that needed to be straightened out now and not later. I resolved to talk to him immediately. When I returned to my flat and walked in the door, I found James packing my things.

"James, what are you doing?"

"What does it look like? I'm packing your stuff and you are leaving with me immediately."

"Just hold on a minute, I do love you and I am your wife, but you do not have the right to tell me what to do. You knew my views about the rights of women before you married me. That has not changed. I believe any woman has the right to follow a career if she wants to.

"That may be how you feel, but I suggest you change your thinking. As my wife you will go along with my wishes."

"James, that statement is unreasonable. You have gone too far and stepped over the line of what I will tolerate. You've made me angry and I'm upset. I suggest you stop what you are doing and leave this flat right now. Leave me alone. I need some time to think. Your actions are totally inconsiderate of me and my desires."

He stopped, turned around and looked very serious. "Melinda Ann, I love you, but I won't stay around this place and see you kill yourself taking care of the scum of London. Nobody cares about these uneducated people. They are no more than street people with no self-pride or abilities. Why are you wasting your time on them?" Well, if he didn't know, I could not explain it to him.

Then he confronted me, "You will go with me now and forget all this nonsense, or I'll leave you by yourself. Whether we ever get back together again is up to you. You'll know where to find me. I'm going to Paris. I have friends there and perhaps they will supply me with the lifestyle I want and need." I knew what he meant. He loved fancy living, big parties, lots of friends to converse with, and especially good-looking women.

CHAPTER THIRTY-FIVE

James did go back to France and it proved to be good in some ways for him, but it was devastating to me. I was still worried about him getting the pox even though fewer cases were arriving each day. I believed that he would be safer in France on his friend's estate. He told me she was a widow woman and was quite attractive. I am not sure why he told me because he could have just gone, but no, for some reason I felt he wanted to make me jealous. It worked.

Since I could not continue my job at the hospital I went to the Quarantine House, which was an annex to the hospital. They were in desperate need of nurses.

Coming home from work one evening, I noticed, at the end of the hall to my left, the door of the flat below me was open. I saw a man sitting in a chair wearing a handsome red and gold smoking jacket. He was reading a book and smoking his pipe. I could see a lamp shinning over his shoulder and the flicker of firelight in the room. The fragrance of sweet lemon tea filtered out into the hall making his room very inviting. I never would have considered going into his flat before because I would have thought it improper.

"Mrs. Sinclair," he called out to me. "You look weary. Would you care for a cup of tea before you climb the stairs?"

"Your fire looks very inviting and a cup of tea is just what I need." I knew I was a married woman, but right then I needed a friend, and this neighbor seemed harmless enough. He turned his head and slowly rose from his chair.

"Mrs. Sinclair, I would be delighted if you would take a cup of tea with me. It is a nice way to end a hard day at work. Please, do come in."

The man had a full head of hair, the color of salt and pepper and curly. He was rather tall with square shoulders. I guessed him to be 10 to 15 years my senior. When he smiled at me I felt completely at ease. He moved toward me with an easy stride and extended his hand in welcome. I entered his flat as I would have a friend's. While we were having our tea I learned that he had retired early, from the academic world of teaching, as a History Professor, to become a full time writer. He introduced himself as Professor Stephen Andrew Hamilton, and added most people called him Andy or Professor. I decided to call him Professor. It sounded less personal.

I needed a friend in the worst way. I was at a crossroad in my life. Should I return to a husband whom I now knew was inconsiderate of my desires and feelings or continue to pursue a nursing career? I considered whether to share my situation or not with this stranger. He seemed like a kind, wise, elderly man who would understand my problem. I felt sure he could shed some light on the subject from a male point of view. I desperately needed to talk to someone! I enjoyed the brief interlude by his fire, but could not bring myself to speak of my problem.

Evening was the worst time of all. Mrs. Peabody, the wife of the desk clerk, often said hello to me and was pleasant enough. She was always fussing about something or cleaning. She never had time to sit with me and chat. I was very lonely and convinced that James meant what he had said. I had dreamed of James with his arms holding me tight and kissing me. Then I would wake up in a sweat calling his name. I wanted him, but I wanted him under my terms.

Several days later on my way home, I stopped and looked over the mail which was on a table in the hall. I observed the Professor down the hall, as he sat by his fire, which warmed the room with a soft glow. It looked like he had been reading, but now he was slumped in his chair with his tea cup and saucer dropped on the floor beside him. I knew something was wrong so I did not hesitate to enter his room. I checked his pulse and listened to his heart. He appeared to have fainted and was very warm to the touch. I opened his smoking jacket and unbuttoned his shirt to give him some air.

Once doing this I ran over to the window and raised it. After a few minutes he regained consciousness, and turned his head toward me. As he looked at me he began to mutter something and then began to pull himself together. About that time Mrs. Peabody, Henry's wife, came out of her flat and looked in at the scene before her. I'm sure, although innocent; it looked very suggestive to her. This put me in a vulnerable situation. She quickly glanced in our direction with a disgusted look on her face, and then went on her way out the front door. I felt a tinge of guilt because I was in a strange man's flat. However, I was a nurse and I was doing my job. I knew what Mrs. Peabody was thinking, but I didn't care. I had merely tried to help someone in need and she could think what she liked.

The Professor stood up with my help and was a bit shaky. "Mrs. Sinclair! I am so sorry you found me in such a condition. Thank you for coming to my rescue. I often have these spells, but after I eat something I return to normal. Would you mind bringing me something to eat? I assure you, I will be better after I have eaten."

"No, of course, I wouldn't mind, but Professor have you ever consulted a doctor about this condition?"

He informed me in no uncertain terms that he had not, and added, "After all, what good are they anyway? They have not been able to stop the pox epidemic, and besides I am as healthy as a twenty year old. For a man my age I am in surprisingly good health. These spells come and go, so don't fret yourself about me. And while you're preparing my sandwich make one for yourself."

I went to a small kitchen area where he had a round table, icebox, and a two burner hotplate. I found some bread, cold meat, and some butter. I made sandwiches for both of us. As I prepared the light meal, I talked about my work in the isolation wards, how sad it was watching patients die, and how tired I became.

"Yes, Mrs. Sinclair, I have watched you leave early each morning and arrive home late and tired in the evening. I do admire you for your work at the hospital. You must be a very dedicated nurse. May I call you by your first name rather than Mrs. Sinclair?

"Yes, of course, that does sound friendlier. By all means, call me Melinda Ann."

"I understand you're married, but I have a hard time believing you are, since your husband does not live with you and never comes to visit you. Are you separated?"

"Well, we're not legally separated. We are just going our separate ways for the time being. I really need a man's opinion on my personal situation. I've considered sharing my problem with you, but I thought you would not be interested or might not want to get involved. Can you understand that?"

"Yes, my dear lady, I do understand. I would like very much to be your friend. That's what you mean, isn't it?" He looked at me in such a strange questioning way that I immediately wanted to set him straight. "Yes, of course, I need a friend, someone I can trust."

"Melinda Ann I assure you, you can always trust me. I admire you for risking your life to save others. I have often wanted to offer you a cup of tea and a meager meal in the evening, but I was sure you would refuse me. I have been so inspired by your noble actions that I have written a poem in your honor."

I was speechless and stood there just looking at him. Why? Why in the world had he written about me? Seeing my reaction he said, "Well, are you going to shut the door and sit down with me or not? You know, I am just lonely. Perhaps we could keep each other company." I guess I must have looked shocked because he quickly added, "Oh, no, not in that way. I'm old enough to be your father. I just want to talk to you and share a cup of tea. Perhaps we could have a game of checkers sometime."

Well, that stopped me cold. His door was still open and there was no one in the hall, so I shut the door and sat down beside him. I sat on the floor at his feet, with him in his chair.

I wasn't sure he was old enough to be my father, but he made me feel comfortable so I began to relax, I even laughed. It was true that after he ate he was fine. When I saw he was in a stable condition, I rose to leave. "Melinda Ann, please stay a while longer I would like to read you some of my poetry." As he read I was overwhelmed at the magic in his voice, the way he spoke with an upper class rich English accent. He was a dreamer and a painter of words. I became lost in the beauty of his words. The flickering firelight was making me drowsy. I soon found myself nodding. When I heard the clock on the mantel strike nine the sound startled me awake. I jumped up, said my goodbye, and fled up the stairs to my own flat. It was a very pleasant evening.

The next morning I was up early before the fog lifted. When I went down the stairs I didn't as much as glance at the Professor's door, but I knew he must be in there. I was wrong. As I closed the outside door behind me, he was coming up the front steps. I bumped into him and nearly fell. Quickly I caught myself by using the stair rail. I couldn't help noticing how handsome he looked, dressed in a casual pair of trouser, a tweed jacket with a white wool scarf wrapped around his neck. He had a smile on his face! When we almost collided he pulled at his tweed cap saying, "Good Morning, Melinda Ann."

I quickly recovered my composure and greeted him. "Professor, how are you feeling this morning?" He beamed at me in a shy teasing way that was a bit charming.

"Just fine, Melinda Ann. Thanks to you and your fine nursing skills."

I must have blushed because he mentioned my cheeks turning pink. That surprised the heck out of me and caused him to chuckle as he entered the building. Before he closed the door he turned to me. "Melinda Ann, please drop in anytime, because it is a pleasure having a new friend." I found I really liked this man. He was kind and gentle, and refusing his company would be hard.

I had made a lot of acquaintances at the hospital, but no true good friends. What contact I had with the nurses and doctors had been strictly professional and not social. The most respected doctor in the hospital was only interested in the training I had received in America and my experiences during the war. He informed me he admired my feelings concerning women in the nursing field. He agreed that nurses were very helpful tending the sick, and assisting in the operating room. But even though he complimented me, I knew that he felt I should consider leaving the profession to rejoin my husband. I couldn't argue with that.

As I thought about this, I realized what a very short time I really had been married. I'd taken my vows to honor and obey him. By refusing to go with James I had jeopardized my marriage. I remembered James' two sons, Alfred and Bradley. Though James hardly talked about them I was sure he loved them. It occurred to me that I had not once considered their needs or feelings. I had been so involved with James and his desires that I had forgotten about them. How inconsiderate of me. When I married James I had also taken on his family hadn't I? I had somehow lost sight of this. I knew I should go to him, but I couldn't bring myself to do it yet.

CHAPTER THIRTY-SIX

One afternoon I was scheduled to work in the Quarantine House. Sometimes I wished it had never happened. This episode changed my life. When I entered these children's world I was shocked at what I saw. Many of them had deep smallpox scars on their young faces, arms and legs. Some were there because they had no place to go. They were well enough to leave the hospital, but many of their parents were either dead or afraid to come to get them. I learned that the youngest of these children would be sent to orphanages. The older youths would be turned out into the streets of London. I was appalled. I believed something should be done especially with the older children. Where were they to find lodging and get food for that matter? How would they ever find work? Wouldn't they be perfect targets for the many criminals who owned some London streets?

My mind was off and running, and by evening I had made my decision to talk to the head nurse at the hospital. Then I would go to the director. There had to be a house or building somewhere in London that could be purchased or donated to this cause. It could be staffed with volunteers and supported by the hospital. I was determined to get some answers. If it were money that was needed, my father had left me quite a sum in the London bank.

After I spoke to the director, I realized it would not be an easy task. I was an American, a woman and not known in England. I would have to contact James in Paris, get him back to London to get his signature on the transaction. I wanted to staff the new home for children with professional people and not just volunteers. It was going to be a monumental project.

Thinking about this tended to absorb my every waking hour and the days passed quickly. All this time I'd not heard a word from James. I began to realize he had meant what he had said. I would have to go to him. The thought of doing that did not make me happy. Why did I have to go to him? Why couldn't he just return to me?

While working on this project I often dropped in on the Professor. I didn't think much about it, but when things slacked off at the Quarantine House I spent more time freshening up before I went home. My hair was combed into a bun. My cape and cap were properly placed. I felt neater and more rested these days since I'd given myself permission to visit him. His salt and pepper hair, small moustache and goatee made him look older than he was. At the same time it showed his stable qualities. He never made hasty decisions. We often shared a light evening meal and delicious lemon tea. He let me express my opinions and often encouraged me to tell him what was on my mind. He even took time to go with me in search of a suitable building for the children's home.

All along, I never suspected the Professor was falling in love with me until he slipped a poem under my door. I read it with mixed feelings. In the poem he explained his feelings for me. He said he loved me and wanted to marry me. He reasoned that since my husband and I were separated and not seeing each other it would be all right to ask me. I'd no idea he was that serious! After I read the poem I was upset and decided to take a walk in the park. I needed to think about what he had said.

The Professor and I had become good friends and I valued his friendship. At times he made me laugh at his foolish jokes. We often took walks in the park when I was too wound up to relax or sleep. I had long since given up worrying about what Mrs. Peabody thought or anyone else for that matter. I will admit James was on my mind less and less. His face was becoming faded in my mind. The truth was that I was being drawn to the Professor! But I had to quit thinking of him and not let myself dream of what might have been. I began to wonder if I had ever really been in love with James. He had swept me off my feet into a whirlwind romance, and I'd never been given a chance to think about our future together.

When I thought of the Professor I knew I admired him, and perhaps even loved him. Not the wild passionate love I had felt for James, but an abiding deep trusting love. A love I didn't know how to express. I had made a mistake. I had married the wrong man, but I must honor my vows. I knew I must refuse to listen to anything the Professor said or had written declaring his love for me. I had to tell him right then that it was my duty to go back to my husband. When I reached the rooming house, the Professor called to me. "Melinda Ann, come and join me for a light supper. I know you're hungry."

I stepped inside the door and closed it behind me. "Professor that was a beautiful poem, but I am not sure I can handle the feelings you have for me. You know we can never be together. I cannot go back on my marriage vows." Saying that, I turned around, walked out the door, stumbling up the stairs feeling deep regret.

What I didn't know was that James had been there. He told me later that, when he arrived, he found my door locked, so he asked for the key which he was given. When he entered my flat he found the poem the Professor had written and unfortunately read it. He had seen me coming in the outside front door and I appeared to be in a good mood so he meant to greet me as I came up the stairs.

When I reached my door it was unlocked and slightly opened, which alarmed me. Hearing no sound or movement anywhere I ventured inside. Once inside I found a lamp burning, the poem from the Professor crumbled on the floor. On the table near the lamp a pair of men's gray suede gloves. I knew at once who they belonged to. My God, James has been here, but where is he now? I quickly pieced together what had happened. He had come in, saw the poem, read it, and became angered. He had crushed the piece of paper, thrown it on the floor, and left in a hurry.

Not bothering to put on my coat I ran down the stairs headed to the nearest pub. Not finding him there, I ran like a crazy woman with my hair flying and my dress becoming wet from the dense, damp London fog. I entered the second pub and there James was drinking. There were two empty shot glasses and a third to his lips.

I ran to James, threw my arms around him from behind and held on tight. He knew at once it was me but when he turned around I don't think he expected what he saw. I was a disheveled-looking woman with no make-up on, with messed-up wet hair curling around my face. My damp uniform was wrinkled and smudges and clung to my body. I was a terrible sight for a man who loved the women in his life to be tidy and well-groomed.

I'm sure I looked awful in his eyes. When my appearance sunk in, he reacted violently and shoved me away from him. The angry push caused me to lose my balance, fall backwards and striking my head on the floor. Then I passed out.

When I came to, my head was in James's lap and he had tears in his eyes. He had not meant for me to fall or to hit my head. As I drifted in and out of consciousness, I became aware that there was two of him. The blow to my head had caused some damage. I felt the blood beginning to soak through my hair and my eyes clouded over.

The next thing I remember is waking up in the hospital with James sitting in a chair beside the bed. The doctor said I had a minor concussion, and a small scalp wound from hitting the floor when I fell.

When my head was clear I was going to tell him I'd booked passage to France, and I was willing to give up my nursing career if that was what he wanted. When I could finally open my eyes, he stood up, looked at me intently and took my hand in his.

"While you were with that man downstairs I was in your flat fuming.

I decided to leave you with this gentleman. After all you were consorting with some strange man with no thought of how it looked or how I might feel about it. I began to wonder if you wanted a divorce. A divorce is unthinkable to me, but I made up my mind to leave you to your own fate.

"Melinda Ann, it is obvious to me that something is going on between you and that man living below you. I should have never left you alone in London. It is entirely my fault."

Damn it, he was being so noble that I wanted to scream at him, but I held my tongue and controlled my voice. "James, I'm your wife and I love only you. You are my husband and the love of my life." I said that to convince myself it was true.

As he spoke, he sat down on the edge of the bed. "My dear, there has been a terrible misunderstanding during our separation. My lady friend in Paris seemed to have destroyed all of our letters to each other. She was jealous of our marriage. The only letter I received from you was the one where you asked for my help. She was jealous of our marriage. The only letter I received from you was the one where you asked for my help, and that is why I returned.

"James, what upset me most was not receiving mail from you. I thought you didn't care about me. I had decided to give up my plans for a children's home in London and even my career as a nurse. I was planning to come to you in Paris. And as to the gentleman in the flat below, as far as I was concerned no matter how it looked, he was just an elderly friend. Divorce had never entered my mind."

"When my hostess revealed what she had done with your letters, I decided to come to London, get you and set things right. You are not to worry about anything now. I will inform the hospital and the Quarantine House of your decision to leave. Trust me, my dearest, I'll take care of everything."

I knew we would be fine now that we were together again. But that last statement, 'I'll take care of everything' bothered me just a little. It was typical James – back in full control, I was hoping we could continue our long-postponed trip to Scotland where my ancestors originated. We would be happy. We would travel together once again as lovers and friends, as well as being husband and wife.

It did not take long for James to finalize our plans, but it wasn't long until we were leaving London. James had seen to the closing of my flat and disposing of what little I had there. We were to train travel once again and see new and interesting country but when I thought all was settled for us to tour Scotland, James changed his mind abruptly and decided that we should stop our travels altogether. He wanted to go back to America to his home in San Francisco.

"But, James." I exclaimed, "I so wanted to see Scotland and we're so close! Have I no say at all in what we do?"

He responded flatly, "We've been gone a long time and I am concerned about the boys."

I had to admit he had a point. There was no arguing this time. We were returning to James' home in San Francisco, and as his wife I would accompany him.

CHAPTER THIRTY-SEVEN

We went back to London and James booked our passage to New York on the next ship out. I was sullen and unhappy the whole trip and rarely ventured out of our cabin. I was hurt and felt betrayed. I soon realized he had taken me away from London because he sensed I might have feelings for the Professor.

When we arrived in New York, James agreed to attend the theatre where Charley was performing. It was because he had read the great reviews in the newspapers. My brother had made it big. He was a well-known actor. It was a joy to know he was fulfilling his dream. I would see him on the stage at last. When we arrived at the theatre, we were treated like royalty. The best seats in the house were ours. Charley had seen to that, which impressed James a great deal. We stayed at the Plaza, the best hotel in New York, according to both my brother and James, which was The Plaza. We shopped in the most expensive stores and ate in fanciest of restaurants. It was just another whirlwind romantic adventure, but no matter how hard I tried I could not be totally happy. That puzzled me.

After a few days in New York, James suggested we return to the west on the train. At least there would be time for us to become re-acquaint, and plan the church wedding, and discuss our future. I was listless and really uninterested in what he talked about, a proper wedding and an elaborate reception. As he droned on and on my mind drifted to the quiet warmth of the Professor's room. What was the matter with me?

James talked incessantly of being home with his mother and sons. I felt like a third wheel. I was beginning to see I would have little say concerning my future. All I could do was accept what was to come and make the best of it.

When I thought of James' sons, Alfred and Bradley, I hoped I would be able to bridge the gap between us. I imagined our becoming friends. If so, maybe someday they would call me mother instead of their grandmother. I wanted my love for James to be rekindled, but I wondered if I would ever be able to accept his total control of my life.

The day finally came when we arrived at the San Francisco railroad station. I dressed in one of my finest traveling suits and worried about how I would appear to James' mother. Would she approve? Somehow I doubted it, but only time would tell.

We were met at the station by his mother and sons, and what surprised me most was that his father was there. I had never heard James speak of his father. In fact, I thought his father was probably dead. When I met the senior Mr. Sinclair, I got the surprise of my life! His father was a hearty man, full of energy and enthusiasm. He spoke with a loud booming voice and was not concerned who heard him. When we were introduced, he lifted me off the ground with a big bear hug, nearly squeezing the life out of me. It wasn't hard to see that he approved and was delighted to meet me. I liked him right away and knew we would get along really well!

The boys didn't say much to either of us. It was as though they were peeved at our being gone so long. His mother made no pretense of trying to hide her dislike of me. She was cool and aloof, hardly looking at me. As we got in the massive Packard automobile she made a remark to Mr. Sinclair that I could not help from overhearing.

"That woman is a southern born country girl! She will never fit in with the San Francisco society. She's not even pretty!"

Mr. Sinclair laughed and commented. "Good, maybe she'll stir that high-toned group of yours up a bit! We've needed some new blood around here for some time, and a little down-to-earth living would be refreshing, too. I like her, and besides, I think she is quite attractive. Priscilla, anyone who can live with our spoiled son has got to be exceptional." When I heard this I was pleased. I knew I had a least one friend in the family.

Their palatial home was situated on one of the hills overlooking San Francisco. The interior looked like a plush hotel with nothing out of place. There were servants everywhere, walking around straightening and cleaning constantly. No wonder Mr. Sinclair was uncomfortable when we arrived. He looked like the home-loving type, not a fancy stuffed shirt. Somehow he just didn't 'fit' in the atmosphere of this fancy house. He excused himself and went directly into the library. Later, I learned this was his hideaway.

As I was given the grand tour by a very proud Mrs. Sinclair, I realized a person could get lost in such a big house. That's when James informed me we would be living here permanently. An entire suite of rooms had been prepared and was ready and waiting for us. A butler and several other servants carried our trunks and cases upstairs. Close on their heels were two maids who began unpacking our luggage before we could catch our breaths. It didn't bother me though because I was exhausted and all I wanted to do was go to sleep.

"James, please make my excuses and say that I will not be coming down for the evening meal. If a little soup and bread could be served up here, I'd be grateful."

This statement was met with one of James' outburst. "Melinda Ann, where do you think you are, in a damn hotel? That behavior is not acceptable in this house. You will dress for dinner and be on time. My mother is quite punctilious and she keeps strict protocol." I couldn't believe what I was hearing and all I could seem to think was how different the customs were between Virginia and San Francisco.

Exactly what did it mean to dress for dinner in San Francisco? I knew I would need some coaching. Immediately I asked one of the maids if I would have a personal maid. She informed me in no uncertain terms. "Quite so Mrs. Sinclair, your maid will be here presently to assist you." Well, dear me, that was a relief!

The young woman who assisted me was a true jewel. At first, she was cautious with her speech, but later she proved to be a very trustworthy friend. When I needed something I did not own, she simply told the elder Mrs. Sinclair and it was ordered and delivered. From that first evening, I never was in the wrong outfit, but I was miserable. I had nothing to do to fill my time. I was expected to read in the library, walk in the lovely gardens, play games with the boys, play solitaire, and go shopping if I wished, I could go out to lunch with the boys, but never with Priscilla which was my mother-in-law's first name. I don't think she wanted to be seen with me.

After a while, Alfred and Bradley came around and accepted me. I adored James' sons. I took them on picnic outings when they were home. Over spring vacation we became rather good friends, but they never dared to call me mother. Their grandmother had made it quite clear that she was the only true mother they had.

I was disappointed, restless and even resentful of this life. James was away during the week days. He worked on major deals for the company. I learned he had lunch at his club every day. On the weekends he played golf and went out in the evenings. Sundays the family went to church together. I'm sure it was just to please his mother. He spent as little time with me as possible. We were becoming strangers to each other.

The only bright spot during this time was Mr. Sin, which he loved to be called, much to the disapproval of Priscilla. When he and I were together he told me stories of his father and grandfather, two scoundrels that he seemed quite proud of. We took long walks together around the gardens and in the city park. He said he found me refreshing with my slight southern accent and bright look on life. When I told him I had been a nurse during the war, he was all ears and wanted to hear all about my experiences. I shared my feelings of deep commitment to the nursing profession. I told him how depressed I felt living in his big house and doing nothing to justify my existence.

One day it dawned on him and he asked me, "My dear girl, why are you here with my son? You're nothing like the woman his mother planned for him to marry. You're a fine person, healthy and intelligent. You should be doing what you love instead of being locked away playing a role that doesn't suit you. I think you're very unhappy. It's clear my son is amusing himself elsewhere and not coming home when he should. I don't know what happened between the two of you, but I'm not blind. If you were ever in love with James, he was one lucky man, but now I feel you're just fulfilling your wedding vows. Yes, I know Priscilla was planning another wedding and a reception for you here in San Francisco. She was going to do it for her self-esteem, but she has not gone through with it. I'm thinking she believes your marriage will not last, so she has dismissed the whole idea."

I stopped in my tracks. Was it that obvious? "Mr. Sin, you and my personal maid, Sherry, are the only people I can be myself with. I'm constantly on my guard for fear I will say or do something wrong with anyone else. Are you aware that when your wife has invited guests, she asks me to leave the room? And when she has her afternoon teas, she is less than cordial to me. You're right! James and I were once madly and passionately in love, but our timing was always wrong. We constantly misunderstood each other. When our wild adventures were over in San Francisco, something changed. Once we were married he treated me like a possession and not a wife. He simply is not been able to see my need to be a nurse nor has he ever understood how I feel about continuing with my research concerning my ancestors."

Mr. Sin knew me very well by this time. He encouraged me to make a decision to leave James. He wanted me to be free to follow my dreams. He finally confided in me.

"Melinda Ann, I know what you're feeling. You may not believe me, but I loved another lady before I met my wife. Priscilla was from the right social family with a name and I was expected to marry well. You see, my dear Melinda Ann, it is too late for me, but it is not too late for you. You don't have any children to hold you here, and before you do, I suggest you run like crazy."

"Do you love my son enough to stay with him a life-time? If not, then let me help you leave. If there is someone else you care about, go to him and be happy. You don't have to tell me if you don't want to, but if you want my help just ask me. I have connections with a number of good lawyers and a divorce could be obtained quietly."

I couldn't believe he had seen right through me and yet I must have told him just enough about the Professor that he probably suspected my true feelings.

"Mr. Sin, I love you dearly and I do still have feelings for James, but as far as deep love, no. That died a long time ago, when he took control of my life."

After sharing my feelings with Mr. Sin I realized how unhappy I really was. I came to a conclusion I would leave James. The quicker I told him the better. That evening James was preparing to go out for the evening as he always did.

"James we need to talk."

"I don't have time can't you see I am about ready to leave?"

"Well tonight you better take time to listen. I don't like my idle life here and I'm not going to stay here any longer."

"Oh you'll be just fine when you become a mother and have children to care for. You will be too busy to complain then."

"James, I do not want to have your children! Besides we have not been together enough."

He whirled around and yelled. "As my wife, you belong here and you will have my children, so make the best of it!"

"That is the point, I don't belong here! I want a divorce!"

"There has never been a divorce in this family! I will not allow one now!"

"Then it will be a first, because I am leaving you in the morning!"

"You are serious aren't you?"

"You're, darn right I am!"

"Then go and don't expect any help from me."

"I don't need you…I never did!'

He looked at me with that school boy expression and I did not find it appealing. His eyes were full of contempt. He turned on his heels, walked out the bedroom door, and out of my life forever.

The next morning I said good-bye to Sherry, as she helped me pack my trunks and carrying cases. The boys were still away at boarding school, so they were spared the final parting. My only regret was leaving the boys and Mr. Sin.

James' mother was there in her finest black dress looking like she was going to a funeral. She had that "I told you so" expression on her face. She said a cold good-bye to me at the head of the stairs and immediately returned to her bedroom. Mr. Sinclair followed me down the stairs and outside to the waiting car.

Mr. Sin, the dear old man, was almost in tears and yet he whispered in my ear. "Don't worry about anything. I'll take care of the divorce. Keep in touch with me. I'll send the papers when they are ready. Go back to London, find that Professor, and tell him you're free. Go with my blessing, child."

I was ushered into the waiting automobile and whisked to the railroad station. Once again I was on my way to New York City, and this time I was free of James. He would never follow me again and at that prospect I felt a little sad. The feeling did not last because I reminded myself how I really felt. I had no love left in my heart for him. I felt only resentment with just twinge of regret where he was concerned. My friend the Professor - what about him? I wasn't sure of my feelings. I did not want to be controlled by any man. I just wanted to be free. Another chapter in my life had come to an end.

CHAPTER THIRTY-EIGHT

When I arrived New York City, I immediately contacted Charley and informed him of what had happened. He was surprised because he had found James to be charming. He had thought James and I would have a good life together. But when I told Charley the whole story he understood why I had to leave James and he agreed it was best.

After eight months, James was only a memory and my life did go on. I stayed with Charley and enjoyed going to the theatre with him as well as other places of interest in New York City. When I felt rested and ready to tackle life again, I shared my plans with Charley. I was going back to England to help establish the children's home and once again seek employment in the hospital. I also told him about the Professor and how I intended to reestablish a friendship with him.

Charley was delighted that I'd planned to go back into nursing. His exact words were, "My dear sister, you have always been a nurse in your heart. James had no right to expect you to give up something that's so much a part of you. I am glad you came to this conclusion, and I have good news. We are taking this show to London, which means you and I can travel together once again."

Crossing the Atlantic Ocean was becoming a habit with me, and I truly loved it. I was prepared to go back to London and to visit the rooming house where I'd met the Professor. Would it be the same? No, nothing is ever the same. Should I wire him that I was coming? Yes…No… I would rather surprise him. Suppose he was not there, and suppose my flat was rented. I had not realized how much I'd admired him, or how my feelings for him had developed.

The Professor was a mature man, not a silly school boy or someone spoiled by wealth and social standing. He was just who he was, stable, self-confident and composed. He, like Mr. Sin, had encouraged me to follow my heart's desire, to reach my lifelong ambition. He was an author and a poet. How could I've been so blind? I must have loved him all along, but my commitment to James had clouded my vision.

Charley and I spent a lot of time together, sharing many memories, some good and some we would like to forget. He had received only one telegram from Aunt Ginny. Birdie and Edward had been married at Kingsley Mansion and hoped to start a family soon. Before we left New York, Charley informed his agent where we could be reached in London. This was just in case Aunt Ginny needed to reach us.

The ship we chose was the RMS Berengaria. She was the pride of the Cunard fleet. This ship had also served as a troop ship until August of 1919. We would embark from New York Harbor and sail to Southampton. She was a massive ship with a crew of 1,180 and the passenger capacity was in the thousands. It was a floating city.

Since Charley and I were traveling together I wasn't concerned about being alone. We had a whole troupe of people traveling with us. The actors were asked to perform in the ship's Lounge several times. The Lounge was elegant, with a stain glass ceiling. It had tall graceful curved windows and painted designs on the walls around the room. In one area, a lovely tapestry was mounted on the wall. The furniture in the room was set on an oriental carpet. There were many small private tables of French design. Each had three or four straight back chairs as well as low curved-back, upholstered ones. It was a perfect place to relax with friends and enjoy a cocktail.

Charley and I reserved a suite of rooms. The most delightful place to sit was on what looked like a sun porch with a sofa, lounge chair, and three occasional chairs. In the middle of the room was a round table with a potted plant sitting on it. On the ocean side there were big square windows with several green potted plants in front of them. It made me feel like I was in a large sunroom.

One of the places the acting troop and I frequented was the Pompeian Swimming Bath. It was designed like something out of ancient Rome.

The room was rectangular in shape with large, standing, fluted columns. The first five feet of each column was covered with bright mosaic tiles. On each side of the bath were benches between the columns. On each end there were steps leading into the water with a rail to hold on to. Like the Lounge, the ceiling was all stained glass. It was most elegant! The water was a comfortable temperature. Charley would not put on a bathing suit for fear his scarred leg would spoil his image. He would however, drop in from time to time to check on us, but always dressed in casual, afternoon attire.

Our days and evenings were filled with activities and I was never lonely or out of sorts. I was extremely happy, and the people around me sensed my excitement with everything I did. I was becoming myself again!

I wasn't paying much attention to the passing days, I was living a life of true luxury with little thought of the future. But I did hold hope that the Professor still had feelings for me. I admonished myself not to get too locked into any plans for the future. I resigned myself to live from day to day.

The one future plan I did think about was the possibility of travel to Scotland. I was excited about the prospect of further researching my family roots. I had to do this alone and now there was nothing to stop me. I had plenty of money and all the time I wanted.

Before I left the plantation, I had read the Kingsley family Bible and learned that in the year 1827 my, Great-great-grandmother Felice had been born in Edinburgh, Scotland. In 1844, at the age of 17 she married Edward Philip Kingsley. He was born in 1820 in London, England, and died in America. I made notes before I left home. I knew little about these people, but their very existence intrigued me, I resolved to find as many living relatives as I could in Scotland. I wasn't sure how to go about this, but I knew Edinburgh would be a place to start. London was the same as I'd remembered it, busy, noisy, and crowded. I loved it! I wanted to go to the hospital immediately, but decided I should reacquaint with the Professor first. It proved to be a good idea. When I arrived at the rooming house, I could hardly contain myself. I ran up the front stairs, opened the door and it was as though he knew I was coming. Looking down the hall I saw the Professor's door was open and just as so many times before he was brewing some lemon tea. I hastened in the open door, stopped and took a deep breath.

"Professor, may I come in for a cup of tea? I've come a long way to be with you." He turned in my direction with a gracious smile. I ran into his waiting arms. The softness of his light sweater vest caressed my cheek as his hands patted my shoulder. Then I looked into his eyes and without a word, he kissed me gently on the cheek.

"You have come back to me! I have waited and prayed you would realize your place was never with James, but with me. Come, sit beside me, and tell me all that has transpired. We have plenty of time."

For once in my life I felt that I was in the right place. But I could not contain myself. I excitedly babbled forth all my experiences and feelings of the past year. I told him how my life had been stifled at the San Francisco mansion and how little I had seen James, and that the only pleasant thing was my friendship with Mr. Sin. He listened patiently, smiling at me often and not interrupting. I felt so at home, just being with him! But finally I came to my senses.

"Do you know whether my flat is still available?"

"Well, I am sure it is. People are slow to move back to the city after the epidemic. Let's go find the manager." And so we did.

When I was settled in my flat, I begin to relax. In the days that followed I went back to the London Hospital and found many of my old friends were still there. I also found out that after I had left London my early effort to establish a home for sick and orphaned children had born fruit. It had become a reality! I was greeted warmly at the children's home and there was even a plaque in my honor. I felt the old compulsion. But before I renewed my nursing career I needed to finish my search for my ancestors. To my surprise the Professor expressed a desire to accompany me to Scotland. While he professed interest in my search, but I suspected he just wanted to be with me. And that made me feel very happy.

CHAPTER THIRTY-NINE

We rode the train to Edinburgh, a picturesque city situated on the hills south of the Firth of Forth. We each took a room in a small hotel on a side street. We placed an advertisement in the newspaper and was rewarded by a phone call from a woman named, Mary Anna Donahue. We set up a meeting with her at the hotel. When she came she brought and old family Bible that proved to be invaluable.

On those old, yellowed pages we found Felice! In fact we found the whole Kingsley family lineage. Mary Ann suggested we go talk to some of the extended family. She invited us to her home which was a distance out of Edinburgh. I was eager to go. Along the drive we observed some wasteland which was overgrown with scattered trees, evergreen shrubs, and purple heather. The temperature was pleasant.

Mary Ann point out that I would now be considered a member of a clan, and that the clans played an important part in the social life of their members. Each year every clan elects a chieftain who makes important decisions for the group.

Mary Anna explained that over the years a lot of changes had been made. Now in the Central Lowlands people lived more like those in the United States and Canada. Usually the houses were built of stone with two stories. Her house was larger than most, with six rooms, each containing large windows. She explained their main occupation was sheep grazing so their farm was the size of a large estate. She told us about her brother, William Scott Donahue, who was unmarried and lived in Glasgow, where he worked in the metal industry.

We were shown to a small quaint spare bedroom. I must have looked a little surprised. I'd expected two bedrooms. At that time, I explained the Professor and I were not married, just traveling companions, and we needed separate bedrooms. This sounded strange to them, I'm sure, but they were gracious and took him to another room. I was so tired that I collapsed on top of the bed. I needed rest and food. I was only there for a few minutes when there was a knock at my door. A brisk walk before the evening meal was expected. The Professor and I were shown around the grounds, fed a light supper of soup and bread. As the light faded from the sky we were sent off to our beds.

The next morning I was awakened early by a number of voices filling the farm house. The word had been sent out that some of their American cousins had arrived. The clan had been gathering since dawn. Walking out of the bedroom I was amazed to see young and old, and even babes in their mother's arms. The aroma of strong coffee and freshly baked bread filled the house. Seeing the people with their ruddy faces told me they were the picture of health. I felt completely at ease, and I even believed I could see the likeness of some of these women to Felice, my Great-great grandmother. I had finally found what I had been searching for all of these years, my roots.

Mary Anna urged us to stay for a few days so that we could all get to know each other. With all the discussion of our family tree, it didn't take long for us all to become good friends. Each member of the clan shared what he knew of their parents, grandparents, and even great-grandparents. All relate some funny, sad, or historical fact about the clan.

Mary Anna's sister recalled their grandmother kept a trunk in her attic that contained some old letters and if she remembered right, they were letters from America written about the time of the American Civil War. My heart nearly jumped up into my throat. I wondered if the letters could have been written by Felice! I asked her if the Professor and I might go to their grandmother's house to look at the letters. She was delighted at the prospect of us viewing the letters, and said she would deliver us on the morrow for a bit of tea and shortbread.

In the morning we dressed warmly, for the weather had turned. Nothing had ever tasted so good as their grandmother's hot tea and shortbread. There was a fire in the fireplace and upon the hearth sat a tea kettle and an old fashioned fire pump. Their grandmother was Mrs. Elizabeth Edna McTavish, who was fondly called Widow Lizzy for short. She was very old and moved quite slowly with her feet shuffling along. She had snow white hair and was bent over. But her eyes sparkled and she didn't hesitate to let the Professor know it was up to him to help her up the two flights of stairs to the attic. Gentleman that he was, he of course graciously agreed. When we arrived at the third landing there was one door leading into a dark room. We went in, lit an oil lamp and found the attic was full of household goods, clothes, pictures, old furniture, wooden boxes, leather trunks and cases. It smelled musty and dusty, but we didn't care. There was one window at the end of the cluttered room and in the middle was a rocking chair covered with an old shawl.

Widow Lizzy was having a great time and enjoyed us being there. This was in a place she said she had not visited in years and it was easy to see why. She was so bent over she was almost always looking down at her feet except when she wanted to make a point. Then she would throw her head back and give one of us a quick glance with those sparkling eyes. We found the trunk and discovered it was tied with a rope, but not locked.

Opening the trunk was a disappointment at first because the top of it contained only some very old baby clothes, wooden toys, small leather shoes, a book or two and a wedding dress. However, digging deeper we found what we were looking for, a packet of letters tied with string. They were yellow with age and partly crumbling, but still intact enough for us to be able to read them. I asked Widow Lizzy if I might hold them and even open one. I felt sure the letters were from Felice because they were from Virginia.

Then we sat down, Widow Lizzy in the rocker, the Professor on a wooden box and I on an old foot-stool. He was as excited as I was. I opened the first envelope and gently pulled the letter out. It was indeed from Felice Kingsley. It was addressed to her brother Peter Cornwall and was dated 1843, around the time the Kingsley Mansion was built. She began by describing their trip to America from England and their arrival in New York City. They had brought horses with them on the same ship, and since they had ample money there were no problems with the crossing. She had brought the horses from England with the intention of breeding a line of strong Thoroughbreds for hunting.

One of the early letters spoke of opening an account in the bank of New York just as they had done with a bank in London before coming to America. It seemed Felice's husband Edward Kingsley was convinced it was a good plan to have money in both countries. Had he not had money, securities, and even gold during the Civil War, he would have lost everything. Being a brilliant, business man determined to not lose what he had inherited, Edward handled his assets well.

The next letter told about their trip to Virginia. They had taken passage on a ship and sailed directly to Norfolk, Virginia. From there they went west into the strange mountain country, bought property, and settled outside of Roanoke.

Once the horses had been transferred to the newly acquired plantation, Felice rode daily exploring the entire property. She donned men's clothes and rode straddle her horse most of the time. Edward Kingsley had to have approved and allowed this behavior. I was beginning to understand he was not over-bearing when it came to his wife. He may have managed their money, but she appeared to be the guiding force of the family.

The letter that talked about the purchase of the property near Roanoke included a rather good pencil sketch of the boundaries. And there were detailed sketches of the mansion itself. Looking closely, I was able to recognize the main house, as well as other small buildings which surrounded it. Even the road leading up to the house was drawn in. The more I looked at the sketches the more excited I became. It was like the ghost of my great-great grandmother was sitting there with us.

When shadows began to creep over the cottage we were reminded that it was getting late and we had to drive back to Mary Anna's. We said our farewells and left, promising to return the next day. In the car I relax leaning on the Professor's shoulder. His arm slid up around my shoulder. He pulled me close and our eyes met. I think we knew at that moment our friendship was leading us into a deeper relationship.

When I retired that evening I was wound up by the day's activity, yet my heart was full of love for the Professor. The following day we were up early and I was extremely eager to continue in my research. When we arrived at Widow Lizzy's, I was surprised to see a number of the clan had already gathered. Some were interested in the letters and wanted to know what I had found in them. Others seemed upset and believed I was delving into matters that were none of my concern. I was puzzled. What had I done to get them so upset? Of course, I soon learned it took very little change in their lives to get them stirred up. I felt the letters belonged to me more than anyone, but a few of the others felt they were the direct descendants of Peter Cornwall and since the letters had been written to him, they had become his personal property and therefore belonged to them.

When I explained I was looking for information about the Kingsley Mansion, the house I grew up in, they were more reasonable. I was reminded that what was written between a brother and sister was considered almost sacred. Anything I uncovered about the clan was to be kept strictly secret, and revealed only to the present day chieftain. Once I had agreed to this, and they were all gathered together, the clan decided to have a celebration eating, drinking, and dancing in true Scottish fashion.

After the celebration we retired for a good night sleep. Early the next morning we returned to Aunt Lizzy's, where we continued reading the letters. I was especially interested in learning about the plantation and Felice's accounts of the coming War Between the States. She had written about the newspaper articles telling about increasing pressure for the South to secede from the Union, but there was no mention of freeing the slaves. If Edward and Felice owned any slaves she did not mention it. From what I could tell, they paid white and black men the same wages to work on the plantation. And yet there was a mention of a Luella, a black woman who helped care for her two children. Felice apparently was with child during the voyage to America and that same year in Virginia she delivered twins!

This was something new! A boy they named James Brightwell Kingsley, and a girl, Sarah Stewart Kingsley, born in 1844. This revelation was like uncovering a ghost in the family. Sarah had a twin brother named James, and yet there was no mention of him in Kingsley family Bible. I had never heard anyone speak of him, and there was no painting of him on the staircase wall of ancestors in the past.

In another letter written in 1856 we learned what had happened to her son. It was a sad day when this young man of twelve was killed. The heart-breaking part was that his father killed him accidentally. They had gone off for a day of hunting. While climbing a fence Mr. Kingsley's gun discharged and shot the boy in the chest. The boy died instantly. His father never got over it, and in his grief he forbade Felice or any other member of their household to mention his son's name again.

This son, James Brightwell had been the only true joy of his father's life, and he had planned to send the boy to the best schools in the south or even perhaps to England. When this tragic event happened, a part of him died. He made Sarah promise she would neither speak of that day fateful day, not ever acknowledge having had a twin brother. At the tender age of twelve years of age she grieved a long time and did not understand why she could not speak of her brother. But she had made a promise and it was not to be broken, not ever.

The plantation had been a place with much social activity where all were welcome, but after the untimely death it became a place for business only. If you were interested in horses you saw Mrs. Kingsley. Any other business Mr. Kingsley attended to in his library or in town. Though Felice was well respected and liked, her husband's behavior soon alienated folks from coming for visits. There were no parties anymore and Sarah suffered a great deal. She felt she was being deprived of a normal life of a Southern plantation girl, and of course that was true. She vowed when she became mistress, there would be parties at the plantation and bright lights in every room.

We came across several letters that talked of the war, which filled every Southerner's mind and heart. The newspapers were full of stories. Felice didn't seem to believe it would really come to division of the country.

Would this not cause great dissension between friends, brothers, and fathers? Much unrest was felt in Virginia as in the other Southern states.

The next letter looked as though it had been read and re-read many times. It was when the war actually began. The Kingsley Mansion was off the beaten track, so they felt relatively safe and determined to wait the war out. What was not obvious was that by December of 1860 the separation of the Deep South from the Union was essential to the preservation of their way of life. However, there was a great deal of sentiment for and against the Unionists, particularly in the Border States.

Well that was true with the Kingsley family. No slaves, no trouble. However, in April of 1860, Virginia seceded from the Union. The Southern states set up a permanent government and moved the capital to Richmond.

This still did not faze the Kingsley family. Their lives continued on in an uneasy peace. It wasn't until early in 1864 that they knew the reality of the war. It concerned them when they were informed that the Yankees were moving toward the Roanoke Valley. The battle that she spoke about was fought at a place where Peter's Creek empties into the Roanoke River. Now it was getting too close to home. Felice told about why the plantation being chosen for a Union headquarters. She speculated as to why this happened. They were noted for two things, not owning slaves and for their fine breed of horses. The Union Army needed horses desperately so General Hunter was sent on a mission to take the entire Kingsley herd.

The next letter I read demanded all of our attention. Felice wrote that a Yankee Colonel appeared with his aide knocking at the door, and she sent my old nanny to answer it. She described the man as a true gentleman in every sense of the word, even though he was a damn Yankee! He was tall and handsome in his military uniform. He asked to speak to the master. Felice heard this and entered the room. She explained her husband was not at home, but he could speak to her. The letter continued as if the two were speaking to each other.

He bowed and said, "Colonel M J Lancaster, at your service, ma'am." He looked at her in a kind of shock, his eyes lighting up when he saw how beautiful she was. He asked her. "Who else is in this house?"

"Only my daughter Sarah, and my old nanny." she replied. Sarah had married young and was staying at the Plantation while her husband, Alfred Andrew Hampton, was in England serving as ambassador for the Confederacy.

Colonel Lancaster told his aide to go out and tell the men to sand by. Felice, being a head-strong woman, started to protest but thought better of it. He demanded she call her daughter and the servant. When he saw this was a young girl and an old woman he relaxed a little. He dismissed them and sent them back to their room.

He turned to her politely and asked if he could see the upstairs. He motioned her to precede him. She had no choice but to lead the way. At the door of the great bedroom she drew back and he walked past her. He turned to her and extended his hand and said, "Won't you join me," with a smile she found rather boyish and appealing. "You seem like a kind woman. Can you understand how a man who hasn't seen his wife in a year would long for the touch of a woman? We are caught up in a war that neither of us asked for. Can't we find comfort briefly together?"

Felice was speechless.

Cautiously he went on. "I have a proposal to offer. My orders are to burn your house down and take your herd of horses. The horses I must have, but I can spare the house if you comply with my wishes."

She sank into the nearest chair. As a defenseless woman she had to admit that her choices were few. If she refused to give in he would take her anyway.

As for the horses she had known something like this could happen. What he did not know was that early in the war she had instructed a few of her most trusted men to take her prize horses deep into the hills, to be reclaimed after the war was over.

If she could keep the house from being burned down the family might survive. She thought she could fight him and consider it rape, but what purpose would that serve? Besides, he might burn down the house anyway. She decided to comply with the man. He was lean and hard of muscle and as he moved toward her he looked like a prince. He took her hand, lifted her up and carried her to the bed. When he touched her it was with gentle hands and pleasant words. She knew then he had not really planned to rape her. He just wanted a woman. She was supposed to defend herself and her honor, but she braced herself to submit. To her surprise her body betrayed her. Although it seemed shameful she felt a passion for this man that she had never met. She pleasured him more than once in their brief interlude.

Colonel Lancaster left her, as she lay in the afterglow of satisfaction, she heard him going down the stairs. Out in the yard he was ordering his men to the stable. He had kept his word. The house had been spared and the horses taken.

The three of us sitting in the attic looked at each other. This was much too private for us to discuss, but we continued reading.

When her husband Edward did return, it was six weeks since the event had taken place, but it was long enough for her to realize she was with child, Colonel M J Lancaster's child. She wondered how she would explain the situation to Edward. She knew she could not. So she conceived a plan to get him intoxicated and into her bed. She was being deceitful and she knew it, but it was the only way to cover what had happened.

When he did come home she told him the Yankees had been there and had taken all the horses. When questioned why they had not burned the house to the ground, she lied and told him she didn't know. She suggested that they should celebrate the house being spared as she brought out the whiskey bottle.

Her plan worked. He became very drunk and ended up in the bed with her - the same bed where six weeks earlier she had been with the Colonel.

Widow Lizzy began to tire and suggested we stop reading for a while and have a cup of tea. She wasn't willing to go down stairs. Instead she sent me to make the tea and to fetch the shortbread. The Professor accompanied me, leaving Widow Lizzy to take a nap in her chair among all her treasured memories.

In the homey surroundings we sat close together looking at the flickering fire feeling a peace I cannot describe. We knew we were falling in love and shared the desire to be together for the rest of our lives. Being together made us content.

After we enjoyed the refreshments, we returned to the attic, served Widow Lizzy her tea and shortbread, and continued reading Felice's letter. It was as though Felice was in the attic with us and we were living her description of events. As soon as it was possible, I told Edward he had fathered another child and that I was expecting. He only looked at me with disgust and commented that I was rather old to be having a baby. Apparently my plan had worked. I had deceived him! If it was a son perhaps that would please him?"

In the letter Felice further revealed that their daughter Sarah had also gotten in a family way before her husband had left for England. Now both mother and daughter were expecting.

The Professor saw I was tiring so he came over to me from his perch on the box.

"Melinda Ann, may I continue reading the letter?

"Please do."

In the letter Felice confided that she never told Edward Kingsley about Colonel Lancaster for fear he would disown her and the child. He had made quite a speech about taking advantage of me when he was drunk. He felt it was his responsibility that I was expecting. He promised to care for our child, and that he would never again take me in a state of drunkenness.

It could never happen again anyway because the coward was leaving. He packed his bags and promptly left for Roanoke with the intention of going to New York."

He knew if he stayed around the plantation he would probably be killed by the Union forces or conscripted into the Southern Army and he liked neither prospect. He felt defenseless women, two whom were expecting babies would not be bothered by either army. The letter went on to reveal that both Sarah and her baby died in childbirth. Sarah had always been weak. This was a difficult and lonely time in Felice's life. Her husband had left, her daughter was dead and she was carrying another man's child.

The letter continued that through the local grapevine Felice heard that Colonel Lancaster had been killed. It had happened while driving a herd of seven hundred horses through the pass near the massive Potts Mountain in Craig County. The big climb killed most of the horses from exhaustion. It was believed that the small Union Army attachment driving the herd encountered Confederate forces while climbing the pass! The Colonel was thrown from his mount during the fight and trampled to death. When Felice heard the news of the Colonel being killed she was stunned, and at the same time relieved because the secret would remain forever with her and the brother to which she was writing. Three weeks later the child was born, and named, Matthew Lancaster Kingsley.

That was the last letter and with no more to read my search had come to an end. I returned each letter to its envelope, bound them up and handed them to Widow Lizzy. She patted my hand, took the packet and put it back into the trunk as a very special treasure. The three of us went down the stairs with the Professor holding her arm and me following. It was time to bid farewell to Widow Lizzy.

When we were driving back to Mary Anna's, the Professor reached over and took my hand. "Melinda Ann, do you understand what we have just discovered?"

"Yes, I think I do …a lot of Kingsley family secrets. Bart wasn't really a Kingsley. He was fathered by Matthew Lancaster Kingsley, the illegitimate son of the deceased Colonel Lancaster."

"Yes, and that means there is actually no one in the family, living at the plantation, who is a real Kingsley"

This was the most astonishing secret of all!

CHAPTER FORTY

In the car on the way to Mary Anna's cottage we discussed our future. There was no mention of marriage, even though it seemed only natural that would be our next step. Without a word the Professor stopped the car, pulled over and drew me into his arms. He kissed me with enough pressure to make my body tingle. I knew then we were meant for each other. When we reached the cottage, a lot of the clan was already there. What we did not know was that a cablegram had been delivered, and being an inquisitive family they had taken the opportunity to read it. I'm sure they were wondering how we would react to such information, so they had gathered to give us support. The cablegram read:

**MELINDA ANN KINGSLEY SINCLAIR STOP
KINGSLEY MANSION BURNED TO THE GROUND STOP
TINNY AND BIRDIE ARE DEAD EDWARD DYING STOP
THIS IS TOO MUCH TO BEAR STOP
AUNT GINNY**

Mary Anna, seeing my distress led us to a small parlor where we could be alone. I needed time to think. The clan gathered silently in the house and in the yard. They were being polite and sympathetic. The people would wait to express their concerns until we emerged from the private room. When she closed the door behind her, I almost fainted. It was too much terrible information for me to fully comprehend. The professor looked at me, took me in his arms, and held me close.

"I don't want to lose you again."

"You will never lose me as long as you want me, but I must go home immediately. And I must wire Aunt Ginny that I am coming. We have to got back to London as soon as possible."

"Yes, you must go immediately, and your family needs to know you are coming. But before you go we need to talk. I've declared my love for you. My darling Melinda Ann, do you want me to go with you? I will you know. I'm not sure how much help I could be, but my just being with you may be of some comfort to you."

"My dear Professor, this is something I need to do on my own, however I had hoped someday you would visit the plantation with me, but now I am not sure. I don't want you to see the Kingsley mansion in ruins."

"Melinda Ann, we've know each other as friends and traveling companions so don't you think it is time you called me Stephen? After all, we both know our friendship is more than casual. In time I hope you'll consider becoming my wife.

I love you more than any woman I've ever known. I was married once and deeply in love. When my wife died I swore I would never go through that pain again. Yet, you came along and changed my life."

Looking at Stephen gave me courage and delighted my spirit to think this very special man truly loved me and no other. Again we embraced, walked out of the parlor, bade a hasty farewell to the clan and thanked Mary Ann for her hospitality. We took the next train from Scotland to London. Stephen decided he would remain there until he heard from me.

Once in London I packed some trunks, carrying cases and closed the flat. Before we parted, Stephen looked at me tenderly and said, "You are a strong woman, Melinda Ann, you can handle this, but if you need me I am here for you and will do anything I can to help." We held each other for a long time and then he kissed me on the lips. I would miss him.

A train took me to Southampton where I boarded the first available ship to New York Harbor. The crossing was a blur. After debarking I was once again on the train to Roanoke traveling alone, deep in my thoughts. My mother's face came to me. She was lying on her bed not wanting to see me. Well, poor dear, now she was dead. My God! What had happened to her? What caused the fire and would take both Mother and Birdie? Aunt Ginny wanted me to come home because I was needed. Needed for support? How could I be of help? Poor Birdie, she didn't win after all. She was dead and had lost everything she so coveted. When and why had the mansion burned? Was it totally destroyed and what had happened to Edward? How could he ever survive such a terrible ordeal? Was the baby a boy or girl, and what happened to the child? There were so many unanswered questions. The sheer shock of it all almost killed me. I wanted to cry out and scream! This could not happen! It was a bad dream and I would wake up. I could shed no tears, but I was numb with grief.

A traveling newspaperman approached me on the train. He said he recognized me as the Kingsley's only daughter. I asked him what had happened since the fire. He filled me in on some very disturbing news, and not in a gentle way. "The story was in all the newspapers, lady. Your brother, Mr. Edward Kingsley, was forced to go to court because the authorities found out his wife delivered a black baby. The story was that he had married a beautiful white woman not knowing she was part black. This woman was raised by your family. Isn't that true Miss Kingsley? I saw the woman once and she was as white as you are and really pretty." With a smirk on his face he added, "Where your brother made his mistake was in marrying her in the first place. He could have just set her up as his mistress. It's commonly done by a lot of Southern gentlemen."

I was stunned and I wanted to slap him. Edward and Birdie's baby black? Impossible! This was my brother he was talking about, so I firmly asked him to get out of my sight. I had heard enough on top of everything else! That meant Birdie had had Negro blood in her veins. How could that be? At that moment, I made up my mind to face whatever was to come with courage and all the dignity I could muster. When I reached the Roanoke station, I was so anxious to be off the train and get to the plantation that I left my trunks and carrying cases with an attendant. I flagged the nearest taxi. The driver was Mr. Jenkins, and old friend of the family. The ride out to the plantation was the longest of my life. I wondered what I would find when I got there? It had been three weeks since Aunt Ginny sent the cable.

As we turned up the road leading to the main house I saw the trees there looked the same and I saw the chiseled stone-marker signifying that this was the Kingsley Mansion. The massive stone and Kingsley name was barely visible through the green vine. Abruptly I saw what was left of the house, a charred shell of what it once was. I thought of Felice and the sacrifice she had made to save it and now it was gone.

When we pulled up in front of the house I sat looking out the window of the taxi. Mr. Jenkins' face was full of concern. "Miss Melinda Ann, I hate to leave you out here all alone."

There was the old weeping willow tree, blackened limbs bent over with its branches touching the ground. Beneath it was a man on a canvas cot. I jumped out of the car. It was Edward! He had suffered terrible burns on his face and hands. I could tell he was in a lot of pain. I quickly ran to his side.

When I was close enough to touch him he spoke to me in a whisper! "Melinda Ann, you've come home, thank God. I'm dying. My burn wounds are deep and I can't bear to have anyone touch me." He began to rattle aimlessly. "The fire was terrible! Mother and Birdie are both dead. It was my fault. I should have hid Birdie and the baby from the authorities. Did you hear the baby was black? There must have been some way I could have protected Mother better than I did." His voice trailed off, he turned away and I could see the other side of his face was burned. I couldn't believe my eyes. My brother was suffering and I could do nothing to help him.

When Charley, Aunt Ginny, and Mick saw me beside Edward they came running. Aunt Ginny stopped beside Edward and quickly looked at him. She came to me and hugged me close to her. "We took him to the hospital right after the fire, but his kidneys were failing. They tried to help him, but it was hopeless. The doctor said he wouldn't live much longer. Edward knew he was dying. He said he wanted to be under the old weeping willow tree when he died. Since we brought him home from the hospital, every day we have carried him on his cot and placed him under the willow. I don't know what to do. I am so glad you are here."

Silence fell over us as we four surrounded Edward. We sat on the grass under the charred limbs of the tree, the same spot where I had said my farewells to Grandmother Lilly. It was a fitting place for me to hear the whole story of the demise of the Kingsley Mansion.

Even though it was difficult for him to speak, Edward still wanted to tell me what had happened. When we were settled he began the gruesome tale. "I was standing right outside the bedroom door when I heard the mid-wife gasp and stammer, 'the poor little boy is a black baby.' When Birdie realized what had happened she screamed and asked the doctor and mid-wife not to tell anyone. She was frantic and even offered them money to keep silent. I rushed in, saw the baby I was stunned…I couldn't believe my eyes! I looked at the tiny baby boy in disbelief. He was so little and helpless, yet I could do nothing for him. I am so ashamed because I ran down stairs to the library and closed the door. I couldn't accept what I had seen."

"The doctor and mid-wife knew this had to be reported. It's against the law in Virginia for a white man to marry a black woman, no matter how white her skin. They did reported it, and in a few days the authorities came and explained to me what had to be done. Birdie and the baby had to leave. Since she was considered black there was no legal marriage. But I would be arrested if I did not comply with Virginia law. Right then I did nothing. I just stood there like a fool, while the authorities watched Birdie pack a few things. She grabbed up our son, wrapped him in a blanket, and left under escort. I didn't know what to do! Birdie said nothing. She first looked at me with sad pleading, but when I didn't lift a finger to help her she glared at me. I felt utterly destroyed." Then Edward dissolved into deep sobs and turned away from us."

Aunt Ginny spoke up. "After a few days we learned Birdie had been taken to a less than desirable part of Roanoke. She was left standing on a corner with her baby in her arms. We made an attempt to locate her and asked questions, but no one in the black community would admit to having seen her. Edward was furious with himself when he could not find her and the baby. He was so much in love with Birdie that he wanted to make some arrangement for her and their child's care. By law Edward was financially responsible for the child, but not Birdie. If she knew she was part black she had deceived him, and he had entered into the marriage innocently. Only a few of the family knew Birdie's background, but we were under oath to Grandmother Lilly not to tell. As of now, we have not been able to locate where the authorities took her and the baby. Edward was like a crazy man. I sent the servants to town every day looking for Birdie and the baby. Then later I wondered what would happen if we found them."

Edward was struggling for breath. As difficult as it was, he opened his eyes and began to speak again. "It was about midnight and I could not sleep. I went down to the library to read. I closed the heavy oak doors. I must have dozed off. I awoke to the acrid smell of thick smoke. I covered my mouth with a handkerchief and threw open the doors and saw that the entire right wing of the mansion was engulfed in flames. I moved out of the library just as it burst into flame. I ran to the foyer and glimpsed a dark figure moving quickly up the staircase torching each one of the ancestor portraits. Choking from the smoke and flame I raced up the stairs as the figure knocked over the small upper hall tables and torched more painting there.

"It was Birdie with a flaming torch in one hand laughing wildly. She looked like a witch with her dark hair flying around her face. She wore a black dress that hung on her like a burlap sack. She was thin as a rail. When she saw me on the stairs she darted into Mother's room just as I passed the flaming portrait of Felice at the top of the stairs. Birdie flew past Mother, who was sitting up in bed with the covers clutched up to her chin, her eyes wild with fear. I moved toward her just as Birdie set the window curtains on fire. Then Birdie turned, ran over and torched Mother's bed. I lunged at Birdie, hoping to get the torch out of her hand, but I was too late. Mother's bed was totally ablaze and she was screaming. The flimsy bedding was engulfed in flame. I couldn't save her. Birdie stood in the middle of the room yelling at me. "If I can't have the Kingsley Mansion then no one will! I hate you and I hope you die!" As she said that a part of the ceiling fell and hit her on the head. She was gone from my sight in a flash of fire!

I felt the intense heat and realized my smoking jacket had caught fire. Somehow I groped my way to the bedroom door and stumbled down the stairs. I was aware that the ancestor portrait paintings were burning fiercely. The heat was unbearable by this time, but somehow I managed to reach the front door. As I crawled and rolled out of the door someone threw a blanket over me trying to smother the flames but it was useless. I tried to tell them to stop and let the damned house burn, but no words came out of my mouth. I must have passed out because I don't remember anymore. It was hell. I'm glad you made it home in time for me to tell you. Now, I just want to die!"

We sat there not knowing what to say. I wanted to touch my brother, I wanted to heal his burns, but I could not. Then it occurred to me, what about the child?"

"Aunt Ginny, what about the baby boy? Do you know where he is?"

"Even after the fire, Mick and I tried to find the baby, but we were not able to."

It was obvious to me Edward's horrible burns would never heal, and he was weaker than I thought. He turned his head and looked at each of us briefly, blinked his eyes open and he was gone. Up until now I had not been able to cry, but it was too much to bear. I wept uncontrollably. The Kingsley family's troubled story had ended in tragedy.

Mick O'Leary pulled off his cap and knelt beside Aunt Ginny and me. He put his arms around her and said, "Now me' darlin' girls, your Mick is here. Remember death is only a part of livin'. One day it will come to each of us. Edward, God rest his departed soul, could not have lived much longer in his condition. You had to let him go. Now it's done, and life must go on."

Charley stood up and tried to give us some words of comfort and ended with: "The Lord is with you dear brother, until we meet again" which left us all weeping. There we were most of what remained of the proud Kingsley family: Aunt Ginny and Mick O'Leary, Charley and me. Only Edwin was missing.

It has been said, people who are dying sometimes hang on until all of their family is present. I am sure Edward would have wanted to see his twin before he died, but he was unable to. His pain was too great and his will to live was gone.

Still sitting there around our brother, looking at his lifeless frame we heard from a distance, an automobile approaching. It turned out to be Edwin.

The car stopped, he burst out and ran to the side of his twin brother. When he saw he was dead, Edwin ripped off his coat, threw it to the ground and covered his face with both hands. The groaning sobs we heard nearly broke our hearts. His grief was so intense.

When it soaked in that Edward was gone and we could do nothing we slowly got up and went to Aunt Ginny's. The question facing us now was … what was to happen next?

Three days later when we laid Edward to rest we gathered again at Mick and Aunt Ginny's house. We talked about the future of the plantation.

I considered then if I should tell them none of us were really a Kingsley, not even Birdie, but I decided I would keep that secret to myself. In a few years Mick and Aunt Ginny would have a splendid line of Thoroughbred horses and would be happy to live out their days in Virginia. Charley would continue his career on the stage, and Edwin would return to Africa, where he had become a successful coffee plantation owner. They all had set plans for their lives. Now I had to figure out how Stephen and I could make a life together in Virginia or in London. .

I had a life changing decision to make. Did I want to remain and help re-establish the horse breeding farm or go back to England? Just weeks ago, I left England, feeling that I would return, resume my nursing career and marry Stephen, but now I was unsure.

The Kingsley Mansion no longer existed and we all agreed that Aunt Ginny's inheritance should be called, O'Leary Stables, which pleased Mick and Aunt Ginny. When our conversation ended about the plantation and the stables, Mick and Aunt Ginny, Charley, Edwin and I went for a walk down the road leading away from the house. Before we returned we stood looking at the old, chiseled-stone marker. It had been placed there by Felice and Edward Kingsley. Now it stood neglected, with the name completely covered with a thick green vine. That stone marker would have to be changed someday, but with what name depended on what I decided to do. As the five of us walked down the road we kicked the dust in the air like children. We were a family and we were together. It really wasn't important what our names were or where we lived as long as we remained a family.

A few days later, Charley and Edwin left, but I stayed with Aunt Ginny and Mick. The more I thought about leaving the more I knew I wanted to build the mansion back, and even better than before. Since I had discovered the original plans in the letters from Felice, I was sure it could be done and I was the one to do it. I was feeling the pull of my roots. I belonged here.

But I was left with a deep quandary, what about the Professor, dear Stephen? How deep was our love? If I went back to London, what could I expect to find there? Would I find true love and contentment? I knew if I married him I would live a quiet life in an English flat. I would return to work and be challenged each day. However, what about my roots here in Virginia?

Looking at the property I owned, and with the opportunity to build something fine, I couldn't bear to leave. My love for Stephen was strange and wonderful. Although true, I wanted to see Mick and Aunt Ginny's horse breeding business succeed, and I wanted to rebuild the mansion. I wanted to restore and revitalize the entire property. I was beginning to understand that I loved Virginia and my home more than I'd ever realized. It was where I belonged after all!

When this realization came to me I wanted to share my plans with Aunt Ginny. "Aunt Ginny I've come to the conclusion I need to stay here in Virginia. I can't explain it. I want to help you and Mick set up the stables for a new Thoroughbred line. We'll build a new practice track and additional stables that will be the envy of every horse breeding farm in Virginia. We'll have the finest Thoroughbreds in the country. I want to rebuild the mansion so that it is more magnificent than before. I can't allow this one elegant home to remain in ashes. When the house is finished we will commission portraits to grace the imposing staircase wall. This time it will start with us, and Charley and Edwin too! Who knows, some of this family may produce children yet! And their portraits will become part of the family gallery."

Looking around and seeing the charred weeping willow tree I vowed to have it pruned back. It had become a symbol of our past family and our strength for the future. I knew it would survive.

Aunt Ginny grabbed my hands and swung me around. "Thank God, Melinda Ann, you've come to your senses. Your home has always been here. This is where you were born and where you belong. This plantation is yours."

At that moment, I was struck with the desire to have my beloved Stephen's arms around me. I knew I needed him. I wanted him to share in this new beginning. Wasn't he more important than this Virginia soil? How could any woman make such a choice? My heart ached for him. How could I keep the plantation, and the love of my life?

I had discarded one man and I was fearful of losing the other. I had to express in a letter my deepest feelings and wait for his response.

Professor Stephen Andrew Hamilton
35 Penbrook Lane – Flat Number 1
London, England

My dear Stephen,

When we are together my world is complete. It grieves me to be so far away, but now that I'm here I know I'm home.

I can't bear to see the house in ruins, nothing but ashes. I've never realized that home really is where the heart is. It has nothing to do with burnt timber. It's rooted deeply in the Virginia soil.

As I sit here under the old, partly-scorched weeping willow tree where my Grandmother Lilly died and my brother died, I feel her spirit calling to me, telling me this land is important. It has put an obligation on me that I can't shake. It is hopeless to expect my brothers to give me any support. They have signed over ownership of the plantation and want nothing to do with it. To them it is just a heap of ashes, but to me it's a vision of a new beginning.

I intend to start a whole new dynasty, but I can't go any further than that until I know your feelings. There is an old, chiseled-stone marker with the words Kingsley Mansion on it. I'm going to erect a new one, but I don't know what name to put on it. Could it be Hamilton?

Dear Stephen how I love you. I love the warmth of your touch and desire a life filled with your presence. My heart calls out to you to come, to share my land, my country and build a new life with me.

Your devoted,

Melinda Ann